Third Reich

What was the relationship between ordinary Germans and Hitler's government? Why did such a dreadful political system find any popular support at all? Who was brave enough to defy the laws of the Third Reich? This book examines decisions made by different social groups to resist or conform to the Nazi regime.

Using accessible language, and drawing on the full range of sources available to historians, Martyn Housden adopts a thematic approach to the subject. He considers, for example, why church-goers failed to reject decisively Hitler's atheistic political movement; what impact the persecution of Germany's Jewish citizens had on the everyday lives of other Germans; why the Hitler Youth held such appeal for young people.

Resistance and conformity in the Third Reich

Martyn Housden

London and New York

Cover image: every effort has been made to contact the copyright holders of this image. In the event of any queries, please contact Suzanne Collins at Routledge, London.

First published 1997
by Routledge
11 New Fetter Lane, London EC4P 4EE

Simultaneously published in the USA and Canada
by Routledge
29 West 35th Street, New York, NY 10001

©1997 Martyn Housden

Typeset in Galliard and Futura by
Keystroke, Jacaranda Lodge, Wolverhampton

Printed and bound in Great Britain by Biddles Ltd,
Guildford and King's Lynn

British Library Cataloguing in Publication Data
A catalogue record for this book is available from the British Library

Library of Congress Cataloguing in Publication Data
Housden, Martyn, 1962–
    Resistance and conformity in the Third Reich / Martyn Housden.
    — (Routledge sources in history)
    Includes bibliographical references and index.
    1. National socialism. 2. Germany—Politics and government—1933–1945. 3. Jews—Persecutions—Germany.
    4. Anti-Nazi movement—Germany. I. Title. II. Series.
    DD256.5.H69 1997   96-18379
    943.086—dc20   CIP

ISBN 0–415–12133–7
        0–415–12134–5 (pbk)

For Gill, Patrick and Alexander

Contents

Series editor's preface

Sources in History is a new series responding to the continued shift of emphasis in the teaching of history in schools and universities towards the use of primary sources and the testing of historical skills. By using documentary evidence, the series is intended to reflect the skills historians have to master when challenged by problems of evidence, interpretation and presentation.

A distinctive feature of *Sources in History* is the manner in which the content, style and significance of documents is analysed. The commentary and the source are not discrete, but rather merge to become part of a continuous and integrated narrative. After reading each volume a student should be well versed in the historiographical problems which sources present. In short, the series provides texts which will allow students to achieve facility in 'thinking historically' and place them in a stronger position to test their historical skills. Wherever possible the intention has been to retain the integrity of a document and not simply to present a 'gobbet', which can be misleading. Documentary evidence thus forces the students to confront a series of questions which professional historians also have to grapple with. Such questions can be summarised as follows:

1 What type of source is the document?
- Is it a written source or an oral or visual source?
- What is its importance?
- Did it have an effect on events or the decision-making process?
2 Who wrote the document?
- A person, a group or a government?
- If it was a person, what was his/her position?
- What basic attitudes might have affected the nature of the information and language used?
3 When was the document written?
- The date, and even the time, might be significant.
- It may be necessary to understand when the document was written in order to understand its context.
- Are there any special problems in understanding the document as contemporaries would have understood it?

4 Why was the document written?
- For what purpose(s) did the document come into existence, and for *whom* was it intended?
- Was the document 'author-initiated' or was it commissioned for somebody? If the document was ordered by someone, the author could possibly have 'tailored' his piece.
5 What was written?
- This is the obvious question, but stating the obvious can be crucial.
- It is sometimes more revealing to ask the question: what was *not* written?
- What other references (to persons, events, other documents, etc.) need to be explained before the document can be fully understood?

Sources in History is intended to reflect the individual voice of the volume author(s) with the aim of bringing the central themes of specific topics into sharper focus. Each volume consists of an authoritative introduction to the topic; chapters discuss the historical significance of the sources, and the final chapter provides an up-to-date synthesis of the historiographical debate. Authors provide an annotated further reading section and a bibliography. These books will become contributions to the historical debate in their own right.

In *Resistance and Conformity in the Third Reich* Martyn Housden analyses the twin concepts of conformity with and resistance to the Nazi regime. How justified were the claims made by the Nazis that they created a consensus in Germany? The relationship between the Nazi dictatorship and the German people, in whose name it claimed to govern, has become the focus of a turbulent historiographical debate that is already providing new insights into the nature of the regime and everyday life in the Third Reich.

What did Hitler's government mean for average Germans? In what ways did they go along with what it demanded of them? To what extent did they reject what it stood for? How can historians ever really start to understand the lives people led under conditions so radically different from those we enjoy today? These questions lie at the core of this study and are explored through detailed discussions of established social themes. The chapters bring out not just the wealth of primary sources available to historians, but also the depth of historiographical controversy that surrounds every facet of the Third Reich. At issue are questions as fundamental as any dealt with by historians; getting to grips with them is more than just playing an academic game. We are exploring the experiences of thinking, feeling human beings. Appropriately, Housden's study aims at being more than a 'bloodless' account of things which could have been done by robots to inanimate objects. By incorporating into the text disarmingly honest postwar memoirs, morally challenging, emotionally charged historical situations are presented in a way which will make readers want to discuss what they have encountered. *Resistance and Conformity* also breaks with the tradition of portraying Germany's Jews as little more than the passive targets of National Socialist persecution. We begin to see these people as integral and active parts of this phase of German history. Ernst

Nolte has complained that the Third Reich is a past that will not pass away. But with so much to be learned from it, and so many records still to be set straight, it is a past that we cannot let slip.

David Welch
Canterbury 1996

Acknowledgements

John Hiden is to be thanked for his innumerable conversations and constant encouragement. Herr Friedrich of the Nuremberg State Archive was kind enough to draw my attention to document 7.7. Generous funding from the British Academy enabled a number of research visits to Germany during which I acquired some of the sources reproduced here.

The following publishers and archives have been kind enough to give permission for more lengthy extracts from their wares to be reproduced:

Berg, for extracts from T. Mason, *Social Policy in the Third Reich. The Working Class and the 'National Community'*, 1993;

Federal Archive, Koblenz;

Professor Dr H.-A. Jacobsen, Bonn;

Princeton University Press for extracts from S. Gordon, *Hitler, Germans and the 'Jewish Question'*, 1984;

State Archive, Nuremberg;

Westdeutscher Verlag GmbH for extracts from T. Mason, *Arbeiterklasse und Volksgemeinschaft*, 1975;

Yad Vashem, The Holocaust Martyrs' and Heroes' Remembrance Authority, for extracts from Yitshak Arad, Yisrael Gutman and Abraham Margialot (eds), *Documents on the Holocaust, Selected Sources on the Destruction of the Jews of Germany and Austria, Poland and the Soviet Union*, Yad Vashem, 1981.

National Socialism | **1**
what was its character and immediate appeal?

Fifty years on, whether we like it or not, all traces of Hitler and his political movement have not gone away. National Socialist insignia and slogans can still be used to shock and insult. Novels and films about the Third Reich can grip the imagination as much as ever. Glance at newspapers and you can confirm that the regime's crimes are still used as a yardstick against which to measure the worst atrocities from around the world. For both those who actually experienced life in Germany from 1933 to 1945 and their relatives, something personal remains at stake when Hitler is discussed. This is doubly so when those involved were somehow perpetrators or victims of the crimes and carnage he inspired. With every anniversary of some event from the Second World War, time and again people have to confront the dual question: what really happened and how should we understand it?

The community of historians which researches into Hitler's Germany cannot provide united answers to some of its most central problems. Why did Hitler and those around him decide to go to war in 1939? Tim Mason **(1993, pp. 307–16)** emphasised a crisis in the German economy; Gerhard Weinberg **(1995, pp. 35, 148)** says it was for reasons of ideology and cold political calculation. Why did this group bring about the Holocaust? Martin Broszat **(1985, pp. 397–414)** blamed the frustration of the German attack on the USSR experienced in autumn 1941; Christopher Browning **(1992, p. 121)** highlights the euphoria of military victory typical of the previous July. And yet, whatever the specifics of even the most shattering of policy decisions, sooner or later we encounter the unavoidable fact that the 'radicalized, political desperados' who ran Germany were not operating in a vacuum **(Broszat, 1986, p. 81)**. Their policies both had implications for and made demands of average Germans. Inevitably we have to address the relationship between National Socialism and the German people. In our first document David Welch explains why this also presents a challenge to historians.

Document 1.1 The Riddle

The popular image of German society under Nazi rule is a confusing one, ranging from the adoration of crowds surrounding Hitler and other leading members of the hierarchy, to the bestiality of the concentration camps and fear of the Gestapo. It is a picture which raises questions crucial to our understanding of National Socialism. What, for example, were the respective roles of consent and coercion in sustaining the regime, and what was the nature of that consent? Behind the façade of national unity was there any dissent or even 'resistance', and, if so, was it terror alone that rendered it so ineffective?

Source: D. Welch, The Third Reich, *1993, pp. 2–3*

To what extent and in what ways did Germans conform to or resist Hitler's politics? Here is the heart of this brief study. Our central chapters will discuss themes relating to several elements of German society: the working class, the churches, youth, members of the conservative élites and the Jewish community. Since racial policy was both the most distinctive feature of the Third Reich and raised issues which cut across most social divides, a further chapter is devoted to this in its own right. Naturally, when dealing with a society so very different to any which exists today, we must be sure that we think about it correctly. As a result, our conclusion takes the form of an investigation into what it meant 'to resist' in the Third Reich. Both to pave the way for the study as a whole and to balance the conclusion, it falls to the introductory chapter to investigate the character of Hitler's politics and to begin to explore how something so outlandish by contemporary standards could ever have had any appeal at all.

So what was National Socialism? Characteristically there is no simple answer. Former director of the Institute for Contemporary History in Munich, Martin Broszat, gave the following definition.

Document 1.2 Dynamism

The ideology and the practical political program of the NSDAP [National Socialist German Workers' Party] was from the very beginning not the result of an original, self-sufficient analysis of the present, or a rational proposal of a system for the future. Nazism was never an idea in the sense of intellectual penetration of political, national, social, or even biological conditions. The chain of ideological dissonances and disappointments which marked the party's path from the outset, are only the reflection of these basic logical disagreements in this so-called Nazi interpretation of life. As an ideology, Nazism is therefore basically different from Marxism with its inner logic. The vague, the accidental, and the conscious discrepancy from the time of the establishment of the NSDAP, belong to the characteristic of its presumed ideas. One could rightfully speak of Nazi ideology as a catch-all, a conglomeration, a hodgepodge of ideas. . . . Insofar as one can speak at all of a genesis of the Nazi conglomeration of ideas, it is less understandable from any one intellectual influence than from the conceptions, examples, sentiments, and resentments which began to form the taste of the masses and the intellectual world of the German nationalist bourgeoisie since the second half of the 19th century. . . . The philosophies of Fichte, Hegel, or Nietzsche did not contribute as much to Germany's pre-Hitlerian intellectual background for National Socialism as commemorations of the victory at Sedan (in the Franco-Prussian War), Bismarckian blood-and-iron quotations, the historical novels of Felix Dahn, and mass editions of sentimental 'house and homeland' poets. The bourgeoisie mistook the arrogant nationalism and race teachings of Paul Lagarde, Julius Langbehn, Count Gobineau, Karl Dühring, and Houston Stewart Chamberlain for knowledge of the world. . . .

If one disregards Hitler's anti-Semitic obsession and the two or three notable fixations of his attitude toward the world, one sees that for Hitler ideology was nothing more than slogans. . . . His conception and description of the ideology and the program of the NSDAP consist of clichés which are hardly original. Hitler's real interest, his total concentration and the demoniacal fanaticism of which he was capable were applied, instead, to questions about effectiveness, timeliness, psychological calculations, tactics, organization, and propaganda. Hitler took a position on the details of ideology and the program primarily with reference to considerations of expediency, and not out of theoretical conviction. . . .

Hitler was not very much concerned with the content of this so-called National Socialist idea and ideology, or with its explanation and consolidation, although he naturally assumed that it represented eternal, 'immutable' verities. His chief consideration was the creation of a movement in competition with Marxism, equally unified and fanatical, of the same discipline and submission, and, if possible, of even greater radicalism and aggressiveness. Hitler attempted to make up for the lack of reasoned ideology, such as that found in Marxism, through organization and manipulation. . . .

. . . . Hitler was not primarily a völkisch [radical nationalist] ideologist. What motivated him was not the missionary zeal of a man who wants to spread definite ideological theories as a new way of looking at the world. We have here the fanaticism of pure aggression, which receives its aims and activity from a fixed opponent-anti-dynamicism – without a substance of its own, guided by the expediency of political dogmas and the totalitarian fighting movement. It is, in the final analysis, an uncommitted fanaticism, without content, believing only in its own irresistible momentum.

Here we see the new element in the Nazi movement. The NSDAP formed by Hitler stood ideologically on the shoulders of the middle class, on the pan-German nationalist and the anti-Semitic völkisch sectarians of the prewar period. In style, organization, and propagandistic dynamism it was, however, avant-garde – formed by Hitler, Goebbels, and their helpers who consciously based it on the wartime and revolutionary experiences of the twentieth century. As a type of revolutionary movement, the NSDAP can be put much more easily on the same historical level as Sorel's teaching of 'the use of force' and on French syndicalism. This also influenced Mussolini and fascism. It also parallels the revolutionary theory and practice of Lenin, and is not on the same historical level with the völkisch or conservative nationalists or bourgeoisie. Hitler's true 'idea' lay in the attractiveness of the presentation, the method of campaigning, and the appeal of agitation, all of which made it possible to cover the lack of an intellectual foundation.

Source: M. Broszat, German National Socialism, 1919–1945, *1966, pp. 32–59*

To Broszat's mind, National Socialism was defined not by its ideology, but by its dynamism, its capacity for cynical manipulation, its aggression and its anti-Communism. Although the argument goes too far (see p. 10), there is still something important here. Right from its inception, throughout the Nazi Party there was always a singular expectation that good Nazis should struggle endlessly, by whatever means necessary, to achieve a stunning victory over their political opponents. It is not just chance that Hitler liked to refer to his political party as a 'movement' (*Bewegung*). He was moulding a political force that was to be nothing less than perpetual motion, constant mobilisation and infinite action.

Nor was this principle confined to the period during which the National Socialist Party was trying to win power. Josef Goebbels distinguished himself during the electoral period 1930–2 by his astute manipulation of Nazism's electoral propaganda. Once in power he became Reich Minister for Popular Enlightenment and Propaganda – his definition of the post is in document 1.3.

Document 1.3 Popular Mobilisation

We have established a Ministry for Popular Enlightenment and Propaganda. These two titles do not convey the same thing. Popular enlightenment is essentially something passive; propaganda, on the other hand, is something active. We cannot be satisfied with just telling the people what we want and enlightening them as to how we are doing it. We must replace this enlightenment with an active government propaganda that aims at winning people over. It is not enough to reconcile people more or less to our regime, to move them towards a position of neutrality towards us, we would rather work on people until they are addicted to us.

Source: Speech by Goebbels discussing the tasks of the newly created Ministry for Popular Enlightenment and Propaganda, 15 March 1933, quoted in D. Welch, The Third Reich, *1993, p. 24*

These were no idle words. Organisations such as the German Labour Front (see Chapter 2) and the Hitler Youth (see Chapter 4) were set up and expanded to mobilise the whole German population. So even though National Socialism always dismissed Marxist ideas of class conflict, we have to agree that it was as 'revolutionary' as any other political force in history. Once again looking to Goebbels for an example, six months after Hitler had become Reich Chancellor, his minister made the following comments.

Document 1.4 Goebbels as Revolutionary

The revolution which we have carried out, is a total one. It has gripped all areas of public life and changed them from the foundations up. It has completley altered and formed anew the connections of people to each other, the connections of people to the state and to questions of existence. It was in fact the breakthrough of a fresh ideology [*Weltanschauung*], which had fought for power 14 years long in opposition, that with the help [of political power] gave a new feeling of state to the German Volk [people]. Whatever has happened since 30 January of this year is only the visible expression of this revolutionary process. But the revolution in itself began here. It has been led to its end point only by [its ideology].

... The system which we overthrew, was most deeply characterised in Liberalism [a doctrine of democratic parliamentarianism, economic freedom and individual rights]. If Liberalism was derived from the individual and placed the single person at the centre of everything, then we have replaced the individual by the Volk and the single person by the community. . . . No individual person, whether he stands at the top or bottom [of society], can possess the right to make use of his freedom at the cost of the national concept of freedom. For only the security of the national concept of freedom vouches for the continuation of his personal freedom.

Source: Speech by Goebbels at the opening of the Reich Chamber of Culture, 15 November 1933, Völkischer Beobachter, *16 November 1933*

The National Socialist revolution demanded the abolition of individuality and the subordination of everything to the good of the nation. In practice it meant that the party's bosses claimed absolute power to legislate about and interfere in even the most intimate spheres of a person's life. Odilo Globocnik was regional SS leader for Lublin in Poland during much of the Second World War. In charge of death camps such as Treblinka and Maidanek he played a pivotal role in the implementation of the Holocaust. Even this position did not protect him from the total claims of the movement. On one occasion an anonymous letter was sent to his superior, Reichsführer-SS Himmler, concerning Globocnik's fiancée. The following is an extract from it.

Document 1.5 A Suitable Wife?

A few weeks ago during my stay in Zakopane I had the opportunity to get to know the fiancée of the SS- and Police Leader of Lublin. Due to the conspicuous [and] absolutely impossible behaviour of the guests at one of our neighbouring tables, the attention of several *Luftwaffe* officers (as of myself) was on a girl who was in the company of a lady, a young girl and several junior *Luftwaffe* officers. As it later turned out, it was the fiancée of *SS-Brigadeführer* Globotschnik [sic]. She was strutting around in the public bar without any embarrassment in the most over-the-top way . . . and she was raising the indignation and horror of all of the guests. . . .

Reichsführer, I have learned to consider the SS- and Police Leader of Lublin as someone with every capability, and have considered him as one of the most idealistic and valuable people [in the SS]. From reasons of *pure comradeship* and with utmost loyalty I would like to ask you to consider whether such common women, who undermine the respect of senior SS leaders by their behaviour in public, are worthy of being engaged to such senior leaders.

Source: Extract from an anonymous letter to Reichsführer-SS Himmler, dated 10 April 1942, Globocnik file, Federal Archive, Berlin-Zehlendorf

Since everyone in the SS was supposed to have future spouses thoroughly vetted, and notwithstanding the fact that Germany was in the third year of war, Himmler made time to take up the matter personally. After an initial exchange of letters with Globocnik, he wrote to his official as follows.

Document 1.6 The Agony Aunt

You question whether your fiancée actually did go into a café with other men. If she did, then break off the engagement.

Be clear that the youth of your fiancée excuses her of no blame what-soever. If the girl is not ready [for marriage] because of her youth, then it could happen that while you would be getting on with your heavy workload (during which time you could hardly worry about your wife) she would disappoint you constantly. Don't take offence at what I have to say – in the end she might even deceive you. Instead of being something to strengthen you, your marriage would be a burden. And worst of all, the time could come when you would begin to doubt whether your children really were your own.

You also write in your letter that you have been told about the story from the other side [i.e., by the fiancée]. From that fact alone, I gather that the warning in the [original] letter really is to be taken rather seriously.

On the whole I can only advise you to break off the engagement.

Source: Extract of a letter from Reichsführer-SS Himmler to Globocnik, 11 September 1942, Federal Archive, Berlin-Zehlendorf

The engagement was broken off and a little later Globocnik married someone else.

It was entirely in keeping with its revolutionary, all-embracing character that National Socialism turned the Third Reich into a true terrorist dictatorship. In the light of the last document, we can readily understand why many people lived in fear that the regime might learn of something (no matter how trivial, no matter whether exactly true) which might cause them to be identified not only as needing marriage guidance, but as a political opponent. Historian W.S. Allen explains how this fear began to affect the way people related to each other in one town.

Document 1.7 Fear and Social Fragmentation

[I]t seems clear that the public in Northeim had a good idea by mid-summer 1933, that even to express oneself against the new system was to invite persecution. In fact, not only were the Northeimers aware of this situation, but by their very awareness they reinforced the actual terror apparatus. Every time someone in Northeim cautioned his neighbour or friend, he was strengthening the general atmosphere of fear.

This happened frequently. A teacher remembered that the mother of one of his pupils complained about the book burning. He agreed with her but also warned her not to try to tell other people, lest she got into trouble. The principal of the high school remembers that he used to buy cigars at a certain store and along with the cigars usually received advice to be careful. The general feeling was that the Gestapo [secret state police] was everywhere. At least five people were identified as being 'Gestapo agents', though in point of fact there was probably only one for the whole town, Hermann Denzler, and that was considerably later. . . .

Thus the Gestapo became extraordinarily efficient by reason of rumours and fears. . . . Given the atmosphere of terror, even people who were friends felt that they must betray each other in order to survive. Thus very early in 1933 there was a case of a Dr Kuno Ruhmann who went to a party and, after one drink too many, sought to entertain people by imitating Hitler's way of speaking. The next morning his hostess reported him to Nazi head-quarters. Word of this spread quickly and soon Northeimers saw that it was better not to go to parties at all. 'Social life was cut down enormously – you couldn't trust anyone any more' [said one townsperson].

Source: W.S. Allen, The Nazi Seizure of Power, *1989, pp. 188–9*

People began to fear that the 'tentacles of the police octopus' ran throughout their communities **(Höhne, 1981, p. 2)**.

The methods used by National Socialism against suspected political opponents were always barbaric. During the Second World War, a secret directive was circulated by the chief of the Gestapo outlining the 'acceptable' methods that interrogators could use.

Document 1.8 Torture by Numbers

1 The sharpened interrogation may only be applied if, on the strength of the preliminary interrogation, it has been ascertained that the prisoner can give information about important facts, connections or plans hostile to

the state or the legal system, but does not want to reveal this knowledge, and the latter cannot be obtained by way of inquiries.

2 Under this circumstance, the sharpened interrogation may be applied only against Communists, Marxists, members of the Bible-researcher sect, saboteurs, terrorists, members of the resistance movement, parachute agents, asocial persons, Polish or Soviet persons who refuse to work, or idlers.

3 The sharpened interrogation may not be applied in order to induce confessions about a person's own criminal acts. Nor may this means be applied toward persons who have been temporarily delivered by justice for the purpose of further investigation.

Once more, exceptions require my previous permission.

4 The sharpening can consist of the following, among other things, according to circumstances:

> simplest rations (bread and water)
> hard bed
> dark cell
> deprivation of sleep
> exhaustion exercises,
> but also the resort to blows with a stick (in the case of more than 20 blows, a doctor must be present).

Source: Secret directive by Gestapo chief Müller of 12 June 1942 regulating 'sharpened interrogation', quoted in H.A. Jacobsen (ed.), Germans Against Hitler, *1969, p. 190*

The very idea of someone sitting down calmly and clinically to put on paper such a set of 'guidelines' is chilling in itself. It also indicates that the true reality of interrogation was often much worse. Document 2.6 (p. 28) shows what could happen even in 1933 when a Communist was picked up by the paramilitary wing of the NSDAP, the SA.

From the very first weeks of the Third Reich, a nationwide system of concentration camps, staffed by party radicals, sprang up across the nation. By late July 1933 the Rhineland alone had 27,000 people in so-called 'protective custody' **(Kolb, 1983, pp. 272–7)**. Conditions in these places were all but indescribable. Deaths of prisoners became so obvious that within months the Bavarian Minister of Justice Hans Frank, himself a National Socialist of long-standing and who in due course became a Reich Minister, felt compelled to launch an investigation into what was going on inside one of the most notorious camps which lay near Munich, namely Dachau. Under wartime conditions, the system of camps was expanded further still. By August 1944, 524,286 people were interned. Of these 145,119 were women and just a few words from one of their female guards says it all.

Document 1.9 The Advantage of Whipping

During my activity as block leader of block 27 in Ravensbrück now and again I had to beat prisoners with my whip. I always only gave them one or two lashes with the whip. I could not hit the internees with my hands because they were covered in lice. . . .

Source: A. Ebbinghaus (ed.), Opfer und Täterinnen, *1987, p. 292*

In practice, and despite what section 3 in document 1.8 says, often a prime aim of both interrogation and internment was to make an individual confess to wrong-doing. In the Third Reich, even the act of admission could take on a particularly inhuman form.

Document 1.10 Not so 'Glad to be Gay'

I admit the following:

'In April 1933 . . . knowing full well what I was doing, I turned to a businessman called Böll with whom I was acquainted. I knew that he personally employed a [male servant] and asked him to find me a trustworthy one. I did this because at an earlier time Böll had already advised me to take on a servant. In this connection Böll explained in general terms that really, at the end of the day, all servants were homosexual and left it open whether Jäger would be similarly inclined.

'In the middle of May 1933 Jäger was introduced to me in Böll's apartment and I engaged him from 1.6.33. At this time I still did not know about Jäger's abnormal tendency. In any case, soon after he took up the post I became clear about his inclination. What led me to this conclusion cannot be put into words. You simply felt something which cannot really be expressed verbally.

'About 14 days after Jäger took up his post, the first sexual acts took place between him and me. . . . I admit candidly, however, that the full conditions of §175 of the Reich Statute Book were fulfilled in individual cases. [Homosexuality was illegal in the Third Reich.] What is more, I admit that in one case anal intercourse took place. This intercourse took place in my bed. . . . We were both undressed during the intercourse itself. . . .

'Furthermore I admit that on repeated occasions oral intercourse was carried out between Jäger and me. Each time it happened in my bed. . . . I cannot say how many times this type of intercourse took place between us, but altogether it may not have happened more often than at most 10 times. . . . The last sexual intercourse with Jäger took place in August 1934. The last time we got together, the sexual act happened once again in the form of oral sex. . . . [The confession is extremely explicit and has been cut heavily.]

'As regards the Krebs case, I admit in addition to my statement of yesterday that I met him in a homosexual pub and that I carried out sexual relations with him repeatedly. I can no longer remember the precise details of the intercourse with Krebs, but still admit the possibility that in one or other case the conditions of § 175 of the Reich Statute Book were fulfilled completely. As I also made known yesterday, I had sexual intercourse with perhaps three other men who were unknown to me. In these cases it was a question of so called "rent boys" who I got to know in different homosexual pubs. I paid the youths 10 RM each time. I cannot tell [you] either the names of the men or the pubs. I admit candidly that also in each of these cases the conditions of §175 were fully fulfilled.

'I had never had homosexual intercourse before the middle of 1932. . . . Since the start of 1933 I have no longer visited homosexual pubs, and have not been a homosexual. I am just as little homosexually inclined. This really is shown best of all by the fact that I have had sexual intercourse with women at every opportunity and have been engaged to be married for several months too. Since my engagement I have not had homosexual intercourse. . . .'

Source: Admission following SS interrogation, 'Author's collection' of documents

It would be sufficiently inhuman if this person was only having to detail so minutely so private an aspect of his life to total strangers. In fact there is every likelihood that he was never even homosexual. An acquaintance later admitted making false accusations to the police while himself under interrogation. In any event, what can the effect of having to make such a confession have been on any individual? National Socialism was irreducibly inhuman and intolerant.

What was the political purpose behind all of this activism and enforced suffering? Increasingly historians are understanding National Socialist ideology differently to Broszat. As a Marxist, originally Tim Mason believed economic and class forces should be of prime importance to the historian. But in a study published posthumously he admitted, rather sadly, that economics could not in fact take you to the core of National Socialism and the Third Reich.

Document 1.11   Racialism

It is becoming increasingly clear that the regime set out violently to reconstitute 'German' society on a biological basis. So numerous and so ruthless were the eugenic interventions and propaganda in this respect that Nazi social policy needs to be understood as 'social racism'. . . . In its implications, this project transcended (though it included) my emphasis on the abolition of class conflict. The creation of an organic 'purified' Volk called for an increasingly radical and comprehensive discrimination between 'fit' and 'unfit', which soon led from the persecution to the physical elimination of many of the latter, especially of the mentally ill. These were measures of everyday life, openly discussed and, euthanasia excepted, openly enacted. They must have resonated through all classes of German society. Beginning with the decisive step of the compulsory sterilization of those suffering from supposedly hereditary diseases in 1933, the regime proceeded to stigmatize and persecute a vast assortment of so-called 'anti-social elements and parasites' on the grounds that their economic costs, their disutility and their 'racial' danger to the community were biologically determined and thus irredeemable. Charity, except towards the deserving poor, was perniciously sentimental and unscientific. Tramps and vagabonds, alcoholics (as long as they were not leading Nazis), homosexuals, the 'work shy' and habitual law-breakers were all under the arbitrary jurisdiction of the Gestapo and the camps by the late 1930s; mulattoes were sterilized; especially vicious was the stigmatization, sterilization and then extermination of the Gypsies, who were designated as hereditarily criminal. Doctors and health administrators were especially fervent advocates of this pseudo-scientific eugenic cleansing, the culmination of which came with the euthanasia actions of the early war years. But even all this was not clear and rigorous enough. During the war the identity of the person who was 'alien-to-the-community' (*gemeinschaftsfremd*) was being worked out as a comprehensive political–eugenic *legal* category: this piece of quasi-constitutional legislation would have defined systematically all the people to be excluded from the 'national community', discriminated against and persecuted. All of this was vigorously and publicly advocated in the 1930s by the Nazi Welfare Organization (NSV), which demanded that 'degenerates' should not be assisted at all, 'worthless' lives should be liquidated, and that the goal of all policy should be to help the fit to become fitter and more numerous. This was not mere rhetoric; it filtered down well before the war into specific acts of eugenic persecution against individuals and families in relatively isolated industrial towns.

The dimension of biologically based social racism is of vital importance for two reasons. First it shows the deep and broad political, ideological and administrative roots of what became the genocidal 'New Order' in Europe. There were competing schools of racist eugenics, but together they made up an irreducible core and a central continuity of Nazi politics. Race-thinking and racial policies in the widest sense were to be the foundation, or goal, of a new social order on a national and continental scale. . . . Second, Nazi eugenics erected a positive stereotype of the useful, worthy member of the community, which carried powerful pseudo-moral overtones. The physically and mentally fit not only possessed an intrinsic biological value (of which the propagandists were certainly more conscious than the people themselves), but they were productive, diligent and dutiful, and thus good potential political material if they could be made aware of their superior worth. Only they, it was incessantly suggested, could contribute – by their work, by their fecundity in the case of healthy women – to the creation of a race/society which was efficient and organically harmonious; efficient on account of its organic harmony.

Source: T.W. Mason, Social Policy in the Third Reich, *1993, pp. 279–80*

National Socialism was specifically an ideologically-oriented, racialist movement. In 1928, writing in his *Second Book*, Adolf Hitler characterised domestic politics in the most unambiguous of terms **(Weinberg, 1961)**. It was said to be 'the art of preserving for the people the basis of [its] power in the form of its racial value and its numbers' **(Schewick, 1980, p. 83)**. Germany's Jews were always going to be the prime victims of this vision as the following remarks, made by Hitler as early as 1922, show.

Document 1.12 Racism at Home

As soon as I have the power, I shall have gallows after gallows erected, for example in Munich on the Marienplatz. . . . Then the Jews will be hanged one after another, and they will stay hanging until they stink. They will stay hanging as long as hygienically possible. As soon as they are untied, then the next group will follow and that will continue until the last Jew in Munich is exterminated. Exactly the same procedure will be followed in other cities until Germany is cleansed of the last Jew!

Source: Quoted in R.G.L. Waite, The Psychopathic God, *1993, p. 363*

Although this was said in private to an acquaintance, in public during the early 1920s Hitler was speaking on themes such as 'Why we are against the Jews' **(Jäckel, 1981, p. 50)**. During the same period, in Salzburg, quite openly he likened Germany's Jews to a disease poisoning the national body politic which needed to be eradicated **(Irving, 1983, p. xxi)**.

Hitler's racialism spilled over easily into foreign policy. Once again referring to his *Second Book*, this was defined as 'the art of securing for a people the living space it needs at a given time in terms of size and resources' **(Schewick, 1980, p. 83)**. The scale of the space envisaged, some 500,000 square kilometres, implied it could only be achieved by war **(Weinberg, 1995, p. 35)**. What was to happen to the non-Germans living in the lands to be seized? From the early 1930s Hitler was sketching the most radical of possibilities to his closest entourage.

Document 1.13 Racism Abroad

'*We are obliged to depopulate*', he went on emphatically, 'as part of our mission of preserving the German population. We shall have to develop a technique of depopulation. If you ask me what I mean by depopulation, I mean the removal of entire racial units. And that is what I intend to carry out – that, roughly, is my task. Nature is cruel, therefore we, too, may be cruel. If I can send the flower of the German nation into the hell of war without the smallest pity for the spilling of precious German blood, then surely I have the right to remove millions of an inferior race that breeds like vermin! And by "remove" I don't necessarily mean destroy; I shall simply take systematic measures to dam their great natural fertility. For example I shall keep their men and women separated for years. Do you remember the falling birth-rate of the world war? Why should we not do quite consciously and through a number of years what was at that time merely the inevitable consequence of the long war? There are many ways, systematical and comparatively painless, or at any rate bloodless, of causing undesirable races to die out.'

Source: Hitler during the period 1932–4, quoted in H. Rauschning, Hitler Speaks, *1939, p. 140*

From every perspective, National Socialism was the ultimate extremist political movement. Highly dynamic, it demanded the most complete control over the individual, was prepared to take the most extreme steps against anyone it perceived as an opponent and, as we can recognise today, encapsulated the most vile, racialist political ends. Herein lay the moving principles of National Socialism and the system of state and government we call the Third Reich.

Why on earth did any German offer the slightest support to such a form of politics? Why did anyone decide to conform to its demands in any way at all? Certainly terror did intimidate very many people, and yet we have to beware of overemphasising its role. Historian Eberhard Jäckel makes the point well.

Document 1.14 The Limits of Terror

It must . . . be stressed once again that Hitler's dictatorship over the Germans in no way only and at no time predominantly rested on terror. Since 1945 this side of the regime has happily been overemphasised for understandable reasons. Not even crimes can be explained in this way. As a rule criminal orders were not followed because of force, seldom what's more, because of the desire to commit a crime, but rather mostly for the sake of obedience, blindness or for some additional kind of advantage. No case is known in which anyone endangered his life or even suffered just serious disadvantages if he refused to participate in a crime, perhaps in the murder of defenceless people [see document 1.21, p. 19]. Likewise membership of the NSDAP, which today for the most part is unrecognised or kept secret, was a decoration which promised advantage and which was forced on nobody, not even really on an unreliable person [as a means of proving his or her reliability]. By contrast party membership was often taken away again. So why the Germans behaved as they did under and towards Hitler, and how they did it cannot be explained by terror (apart from in the case of those who were persecuted).

Source: E. Jäckel, 'Hitler und die Deutschen', 1983, p. 712

In July 1932, almost 40 per cent of the population voted for Hitler of their own accord. Once the Third Reich was established, millions joined the party and its affiliated organisations. The nation managed to wage a colossal war against much of the rest of the world for several years. All of this cannot be explained as through terror alone. So what can we say about the other forces which might have encouraged Germans to work alongside National Socialism?

The most emotive issue is that of racialism. Were many Germans drawn to Hitler because they shared this prejudice? At least some people did take up the racial crusade with an enthusiasm which could only have been born of true belief (see document 7.9, p. 148), but how typical were they? Once again referring to W.S. Allen's study of Northeim we find one answer.

Document 1.15 The Civilised Side of Prejudice

Social discrimination against Jews was practically nonexistent in the town. Jews were integrated along class lines: the two wealthy Jewish families belonged to upper-class circles and clubs, Jews of middling income belonged to the middle-class social organizations, and working-class Jews were in the Socialist community. Yet abstract anti-Semitism in the form of jokes or expressions of generalized distaste was prevalent, approximately to the extent that these things existed in America in the 1930s. . . . Northeimers were drawn to anti-Semitism because they were drawn to Nazism, not the other way around. Many who voted Nazi simply ignored or rationalized the anti-Semitism of the party, just as they ignored other unpleasant aspects of the Nazi movement.

Source: W.S. Allen, The Nazi Seizure of Power, *1989, pp. 84–6*

The argument finds support in Peter Merkl's analysis of why long-standing Nazis joined the party. Fewer than 20 per cent of his sample of 'old guard' members showed signs of being truly radical anti-Semites. Although the views of the others could be classified as either 'moderately' or 'mildly' anti-Semitic, they did not demand the active persecution of their country's Jews **(quoted in Gordon, 1984, p. 56)**. One of the paradoxes of history is that people supported this most radical of racial movements for reasons that involved more than simply racism.

So where else should we look for the movement's mass appeal? Since the mid-nineteenth century, German society had been undergoing profound changes. The industrialisation and concomitant modernisation of the country involved, among other things, the creation of ever more massed and ever better organised labour forces. The burgeoning working class increasingly seemed to pose a threat to the traditional power and prestige of the middle classes. The situation reached a crisis point during the Depression years following 1929. By 1932, there were 6 million unemployed. Under the extreme conditions, people from all walks of life were left feeling more vulnerable than ever. Workers generally looked to the German Communist or Socialist Parties to solve their problems. Together these won between 36 and 40 per cent of the votes cast in national elections between 1928 and 1932. Members of the middle classes, however, looked in disproportionate numbers to National Socialism to solve their problems. The trends are reflected in the Nazi Party's membership statistics. In the early 1930s, workers comprised 45.9 per cent of the German population, but only 28 per cent of Hitler's party. By contrast, white-collar workers made up only 12 per cent of society, but 25.6 per cent of party members. For self-employed people the statistics were, respectively, 9 per cent and 20.7 per cent; for civil servants 5.1 per cent and 8.3 per cent **(Taylor, 1985, p. 19)**. The fears of the middle classes which lay behind the numbers and historical processes are explained by one of Northeim's citizens in document 1.16.

Document 1.16 Fear of Communism

I came to Northeim in 1925 from Berlin, where I had lived for thirty years and where I returned for a few weeks during my vacation every year. I observed many things in Berlin which could not be noticed – or only to a lesser degree – in small towns. I saw the Communist danger, the Communist terror, their gangs breaking up 'bourgeois' meetings, the 'bourgeois' parties being utterly helpless, the Nazis being the only party that broke terror by anti-terror. I saw the complete failure of the 'bourgeois' parties to deal with the economic crisis (6 to 7 millions out of work, the Reichsbank discount up to 15 per cent). Only national socialism offered any hope.

Source: W.S. Allen, The Nazi Seizure of Power, *1989, pp. 84–6*

Nor was support for National Socialism only an urban phenomenon. It drew weighty electoral support in some rural areas adversely affected by the disastrous economic climate. Traditionally much of village life had been typified by mutual help and a genuine sense of community. Mounting financial hardship changed all of this. Between 1927 and 1932, 27,000 farms throughout Germany were sold **(Grunberger, 1983, p. 22)**. The tougher things got, the less easy it was for farmers to find time to help each other. As different types of farms were hit to differing degrees, the more obvious became the differences between rich and poor. Village life began to fragment. Historians Wagner and Wilke, who have studied life in the village of Körle in Hesse, believe National Socialism was able to turn all of these growing problems to its advantage by applying its revolutionary ideology, in which notions of blood, land and national unity all played important parts.

Document 1.17 Village Communities

The 'victory train' [of the NSDAP] had deep roots [in the local community] and is to be explained in one respect through the organisational 'renewals', which the party brought into village life, and the fact that the ideology of the National Socialist movement drew extensively on the elements of the ideals which predominated in the village about a united community. The same ideas were now being implemented in another form, by other people and with an altered orientation.

While the older generation which had a conservative orientation saw the solution to the conflicts and problems – economic crisis, maintenance of the family farm, loss of authority, loss of social status, etc. – as guaranteed only through a return to the *Kaiserreich*, the ideas of the National Socialists, that these problems were only to be solved in a 'new social order', found fertile ground among the younger generation of cow and horse farmers. . . .

The values of village society and of the household were made by the National Socialists into the central momentum of their ideology.

Source: K. Wagner and G. Wilke, 'Dorfleben im Dritten Reich', 1981, pp. 92–4

Under the circumstances we can appreciate that campaign posters such as the one shown on p. 17 would have had a particular appeal in the countryside. The woman has a rustic style headscarf and the man could just have come in from working in the fields. The top slogan reads, 'The NSDAP is securing the National Community'; the bottom one says 'National comrades, if you need advice and help, go to your local [NSDAP] branch'.

Document 1.18 Rural Idyll

[See illustration on facing page]

National Socialism was promising the reparation of the village community and the creation of an idyllic rural life.

As the young people of Körle recognised, and as we should expect of a truly revolutionary party, the prospect was never just of 'setting the clock back'. Individuals could find in National Socialism a means to breaking all manner of traditional shackles. For some people it provided a gateway to greater personal fulfilment. In due course Hitler's movement certainly implemented a number of policies at odds with the advancement of women in society **(see Burleigh and Wippermann, 1991, ch. 8; also Bock, 1986)**, but this was not the entire picture, as historian Claudia Koonz shows.

Document 1.19 Personal Fulfilment

A housewife speaking to apathetic passersby on a street corner, was confronted by an outraged businessman. As a good Nazi woman, he said, she ought to be home serving dinner to her family. Sneering at this 'bourgeois heckler', she retorted, 'The nation is in peril! I cannot remain happy and carefree at the suppertable when Mother Germany weeps and her

Source: Wiener Library, London

children die. Germany must live on, even if we sacrifice our lives!' . . . The Nazi movement, like a religious crusade, imparted a crisis mentality to its adherents and empowered them to behave in new ways. While claiming to care only for the community, they discovered their individuality and exercised broad influence within their own milieu. An account by a former SA man [Stormtrooper] shows how women shared a sense of danger with the men. 'I would like to say a word which will tell you something about the National Socialist spirit of our women. We were not allowed to carry weapons, and when the police showed up, they could not find any on our bodies. The weapons had all fallen under the skirts of the women present. My mother alone had six of those things inside her clothes.' . . .

These autobiographical sketches testify to women's discovery of selfworth and faith. . . . In the service of this selfless crusade, Hitler's followers discovered their selfhood. Hundreds of thousands of 'nobodies' began to feel like 'somebodies'.

Source: C. Koonz, Mothers in the Fatherland, *1987, pp. 78–9*

Once in power, National Socialism began to reshape the country. The process offered extensive opportunities to all manner of Germans. There was a major drive to overcome unemployment through programmes of public works. Also, the army was expanded massively from 100,000 men in 1933 to 1.4 million by 1939. As a result, joblessness became a thing of the past. But the opportunities offered in the Third Reich involved changes of quality too, as the following statistics concerning the army and SS show. In 1920, 61 per cent of generals came from aristocratic families; by 1936 the figure was only 25 per cent. During the Second World War, twenty-one out of twenty-six colonel-generals and 140 out of 166 infantry generals were middle, not upper, class **(Grunberger, 1983, p. 182)**. New, party-based institutions took on considerable significance in society and came to offer their own kinds of opportunities. While at the start of the Second World War 50 per cent of junior army officers still came from traditional 'military families', only 5 per cent of comparable SS officers did. Likewise, only two in five SS officers had passed their final school examinations **(Grunberger, 1983, p. 181)**. In other words, appointments to important positions less than ever were decided according to traditional criteria such as family background and educational qualifications. More important became commitment to Hitler's politics. Here was an important and popularist incentive to conform to the demands of the Third Reich.

National Socialism, then, offered solutions to economic and personal frustrations. It promised an harmonious society and delivered substantial opportunities. In short it appealed in ways which we can readily understand even today – which in some respects we might even consider 'normal'. Historians have been able to trace normality to the most inhuman areas of the Third Reich. Consider the following extract from a police report which explains why one individual denounced another.

Document 1.20 Personal Vendetta

36th Police District, Hamburg, 21 September '42. Female armaments worker M. arrested for the Gestapo . . . on account of breach of labour contract and on account of prostitution [prostitution was illegal in the Third Reich].

On 21.9.42 at around 22.30 the ship's stoker V (who lives in Hamburg 6 . . .) appeared in the 36th police district and reported that in the pub 'Grenzhaus', Reeperbahn 163, he saw a woman who the Gestapo were looking for, and from whom he had got a sexual illness. The 36th district sent an officer at once to the named bar. He brought the identified armaments worker M. (born 1910 in Hamburg, currently without an address) into the 36th Police district. She was sober. An inquiry at the police record department showed that the armaments worker M. was sought by the Gestapo . . . for breach of labour contract and also on account of suspicion of sexual illness by [department] 22.K. Upon arrest the accused M. made the following written statement.

'I haven't been working for the past 9 weeks because I earned too little. During this time I practised prostitution. I did not know that I had a sexual illness. I have still not noticed any sign of it. I had the intention of settling in a brothel and going on with prostitution. I do not have an apartment.'

Read by herself and found to be correct. Signed, M.

Witnessed with the remark that the accused M. was imprisoned for the Gestapo and 22.K. . . .

Source: Police report in A. Ebbinghaus (ed.), Opfer und Täterinnen, *1987, p. 91*

By helping the Gestapo in the enforcement of anti-prostitution laws, the stoker was conforming to the demands of National Socialism, but why? There is no sign that he supported the government for political reasons. It is more likely that he was simply 'getting back' at the woman for giving him a sexual disease. In this case, conformity was born of a rather understandable personal vendetta.

There are even 'normal' perspectives on the Holocaust. When he wrote about a mobile killing unit which toured Poland shooting Jews, Christopher Browning called his study *Ordinary Men*. He tried to account for the behaviour of these individuals in the following way.

Document 1.21 The Decision to Shoot

80 to 90 per cent of the men proceeded to kill, though almost all of them were horrified and disgusted by what they were doing. To break ranks and step out, to adopt overtly nonconformist behaviour, was simply beyond most of the men. It was easier for them to shoot.

Why? First of all, by breaking ranks, nonshooters were leaving the 'dirty work' to their comrades. Since the battalion had to shoot even if individuals did not, refusing to shoot constituted refusing one's share of an unpleasant collective obligation. It was in effect an asocial act vis-à-vis one's comrades. Those who did not shoot risked isolation, rejection, and ostracism – a very uncomfortable prospect within the framework of a tight-knit unit stationed abroad among a hostile population, so that the individual had virtually nowhere else to turn for support and social contact.

This threat of isolation was intensified by the fact that stepping out could also have been seen as a form of moral reproach of one's comrades: the non-shooter was potentially indicating that he was 'too good' to do such things. Most, though not all, nonshooters intuitively tried to diffuse the criticism of their comrades that was inherent in their actions. They pleaded not that they were 'too good' but rather that they were 'too weak' to kill.

Such a stance presented no challenge to the esteem of one's comrades; on the contrary, it legitimized and upheld 'toughness' as a superior quality. For the anxious individual, it had the added advantage of posing no moral challenge to the murderous policies of the regime, though it did pose another problem, since the difference between being 'weak' and being a 'coward' was not great. Hence the distinction made by one policeman who did not dare step out at Jósefów for fear of being a 'coward' but who subsequently dropped out of his firing squad. It was one thing to be too cowardly even to try to kill; it was another, after resolutely trying to do one's share, to be too weak to continue.

Insidiously, therefore, most of those who did not shoot only reaffirmed the 'macho' values of the majority – according to which it was a positive quality to be 'tough' enough to kill unarmed, noncombatant men, women and children – and tried not to rupture the bonds of comradeship that constituted their social world.

Source: C. Browning, Ordinary Men, *1993, pp. 184–5*

The killers conformed, it is said, due to the very normal characteristics of machismo and peer pressure.

Some historians have welcomed this ability to find normality in the history of the Third Reich. As Martin Broszat put it, the '"normalization" of our historical consciousness cannot in the long run exclude the Nazi period, nor can it succeed in bypassing it' **(Broszat, 1990, p. 87)**. But how far should we take the argument? Are we beginning to imply that conformity to the demands of National Socialism really was nothing other than 'normal'? While 'ordinary' social and psychological factors surely did play a part, they leave something missing. The point remains that it is far from 'normal' for people either to solve their problems through an alliance with such a dreadful political movement or to carry out the horrific crimes committed. Talking of specifically the Jewish Question, former Chancellor of West Germany, Willy Brandt, made the following comments.

Document 1.22 Good Neighbours

Still, the question is this: what prevented, what hindered those who had gone to school with Jewish neighbors, who had worked with them in offices, schools, factories and hospitals, who had spent leisure time with them in coffeehouses or at the '*Stammtisch*' [regular table in the local pub], what kept them from standing up for their friends and neighbors of Jewish faith?

Were they, were we all, so 'ill equipped' . . . [to withstand the onslaught of National Socialism]? . . . Anti-Semitism was both overt and covert in Sonderburg. The normal thing to do was to get along with one another, to live and let live. When does this principle turn into 'minding one's own business'? At what point does laissez-faire turn into indifference, indifference into disrespect?

If history proves anything it is that too few people made conscious choices against evil. If there is any lesson to be learned from the extermination of millions of Jews, it is that decent men and women learn to make choices in favor of the good, and to do this before criminal power is established and gets stabilized. It is the one lesson history must teach, so that it does not repeat itself.

Source: W. Brandt, 'Foreword', 1984, pp. vii–viii

Even Christopher Browning's 'ordinary men' had consciences they should have heard. In the final analysis, when we try to explain why people conformed to National Socialism, we are grappling with something that remains abnormal, something that we are still in the process of trying to understand. It is a topic we will return to time and again throughout the book.

We should end this chapter by referring to Willy Brandt's final paragraph. Decent people should make choices for good. In the context of the Third Reich, this meant not conforming to but trying to oppose the government. Is it true, in all circumstances and in all ways, that in Germany at this time 'too few people made conscious choices against evil'? And what were the sources in society that might have supported anyone considering taking such a stand? The discussion in the next six chapters takes its structure from the potential social forces supportive of opposition that existed at this time.

Chapter Structure

Possible sources of support for opposition to the Third Reich	Chapter
Left-wing politics	The workers: class action?
Christian morality	The churches: opposition born of belief?
Teenage rebellion against authority	Youth: rebels for which cause?

Traditional values

Conservative élites: successful opposition from the men of 20 July?

People who were defined by the regime as its opponents

Germany's Jewish citizens: like lambs to the slaughter?

Widespread rejection of extreme anti-Semitism

Exploring the inexplicable: what was the relationship between ordinary Germans and racial policy?

The government of the Third Reich could never ignore the German workers. They accounted for 40.3 per cent of people living in Bavaria in 1933, for instance **(Kershaw, 1983, p. 66)**. Hitler knew that he needed such a large proportion of the population on his side, as can be seen from the statement he made to a government meeting just six months after the seizure of power.

Document 2.1 Trust

The people, you see, will be the decisive factor. They must believe in us with such unquestioning trust that, even if an obvious mistake were actually made, they would never dream of the consequences; rather they would swallow defeat like a well-trained army and say: 'Let's have another go at them and this time pay them back with interest.' That is the attitude we need in order to get out of a dreadful situation. Otherwise we would be stuck there forever.

A people has to be taught to march through thick and thin with its government, it must be instantly susceptible to every psychological factor, able to be whipped into a frenzy, and be inspired and roused. If this is not possible, then all our efforts will be in vain, we will be forced to surrender.

Source: Hitler to the General Council on the Economy, 30 September 1933, quoted in T.W. Mason, Social Policy in the Third Reich, *1993, pp. 179–80*

Factory workers would have to produce the armaments Hitler wanted. Working men would be his soldiers. Their loyalty was imperative. As one author has put it, ideally these people were expected to become a mass of 'heroic robots' **(Allen, 1985, pp. 860–1)**. But as indicated already (pp. 14–15), they were often less than obvious allies for the new government.

It was not just luck that during the Weimar period the workers had given their most weighty support not to the National Socialist German Workers' Party (NSDAP) but to the German Communist Party (KPD) and the German Socialist Party (SPD). In the 1930 Reichstag elections, the SPD had captured 24.5 per cent of the national vote and the KPD 13.1; in the November 1932 elections they won 20.4 and 16.9 per cent respectively. Outside Russia, the German labour movement was the largest in the world **(Peukert, 1991, p. 40)**. In 1933 its long and proud tradition presented a real obstacle to Hitler's aims. How, then, did the German workers face up to the new National Socialist regime?

An objective assessment of the KPD's actions faces particular problems. Historians writing in the former East Germany (GDR), for example, took it as an article of faith that the German Communists always formed the very centre of all significant resistance efforts against National Socialism.

Document 2.2 The KPD and the GDR

In the battle against German imperialism and militarism which developed during the November Revolution of 1918, the KPD, as the champion of the German working class, represented the interests of the working people constantly and consistently. At any given time it acted in the spirit of proletarian internationalism, proved itself to be a faithful ally of the Communist Party of the Soviet Union and of the Soviet Union, and to be a reliable part of the revolutionary world movement. . . .

Under the leadership of the SED [German Socialist Unity Party], which incorporates all the revolutionary traditions of the German workers' movements, the goals of the anti-fascist resistance movement were realised in the GDR in full measure. The ideals and the legacy of this battle are fostered in the socialist GDR and all people, in particular the young, are entrusted with the history of anti-fascist resistance. . . .

Led by the KPD, the working class was the main social force in the anti-fascist battle. The most active and the most deliberate fighters against the fascist dictatorship came from its ranks. They gave character to the fight for a new, democratic, anti-imperial order and influenced the most diverse orientations and oppositional groupings of the anti-fascist resistance movement. Bit by bit, anti-fascists and Hitler-opponents from different classes and [social] strata joined in.

Source: M. Pikarski and G. Uebel, Der Antifaschistische Widerstandskampf der KPD im Spiegel des Flugblattes 1933–1945, *1978, pp. 5–12*

The book was published by the Institute for Marxism–Leninism of the Central Committee of the SED and a very obvious political agenda was at work here. The authors were trying to trace a direct line from the German revolution of 1918 to the KPD, the resistance to the Third Reich undertaken by it and then to the governing party of the GDR (i.e., the SED). The aim was to legitimise East Germany's Marxist political system and the nation's close ties to the Soviet Union. So was the KPD really at the very centre of working-class (let alone national) opposition to the Third Reich?

When the NSDAP came to power, the KPD expected the working class to mobilise against the new government. Party functionaries debated what form this should take. The following document is a description by two historians of a KPD meeting in Bremen. The minuted views of some of the Communists present are quoted directly.

Document 2.3 Strike or Coup?

[Among members of the KPD, in early 1933 the] . . . feeling still predominated that the position could be mastered, as for instance the words of functionary Wilhelm Beyes show:

'The fascists are powerless if the entire working class rebels against the present system. The SPD workers and the trades union members must be made aware of the danger which is threatening [them]. . . . Only in this way, with all of the comrades at their posts, can the return of [another] 20 July be prevented.' [On 20 July 1932 Reich Chancellor von Papen had taken up emergency powers in Prussia.]

Oskar Eichentopf argued on the other hand, as did various other functionaries, in favour of armed struggle:

'The KPD must show the bourgeoisie that it is willing to fight. Everyone must have overcome the fear of death long ago. It's no pity if a comrade is shot since he has nothing to lose. Wherever a comrade would be shot, 100 [more] would appear in his place. If the fight is led courageously, it will have to succeed in overrunning the police and the SA. If a few Communists are killed in the process, it doesn't really matter.'

Source: I. Marßolek and R. Ott, Bremen im Dritten Reich, *1986, p. 106*

Was it to be a mass uprising by the whole of the working class, or an armed coup?

Taking the option of mass working-class action first, Communist newspapers such as the *Ruhr Echo* did call all workers on to the streets as the Nazis seized power. Certainly there were no small number of popular anti-Nazi demonstrations on the night of 30 January, for example, in towns throughout the Ruhr such as Düsseldorf, Dortmund, Cologne, Solingen and Bochum. Unfortunately for the KPD, not only were these dealt with easily by the police, but also it seems that they were more the result of genuinely spontaneous anti-Nazi feeling than specifically Communist instigation. In fact, we have to question how much influence the KPD had over any German industrial workers at this time. For example, although the KPD had about 300,000 actual party members, 80–90 per cent of these were unemployed **(Peukert, 1980, p. 34)**. Even in larger factories there were only ever a dozen or so Communist activists, as opposed to voters **(Peukert, 1980, p. 64)**. In reality, Germany's Communist Party had a very slender grip on the industrial workers and was hardly in a position to coordinate mass action by them.

With the National Socialists in charge of government, and hence in control of the system of law and order, KPD agitation, whether or not it was really effective, was used as a reason to ban all Communist publications. The regime began persecuting known and suspected Communists with so little mercy that historian

F.J. Heyen has spoken of the regime 'trying out' its methods of dictatorship on these victims **(Heyen, 1967, p. 83)**. The homes of Communists were searched, even if this often proved a waste of time. The following is a police report of a set of raids.

Document 2.4 Police Raid

Concerning: the action against the Communist [functionaries] in Eutin, Fissau, Groß-Neudorf and Groß-Meinsdorf on . . . 9.2.33 from 12 to 15.30 hrs. In commission of the government of Eutin, with the help of the police from Malente, Eutin and Bad Schwartau, an action was undertaken against the Communists in the named places. Basically the apartments of the political leaders and the functionaries were searched.

Printed materials of the most varied sorts were found and seized at the home of the KPD leader in Eutin, worker August Salhof, born on 6.7.1890 in Demzin. In addition, several more things were seized: 1. one revolver; 2. one bag with shot pellets; 3. one stamp with a pad; 4. one accounts book with receipts; 5. printed material (of a highly treasonable nature and Bolshevist content). . . .

Police inspector V. from Malente searched 1) builder Ernst G. [and] 2) electrician Ludwig G. in Groß-Meinsdorf. Both are members of the KPD. A side arm (a military weapon) was found and seized. Papers of a highly treasonable content and special material of a Bolshevik complexion were not to be found. . . .

The searches made in Fischau at the homes of Hermann B., Karl K. . . . Heinrich P. and Z. produced no results. All of the named people are members of the KPD. . . . The search of the home of the worker Friedrich Hamer in Groß-Neudorf produced nothing special. Only membership books, accounts books and song books were found and seized.

Source: Report of the town police to the government of Eutin, 10 February 1933, quoted in L.D. Stokes, Kleinstadt und Nationalsozialismus, 1984, pp. 388–9

The report makes clear how ill prepared the Communists really were in 1933 for serious opposition to so unscrupulous a phenomenon as the Third Reich. In particular they lacked the sort of weapons required for an armed uprising against well-trained and equipped police and military forces backed by National Socialism's own paramilitaries. Talk by the likes of Oskar Eichentopf was totally naive **(see document 2.3)**. Wisely the KPD central leadership never actually called for an armed revolt.

The reality of the Communists' incapacity for serious rebellion did not prevent the government using the Reichstag fire, caused supposedly by a half-mad Dutch Communist called van der Lubbe, as an excuse to tighten dramatically its grip on power and heighten the persecution of the Communists. The fire occurred on the night of 27 February 1933. The next day, the Presidential Decree for the Protection of the People and State (the so-called Reichstag Fire Decree) was promulgated and suspended all manner of personal liberties previously guaranteed by the Weimar constitution. At once 10,000 Communists throughout Germany were arrested, 1,500 in Berlin alone **(Merson, 1985, p. 32)**. On 3 March Ernst Thälmann, the party's leader, was arrested. Even though the party polled 4,850,000 votes (over 12 per cent of those cast) and won eighty-one seats in the Reichstag election of 5 March, the very next day all KPD activities were banned. On 9 March all of the party's Reichstag seats were cancelled.

The persecution became ever better organised. Historian Detlev Peukert explains how initiatives carried out by the police, often supported by the likes of the SA, were used to intimidate whole working-class communities.

Document 2.5 Policing to Intimidate

[Initially] arbitrary attacks by SA troops on the working-class neighbourhoods were replaced gradually by systematic raids which went on until Autumn 1933. Armed formations cordoned off whole working-class quarters and searched from house to house. These raids had just about the same character everywhere. . . .

Police, SA, SS, *Stahlhelm*, the fire brigade and emergency services blocked off entirely the part of the town [to be searched] or several streets in the quarter. Control posts were set up at the entrances to the residential area which registered people who wanted to go to work or to school and searched them for weapons, Marxist literature or hidden materials relating to workers' organisations. Bit by bit units combed through one apartment after another, searched the cellars and rooftops, sheds and greenhouses. In this way they flushed out illegal living quarters of Communists who were on the run, likewise any hidden Communist printing presses; in January and February office materials, pieces of writing, maps, typewriters, printing equipment and not least of all apparatus from workers' sports clubs and instruments from workers' music groups were seized. The National Socialist press made particularly great play of the few pistols, arms and hand grenades that were discovered and which made plain the dilettante and inadequate character of the Communist preparations for civil war. The raids were accompanied by imprisonment and physical assaults.

Source: D. Peukert, Die KPD im Widerstand, *1980, pp. 90–2*

An extreme sort of violence could be meted out to any Communist who fell into the hands of Nazi organisations. Their treatment puts the modern reader in mind of the atrocities later committed against Europe's Jews. One documented example concerns Communist motor mechanic Oskar Pflaumer. He was arrested by two SA men near Nuremberg on 17 August 1933 and died in police custody, supposedly complaining of stomach pains. Certainly he had been beaten up with truncheons, but there was more to it than that – as the coroner's report showed.

Document 2.6 Death in Custody

2 If the heavy bleeding, as must be supposed, was caused by painful mistreatment, then it was enough to cause death through shock. (Fat embolism?)

3 Apart from the accumulation of fat which was rather over-developed for the age of the dead man, and which also affected the heart, there were no special conditions in the constitution of the dead man which were associated with this presumed death due to shock.

4 What type of mistreatment had taken place cannot be said with certainty on the basis of the autopsy. But the positioning of the bleeding which is formed like riding britches lets us suppose that probably the dead man had been bent over. The collection of blood under the soles of the feet leads us to assume a mistreatment similar to Oriental 'Bastonade' [a type of torture].

Source: Section from the coroner's report, 18 August 1933, full document is in the Nuremberg State Archive, KV Anklage D–923

Oskar Pflaumer had been tortured to death while in official custody. When the matter was brought to the attention of the National Socialist Minister President of Bavaria, Ritter von Epp, he quashed an inquiry. As would later be the case for the Jews, someone labelled a threat to the Third Reich could expect neither protection nor mercy in the Third Reich.

The final nail in the coffin of the KPD as a coherent threat to the Third Reich was the arrest of its Central Operational Leadership in Berlin in March 1935. The group was never reconstituted. That same October, one Communist leader still at large (Walther Piek) reviewed what had happened to the 422 leading KPD functionaries of January 1933: 219 had been arrested, 125 forced to emigrate, twenty-four had been murdered and forty-two had left the party. Of the 140 still at liberty, only twelve had avoided arrest at some time or other. What is more, the persecution of ordinary members continued. A total of 14,000 Communists were arrested in 1935, 11,678 in 1936, 8,086 in 1937 and 3,800 in 1938 **(Merson, 1985, pp.182–3)**. By 1945, more or less half of the KPD's 300,000 strong membership of 1933 had been persecuted in some way, 25,000–30,000 of them having been either murdered, executed or found dead in a concentration camp **(Merson, 1985, p. 309)**.

Although it too was a Marxist party, the challenge of the SPD was rather different. A split between the KPD and SPD had become entrenched after the decision of the Communist International of 1928 not to cooperate with the Socialists. The division reflected the fact that, while the KPD was in direct competition with the NSDAP as offering an alternative type of revolutionary and totalitarian politics, the SPD had been one of the staunchest supporters of Weimar democracy. Believing its party the guarantor of the Weimar constitution, the SPD leadership tried initially to pursue legal opposition. On paper, its prospects looked good. The party itself had 1 million members in 1933, affiliated trades unions had 4 million. About one-fifth of the nation backed it at election time. What is more, in some respects its supporters were treated more leniently than the Communists – relatively speaking: 1,374 SPD members were arrested in 1936 and 733 in 1937 **(Merson, 1985, pp. 182–3)**.

Of course, in the run up to the election of 5 March 1933, SPD activists were busy debunking National Socialist politics and the mythological reading of German history that went with them. The following is a police report about an SPD meeting attended by 3,000 people, forty of whom were in the uniforms of the SPD's paramilitary group, the Reichsbanner.

Document 2.7 Socialist History

The speaker talked about the year 1918. Reich Chancellor Hitler speaks today, not as a Chancellor, but rather as a party man. Hitler forgets everything that was achieved in the 14 years [of the Weimar Republic]. His loss of memory really seems to be so great that a person doesn't know any more why 9 November 1918 happened. [The day on which the Kaiser abdicated and revolution broke out in Berlin.] This day did not happen because foreigners made promises which made the German people lay down their arms. Wilson promised the German people welfare and peace. The German people was starving and the army had become tired. Crown Prince Rupprecht had entered in the war diary as early as September 1918 that the position was very critical and that a peace offer had to be made. Even the great leaders who were left spoke of [the need for] a peace treaty. This is the historical fact. We cannot therefore make the men of November 1918 [who led the German revolution] responsible [for the lost war]. . . . It was the breakdown of the imperial system. . . . No one expelled or hunted down the Kaiser. He simply fled because the imperial system had left behind a field of wreckage. . . . Now the men came to save the land and to build it up again. These people today are called November criminals. The German working class was Germany's saviour and its richest son was unfaithful.

Source: Police report from Frankenthal dated 4 March 1933 on SPD meeting of previous night, quoted in A. Doll (ed.), Nationalsozialismus im Alltag, *1983, pp. 68ff.*

Even when the persecution of SPD activists began to bite, the party leadership resolutely tried to respond in legal ways. These were thoroughly inadequate and showed the SPD leaders to be totally out of step with the situation facing them, as an historian explains in document 2.8.

Document 2.8 Underestimation

The most eloquent document on this was a set of instructions sent out to the SPD locals in District Hannover on March 23, 1933. It was filled with instructions about sending for handbooks on Socialist policy in communal affairs and filling out questionnaires; in short, carrying on business as usual. The only reference to Nazism was contained in paragraph seven:

'Will the election of our village and town representatives be approved? That is a question which is repeatedly being asked. The question is unanswerable because we do not know what this government will do. However, in any case we must, now as always, select trustworthy comrades as village representatives wherever we have a minority. Should they later not be sworn in, then we will take a position on this. Under no circumstances should we value our rights cheaply.'

This at a time when SPD leaders were having their houses searched for weapons! This when officers of the Reichsbanner were being herded into jail by Stormtroopers, beaten in the prisons across Germany, cast into Nazi concentration camps! The SPD, the only defenders of democracy in Germany, the men who should have been gathering guns and calling the general strike, or at least developing an underground with passwords, false names, and the other paraphernalia of effective covert resistance, were instead being urged to keep the party files in order, to avoid bookkeeping errors, and above all to purchase the latest pamphlet on parliamentary tactics in village councils.

Source: W.S. Allen, The Nazi Seizure of Power, *1989, p. 192*

The SPD carried its opposition into the Reichstag. Undeterred by the banning of KPD deputies as well as the imprisonment or exile of twenty-six of their own, and amid a welter of National Socialist intimidatory tactics, ninety-four SPD deputies attended the Reichstag sitting of 23 March (by chance the same day as the above party circular appeared and now held in the Kroll Opera House) to vote against the Enabling Law. The law, which eventually was passed by 444 votes to the ninety-four of the Socialists, authorised the Reich cabinet to make laws regardless of the Reichstag. As the following newspaper report shows, the party's leader Otto Wels spoke out bravely but, as if symbolic of his whole party's weakness, was easily swept aside by Hitler.

Document 2.9 Unequal Contest

Mr Wels spoke for the social democratic party which does not agree with the Enabling Law. The veiled voice sounded very serious. Repressed pathos, moral justification, moral appeal. A speech in the most difficult situation imaginable – decent, brave, at times even slightly aggressive. One felt the whole misfortune which has today come over this well-meaning but luckless party. The social democrats applauded, the remainder of the house was silent. The Reich Chancellor made notes. The social democratic leader demanded justice and humanness, his motto was 'defenceless is not to be without honour'.

During the last words of Wels' speech, the chancellor jumped up and hurried to the rostrum. A thunderstorm burst over the social democratic party, the like of which we have never witnessed in all the years in the Reichstag. How Hitler can debate! Without trouble he found the arguments to talk down the opposition amidst the stormy applause of the brown shirts. We beat you with your own weapons. . . .

Source: Frankfurter Zeitung, *24 March 1933, translation in the Nuremberg State Archive, KV–Anklage 2579–PS*

On 2 May trades union offices were occupied by Stormtroopers. On 22 June the SPD agreed to being dissolved. Left-wing political leaders resigned themselves to setting up leadership centres abroad. Both the SPD and KPD had done this by 1935. Finally recognising their true enemy, the Communists now authorised cooperation with the SPD. But with their party organisations within Germany essentially destroyed, what could the remaining Socialists and Communists do?

They showed solidarity whenever possible, for instance at events which could not easily be banned. The following extract is taken from a police report.

Document 2.10 Funeral of a Communist

Concerning: Communist demonstration on the occasion of the burial of Adam Schaefer from Mainz-Kostheim who had been a prisoner in protective custody in Dachau.

The investigations instituted into the above affair have so far discovered:

On 24 March 1937 Adam Schaefer (a prisoner in protective custody in Dachau concentration camp, who was born on 25 August 1907 in Mainz-Kostheim and who was in the camp due to expressing anti-state opinions) was shot by an SS guard whom he attacked. At the expressed wish of the parents, the corpse was transferred to Mainz-Kostheim, where the funeral took place on 29 March 1937. Even before the corpse had arrived, the rumour was around Mainz-Kostheim that Schaefer had not been shot but beaten to death and that this was the reason even the parents refused to open the coffin.

About 800 people were present at the burial itself. At issue here were almost exclusively opponents of the state. About 40% were known former associates and members of the SPD and the Centre; perhaps 60% were former Communists. Since then even funeral celebrations of prominent personalities have not shown such a high number of participants in Mainz-Kostheim. What is more, participants had appeared from far removed suburbs and even from Mainz itself. The Communists stood pretty much together during the ceremony at the graveside. . . .

After the end of the religious ceremonies at Schaefer's graveside, M . . . appeared out of the ranks of his likeminded comrades [and approached to] about 2 metres from the graveside. From here he threw a wreath on to the grave with the words 'Rest in peace'. His whole demeanour in carrying out this action was such that everyone had to recognise the symbolic purpose which lay behind it. The big turn out at the funeral and the laying of the wreath for all the world to see should be taken as proof that the KPD is not dead, but rather continues to exist illegally.

As a result, M . . . was taken into protective custody at once. . . .

Source: Report of the State Police Office, Darmstadt, to the Gestapo office on 21 April 1937, quoted in T.W. Mason, Arbeiterklasse und Volksgemeinschaft, 1975, pp. 315–16

There was local reorganisation. Communists spent time trying to construct cells of like-minded people for the future. By 1939, they had created these in eighty-nine factories in Berlin **(Merson, 1985, p. 225)**. Former SPD people kept up contact through extensive, informal networks of sporting and social clubs. In document 2.11, historians explain the activities of female Socialists in Bremen.

Document 2.11 Political Parties – and Outings

After a first meeting in the open air baths . . . in June 1933, the women organised communal outings on bicycles or on foot, but also by motorboat to Worpswede or by train. More than 70 women altogether took part in these outings. In the winter months, when these journeys were no longer possible, they met at birthday parties. In many of the months, two or three such parties were held around and about. They were attended by ten to fifteen friends at a time. Someone from the narrow leadership circle of the illegal organisation then gave a short political speech. Information was exchanged at the end. But it was just as important that these regular meetings over coffee and cakes gave the women the feeling that solidarity was being maintained. The problems of everyday life which the women discussed were also political. How should you act in the face of Nazi spying in the streets? How could you prevent your own children joining the Hitler Youth?

Source: I. Marßolek and R. Ott, Bremen im Dritten Reich, 1986, p. 218

Since they generally did little to draw attention to themselves, in this way thousands of Socialist dissenters maintained contact with each other, often for years without Gestapo detection **(Allen, 1985, pp. 858–9)**.

More dangerous were efforts to distribute anti-Nazi publications. Frequently these were printed outside Germany and smuggled in. Communist networks had presses in Zurich providing literature to southern Germany (Munich, Stuttgart, Ulm), Prague to central Germany (Hannover, Magdeburg, Leipzig, Dresden and Berlin), Brussels and Amsterdam to the Ruhr (Dortmund, Cologne, Düsseldorf) and Copenhagen and Malmö to the north coast (Bremen, Hamburg and Danzig) **(Pikarski and Uebel, 1978, p. 22)**. Political booklets were often concealed inside apparently innocuous printed covers, suitable perhaps for a gardening manual or a leaflet advertising a bank. A truly massive effort was expended here. Communist presses produced over 600 different titles between 1933 and 1945. In 1934 1.25 million and in 1935 1.65 million illegal Communist leaflets were seized by Nazi authorities at the border. Goodness knows how many actually got through **(Merson, 1985, p. 116)**. As regards Socialist publications, between 1934 and 1936 over 200,000 people in Germany were able to read each edition of *Socialist Action*.

Of course, not all left-wing leaflets were professionally produced. The following specimen was handwritten and circulated among motorway construction workers in Bavaria in 1935.

Document 2.12 The Red Helpers

MOTORWAY WORKERS

What has the Third Reich done for you?

Slavery and forced labour. Starvation wages and a new unheard of terror against every worker who does not bow down to these coolie-conditions without resistance. Thousands of workers are sitting in concentration camps because they mustered the courage not to die slowly on command. Class comrades! Prove to the fascist hangmen that the imprisoned comrades are blood of your blood, that the victims of Hitler's barbarism are not forgotten. Unite in the Red-Helper-Groups and give regular support to those who are in prison and to their families.

District leadership RH.

Source: M. Pikarski and G. Uebel, Der Antifaschistische Widerstandskampf der KPD im Spiegel des Flugblattes 1933–1945, *1978, document 54*

The simplest of messages reminded others that there were alternatives to National Socialism.

More dramatic were the wartime efforts of Red Orchestra. This was an organisation of German Communists. With its Berlin section made up of senior civil servants, as opposed to more ordinary 'workers', it conspired to supply Russia with military intelligence and to aid Russian agents. Its actions were uncovered by the police in 1942 and eventually its members were executed. After the war, a lawyer who had been involved in the prosecution of Red Orchestra described the case to American authorities.

Document 2.13 Red Orchestra

The information which was sent to Russia [by Red Orchestra] concerned events from the military and economic life of Germany. It included quite secret things which those concerned managed to find out about by virtue of their ministerial connections. If I'm not mistaken, [Arvid] Harnack [a civil servant in the Reich Ministry of Economics and a leader of Red Orchestra] had given the Russian 'Erdmann' [the codename of their Russian contact] a discussion paper about German armaments. From now on, precise data about German aeroplane production was passed on. It was laid out according to planned and actual production, as well as according to the different types of planes. The businessman Graudenz [another member of Red Orchestra], who had to carry out dealings with the office of the General Aeroplane Chief in the Reich Ministry, had obtained this information through an airforce engineer. In another case Graudenz tried to warn the English intelligence service through Switzerland of planned German measures against English convoys to Murmansk. In addition, the Soviet intelligence service was told about new aerial weapons, of planned German attacks in the East, of the prospective use of volunteer Russian units, of air support and so on in the Caucasus, of the use of German parachute agents, of commando projects behind enemy lines and more of the same. . . .

Other information concerned industrial sites and industrial production. As far as I could gather, the actual extent of the treason was greater than what was actually discovered. The value of the information given to the Russians cannot be overestimated. Its effects on the train of military events must have been significant.

From time to time Russian agents appeared in Berlin in order to get supplementary material and to give new instructions.

I remember that in the course of 1942 a series of Russian parachute agents was used too. It was a question of German emigrants and prisoners of war who had been recruited by the intelligence services in Russia. They were kitted out with every technical and special requirement – in particular the most modern small radios – and were dropped by Russian planes into the outskirts of Berlin. They were provided with contact addresses, were sheltered by members of the Schulze-Boysen group [Harro Schulze-Boysen was a leader of Red Orchestra and a civil servant in the Reich Air Ministry] and when they left them, they were told about the essentials of the radio system. One of these agents was arrested. Through him a successful radio game was played with the Russian intelligence service for a few months. As a result, we discovered several other agents who were caught. . . .

Source: Extract from an interview with Dr A.K. in August 1948, full document is in the Nuremberg State Archive, KV–Anklage K144a

Even though their party organisations had been broken up within Germany, groups of committed Communists and Socialists clearly did not just give up in the face of the Third Reich. But to what extent was all their activism matched by the German working class as a whole?

Most probably it was not. Referring to particularly Communist activists, historian Detlev Peukert explains part of the reason why.

Document 2.14 The Rarity of Activism

The high visibility of life in the mining colony, the works camp, the tenement blocks and public knowledge about the political views of the party members had become constituent aspects of the proletarian way of life in the industrial centres. After 1933 precisely these conditions of life limited resistance activity. Every visit, every unusual event which did not correspond to the tried and trusted ways in the workplace, in terms of what was bought or in the local pub, was registered by neighbours who were not always thoroughly well-wishing. Their impressions were passed on in an unfathomable flood of groundless suspicions, banal information and 'hot' tips to the Gestapo as well as to the SA's intelligence wing, to the NSBO, to the DAF, to the SD or to the responsible National Socialist political leaders and officials. Only a few denunciations were really of use to the police. Nevertheless the chances of staying undiscovered went down for a Communist living illegally with every day of his stay in the neighbourhood of his nightquarters or his contact address.

Source: D. Peukert, Die KPD im Widerstand, *1980, pp. 122–3*

Close-knit communities and the presence of informers made left-wing agitation highly dangerous. Committed action in support of left-wing convictions had to be the exception rather than the rule.

Marxist historian Tim Mason took this rarity of overtly political action as the starting-point of an attempt to reinterpret the way class-based opposition to the Third Reich must have developed.

Document 2.15 Opposition of a Whole Class?

I would like to start by drawing a distinction between the political resistance of the working class under National Socialism and that which I want to call Worker opposition.

To political resistance belong only the unequivocally politically conscious actions of members of persecuted organisations, i.e., the illegal, conspiratorial activities of those groups and individuals, which strived to weaken or overthrow the dictatorship in the name of social democracy, Communism or trade unionism – that is to say, political activity which was characterised by a rejection and challenging of National Socialism based on [political] principle. But this heroic, tragic battle in the underground in no way exhausts the role of the working class in the Third Reich. *Alongside* the dogged propaganda work of the illegal groups, from 1936 on economic class conflict was revived once more in industry on a broad front. This happened in forms which did not have an unequivocally political character, as they concerned the demonstrable motivations of the participating workers. In many cases it is not immediately possible to establish a *conscious* political factor in the behaviour of the workers. What is more this battle about the fundamental economic interests of the working class does not even seem to have been organised in any way. It expressed itself in spontaneous walkouts, in collective pressure on employers and on National Socialist institutions, in opposition of various types against workplace regulations and state rules, in go-slows, staying off work, taking sick leave, expressions of displeasure, etc.

This refusal of the working class to subordinate itself fully to the National Socialist system of dictatorship can be called *opposition*: it made use of the contradictions within the capitalist economic order and of the dictatorship, and sharpened these contradictions; it expressed itself in the grey areas of fascist legality and described a massive challenge to the regime – but not one based on principle. This distinction between *Opposition* and *Resistance* of the working class does not grow out of the pursuit of analytical clarity for its own sake, nor is it a matter of creating purely academic concepts. It is based on the actual historical experiences of the working class, which are of central importance for an analysis of this entire theme, for the factual separation of the illegal resistance groups from their class was a decisive success of the state-political terror in the Third Reich.

Source: T.W. Mason, 'Arbeiteropposition im nationalsozialistischen Deutschland', 1981, pp. 293–4

Admitting the fundamental separation of left-wing activists from their class comrades, Mason sought to redirect the search for working-class opposition away from political organisation and towards ordinary people rebelling against the concrete conditions of everyday life.

To this way of thinking, widespread worker opposition became most obvious during the government's drive for rearmament between 1937 and 1939. On the one hand, government concern with weapons production meant that fewer resources were available for consumer goods; there was less in the shops to buy **(Mason, 1993, p. 181)**. On the other hand, with the pace of industrial production quickening and the previous unemployment problem having been overcome, by the end of 1938 Germany was actually short of about 1 million workers **(Mason, 1981, pp. 296–7)**. Under these circumstances, to Mason's mind, ordinary workers found both reason and opportunity to follow their own interests, to act together against the unpleasant practical consequences of National Socialist policy. There is indeed some evidence that during these years ill-discipline increased in the workplace. The following extract is from a police report.

Document 2.16 Trouble at the Steel Mill

Concerning: Unrest among draftees, especially at the 'Middle German Steel Works', Groeditz. . . .

There have been complaints for several months about inadequate work production at the armaments firm of 'Middle German Steel Works' in Groeditz, district Grossenhain (which has a workforce of about 6,000 people). Absence from work without good reason and unnaturally high reports of sickness led to a situation where temporarily up to 1,200 workers were missing. In several cases damage to machinery caused suspicion of sabotage. Since October 1938 the Gestapo has become involved in about 50 cases. . . .

State police discussions established that the main mass of those unwilling to work were around 300 draftees who had been sent to the works from different districts of the *Erzgebirge* in the middle of November. Their behaviour may first of all be explained by the fact that they are a very unfavourable selection. Many of them had neither the character nor the political background which made them suitable for use in the armaments industry. The regional labour office at some time has therefore requested the labour offices in question to deal with the selection of draftees more carefully in the future.

Above all, however, there have turned out to be social–political deficiencies in the treatment of the draftees. These are first rate danger areas from which can be derived most of the lack of desire to work and [the desire to create] unrest among the workforce and which therefore require urgently to be abolished completely for reasons of state policy.

1 At the end of January 1939 the officials of the Gestapo established that some of the draftees had been put up in an emergency camp in a hotel room in improper and unhygienic ways. At my instigation the Reich Trustee of Labour immediately cleared out the room and put the workers up in private quarters. In addition he encouraged the factory to put up living barracks to which no one could object. Only when these are finished will the works be in the position in this respect to receive draftees in an unobjectionable way.

2 The period of service ran out between 16 and 23 May 1939. Only on 12 May 1939 were the draftees informed, in part by post, about a fresh [labour] obligation to last for a further six months. . . . This newly extended obligation has led to the formation of mobs, demonstrations, isolated cases of downing tools and a general heightening of the lack of desire to work. The joy of work now suffers especially from the fact that the draftees do not know when their obligation will end and their release follow.

3 According to the valid regulations . . . the draftees do not get paid in line with their previous job, but rather are paid according to the rate of the work

into which they are drafted. This regulation has led to a situation where a great number of draftees now earn substantially less than in the workplace from which they were drafted. In principle I am in agreement with the Reich Trustee of Labour that a financial sacrifice should not also be demanded of the draftee who in any case is forced into a substantial sacrifice. . . .

Under these circumstances we can understand why Marxist propaganda or at least that of a comparable disposition is being encouraged. Two former Communists were arrested in the works at the start of June. They had been interested in the works in a particular way, as specified in the instructions given out by the KPD [presumably this means sabotage or espionage].

H . . . , Karl Albert, lathe operator, born 8 January 1907. . . . Former member of the Red Sport Unit; punished in 1933 on account of Communist activity. Still suspected today of illegal Communist activity.
S . . . , Ernst Rudolf, machine fitter, born 26 October 1914. . . .

They frequently registered sick, often did not pay attention to their drills, thereby causing a substantial loss of productivity, and have stirred up their colleagues at work to achieve less and to feel no guilt. An imprisonment order against both has been issued by a lawyer.
By reason of these discussions another 6 workers had to be arrested on account of similar actions. They admitted to having been stirred up by H . . . and S. . . .
. . . According to my conclusions, the situation in the Middle German Steel Works, Groeditz, as it is described here, is no isolated phenomenon. It must, however, give considerable cause for concern as regards the political development of the workforce. It will become much more earnest as the possibility of war comes ever more into consideration.

Source: Report from Dresden police to Gestapo of 29 June 1939, quoted in T.W. Mason, Arbeiterklasse und Volksgemeinschaft, *1975, pp. 722–5*

Mason believed the stand-off described so graphically between on the one side government, employers and police, and on the other side the workers constituted 'a new form of class war' **(Mason, 1981, p. 310)**. But if there really was such deep-seated resentment among the workers as a whole, why was there no great proletarian uprising, especially in the later stages of the war? Mason made the following admission in a book published posthumously.

Document 2.17 Wartime Conundrum

The behaviour of the German population, civilian and military, from early 1943 to May 1945 remains to me in the end incomprehensible. In circumstances in which the war was obviously lost and the 'Hitler Myth' was crumbling, there was obviously much room for give-and-take between the regime and the people, for those small concessions to carefully expressed opposition and grievances, to which I attach so much importance in accounting for the stability of the regime up to 1940. In particular my reading of the late 1930s suggested that there should have been more acts of resistance, especially by the workers, than there in fact were. The clear lesson of the last years of the war is that quite other factors were at work in mediating the relationship between the regime and the people than those to which I have given especial importance.

Source: T.W. Mason, Social Policy in the Third Reich, *1993, pp. 276–7*

As Mason puts it a little further on in the same book, something 'seems not to add up' **(Mason, 1993, p. 330)**.

So how can we explain a set of workers who were obviously ready to show disapproval of the system but who never turned their dissatisfaction into something more concerted even when the situation was favourable? Looking again at document 2.16 provides a clue. The reporting police official is clear that the workers had very good reason to complain. Their accommodation was poor, they found they would have to work away from home longer than they had hoped and many even suffered a cut in wages relative to what they had been used to. It was no wonder that two Communist agitators (out of a factory of 6,000!) found people willing to listen to them. But this does not mean that the average worker needed to embark upon a course of resistance to the Nazi state *per se*. Much rather he could settle for trying to improve his conditions and prospects within its framework. Some certainly chose this path (see p. 157). In fact, historian Ulrich Herbert argues that with memories still fresh of the high unemployment rates of the Depression years, even in the late 1930s first and foremost the majority of people were happy just to have jobs **(Herbert, 1983b, p. 88)**. The protests of 1937–9 need to be understood in this context. As Herbert found in a series of interviews with former Ruhr workers, so long as their circumstances did not become extreme, often they were prepared to make the most of their lives.

Document 2.18 A Worker Remembers

Interview with Willi Erbach, a metal worker.
You couldn't say anything; the shop steward was always standing behind you. Now it all wouldn't have been so bad, we would have been able to come to terms even with all of that – if you resigned, what were you going to do then, you thought about your enjoyments in life. . . . There were no conflicts in the firm at that time, everyone was in the DAF (German Labour Front), since you couldn't risk anything. . . . When you did your work – There weren't any conflicts, you just had to get on with your piecework – [there were] strict controls. You know German craftsmanship, which used

to be good and is just as good today – I hope that it's just as good today, and after all you wanted to earn money.

Source: U. Herbert, 'Die guten und die schlechten Zeiten', 1983b, pp. 74–6

A variety of deliberate strategies were designed to promote support for the regime among average German workers. The following example is drawn from the public opinion reports compiled by the SPD in exile and shows an example of a bold, populist propaganda gambit by a Nazi leader in front of a large workforce.

Document 2.19 Anti-Capitalist Rhetoric

MAN [a lorry firm] – Nuremberg: (4,500 employees) The boss gave a talk to one of the last workforce meetings. He had hardly been speaking for 10 minutes when the 'leader of Franconia', Julius Streicher, who was also present, came up to the speaker's platform, and shouted at the boss of the factory: 'Get off!' and then he began speaking himself. He referred to those present and, with the agreement of the workforce, explained more or less as follows: 'This man is one of the exploiters, he's a typical representative of the capitalist system, against whom we National Socialists have declared war.' He gave an extraordinarily anti-capitalist speech. The boss had to listen to it as well.

Source: Deutschland-Berichte der Sozialdemokratischen Partei Deutschlands (Sopade) 1934, *1980, p. 134*

It was well known that the National Socialist Party itself had a radical, 'socialist' wing, capable quite genuinely of championing working-class causes – even if it was were not always successful. Just like document 2.19, the following extract is taken from the SPD in exile's compilation of public opinion reports.

Document 2.20 Anti-Capitalist Action

In the following reports about resistance movements inside the working class it is worth remarking that in different cases the resistance has come from SA or SS people. . . .

Rheinland: A mineworker from mine X reports: a face worker in our department today earns 5,50 Marks per shift. We must, however, work hard for that and we are constantly urged to produce more. The system of slavery is worked out in the smallest detail. The necessity of constantly having to produce more is always justified with reference to the possibility that one day the mine will have to close. The many appeals and complaints from the workers to the trustee led the pit foreman to say: 'Good, you'll get one Mark more.' But the firm's manager refused. With that, 23 workers went on strike, five of them even walked out. They were dismissed at once. The 5 were SA people. The firm's manager told them, they should be glad they were 'old fighters', otherwise they'd have been sent to a concentration camp. This first unfortunate attempt at united action in our mine has had a very instructive effect. The Nazis in the firm have become very quiet.

Source: Deutschland-Berichte der Sozialdemokratischen Partei Deutschlands (Sopade) 1936, *1980, pp. 87–8*

National Socialist attempts at least to appear to take on board the interests of the workers were a matter of government policy. On the same day the traditional trades unions were banned (2 May 1934), the German Labour Front was established. By 1935 it had 16 million members **(Mason, 1993, p. 156)**. Even if many of the members were sceptical about the precise motives behind this body, still very many did appreciate the advantages it brought. For example, in November 1933 the spin-off organisation *Kraft durch Freude* ('Strength through Joy') was set up to improve the quality of workers' leisure time. In a period when tourism was much less extensive than it is today, the impact of its posters advertising the mere possibility of average workers visiting the Norwegian fjords on trips arranged by that organisation conveyed a powerful message.

Document 2.21 *Kraft durch Freude*

[See illustration on p. 42]

Naturally 'Strength through Joy' organised many more trips within Germany than abroad, but even these found considerable popularity both among workers and those whose income relied on holiday-makers. Once again we can find evidence among the reports of the German Socialist Party in exile.

Document 2.22 Holidays for the Workers

Southern Bavaria: The KdF outings are exerting a considerable influence on the community. According to the corroborating reports of everyone concerned this is a positive achievement by the regime. The popularity of these trips has an ever greater effect. Their cheapness is astonishing. Here are several examples:

(Chiemgau) The '*Kraft durch Freude*' trips are really popular here. The numerous visits which the mountain villages get from them is stimulating our tourist trade considerably. In all cases this is something that has to be recognised. A few days ago I met a married couple from Cologne. For an 8 day stay in Frasdorf, including the journey there and back, costs and apartment, two people had paid 60 Marks. Otherwise the journey alone with a holiday card would have cost 100 Marks. In any case a worker earning 53 Pf per hour cannot manage it on his own. In any case, thanks to '*Kraft durch Freude*', a lot of people from simple backgrounds are now enjoying lovely holiday trips. This success is making a not inconsiderable impression. But the Nazis also use it well for their propaganda.

Source: Federal Archive, Koblenz

1,200 workers from southern Bavaria went to Spitzbergen. The trip lasted 10 days. Inclusive of board, the whole trip cost 76 Marks per person. 900 men from Munich, among them a lot of workers from the town firms and BMW, went on an 8 day trip on the Mosel. The trip cost 35 Marks per person. The town workers got an additional supplement from the town administration, so that the whole trip cost only 7 Marks. The participants got a glass of wine with each midday meal. At one place on the Mosel, there was a wine tasting at a public spa, and the participants of the trip were allowed to drink to their hearts' content. You can imagine how enthusiastic the participants were!

Source: Deutschland-Berichte der Sozialdemokratischen Partei Deutschlands (Sopade) 1934, *1980, p. 525*

Official statistics showed that 2.3 million people took KdF holidays in 1934. The figure was 10.3 million in 1938 **(Mason, 1993, p. 160)**.

If this wasn't enough, the National Socialists also developed a number of particularly important industrial plants as 'model factories'. One of these was the aeroplane plant of Focke-Wulf outside Bremen. Historians Marßoleck and Ott describe how the workers responded to the conditions they found there.

Document 2.23 Model Factory

[W]orkers who came from other lines of work were retrained as lathe workers or welders. For the most part they were recruited outside of Bremen. In particular, notwithstanding a wage freeze, Focke-Wulf paid wages that were over the odds and as a result attracted workers from other firms. . . .

Based on a preliminary evaluation of the Focke-Wulf factory newspaper, the first edition of which only appeared in March 1939, as well as by reason of conversations with members of the Focke-Wulf workforce from that time, we can gain a picture which (in spite of all the speculation and lack of clarity) does tell us something about the everyday life of workers and their attitudes. Focke-Wulf was a model NS factory. Through the construction of works' housing estates, through a network of social initiatives, through medical care provided by the firm, through cultural events for the members of the factory and through relatively high wages, the firm's management obviously succeeded in binding the workers to the factory. For instance, the firm had an extensive programme for sport which extended from football and hand-ball, through gymnastics and fencing to tennis. If the latter type of sport really was intended more for the senior employees – courts rented by the firm were available to them everyday, but only for three days for other members of the workforce who paid very much lower rates – then the very fact alone that the 'white' sport was even offered to the workers on principle, did have its effect.

Apart from the ample offers from the KdF . . . we should mention the factory's own library, the new acquisitions of which were advertised in the works' newspaper. Quite in the spirit of NS ideology (according to which the firm's boss bore considerable responsibility for his workforce), in October 1938/39 the manager alone gave 30,000 RM to the Comradeship Insurance Scheme. Assistance was donated from this scheme on the occasion of births and school leaving, sickness and death, and in the case of chance emergencies. Free lunches, bonuses or the financing of KdF trips were also accepted. The following 'thank you letters' printed in the factory's newspaper document that these achievements were not without their propaganda effect. Even if you bear in mind that these letters were selected particularly for propaganda purposes, they may still reflect the opinion of those involved:

'I would like to take this opportunity to give my warmest thanks for the support paid to my wife and children during my illness. Since my family received no [state] subsidies and only had sickness benefit to live on, the support from the Comradeship Insurance Scheme meant a great deal to us.'

'. . . We want to give our most sincere thanks for the granting of an allowance to buy clothes for my daughter's forthcoming school leaving. . . .'

'The undersigned colleague received a holiday to the Mosel from the Focke-Wulf works, and I would like to say thank you very much indeed for that. The holiday went much too quickly. Everyone will think back with pleasure on the lovely time and be thankful to our leader Adolf Hitler who set up this splendid organisation.'

'. . . I would like to take this opportunity in the first place not to forget to give my deepest thanks to both the works and the firm manager for giving me this chance of getting to know . . . the beauties of our homeland in the company of workers.'

'. . . I could never have believed that I (a severely injured war veteran and father of four children) could have such fun. I would like to thank the Focke-Wulf firm very much indeed.'

Nor should we underestimate the pride Focke-Wulf workers had in 'their' aeroplanes. The fascination of technology, bound up with the feeling of participating in the pioneering activity of the constructors and engineers, facilitated the identification of the workers with 'their' firm and above and beyond that with the system. It was not for nothing that reports about the newly constructed aeroplane the 'Condor' appeared in each edition of the works' newspaper in 1939. These flights went on worldwide, and prominent actors like Heinz Rühmann and A.E. Böhme or Kurt Tank flew the machines personally. Further inventions or pathbreaking new things were reported. With their appeal to pride in one's own labour the National Socialists could link up with the traditional labour ethos of the specialist worker, especially even of the socialist worker. [As a result] they found a corresponding resonance.

Source: I. Marßolek and R. Ott, Bremen im Dritten Reich, *1986, pp. 152–3*

The picture of the relationship between the working class and the National Socialist government is obviously much more complicated and differentiated than that of the typical worker gradually becoming a simple opponent of National Socialism because of the unpleasant conditions of everyday life. On the one hand, at least some people were quite prepared to get on with their lives as best they could even when conditions were less than ideal. On the other hand, the National Socialist movement offered both avenues through which workers could vent at least some complaints and also provided social improvements designed to bind the people into the system. Even if conditions did degenerate at times, many workers could still have interpreted these in the light of the far worse hardships of the still recent Depression years. In any case experiences varied depending on where different people worked. Under the circumstances, sweeping generalisations about the relationship of the workers to the Third Reich are difficult. If anything, the average worker would have been aware that the overall system offered both good and bad experiences: bad in so far as he might have been working for longer hours under close supervision and also because there was the risk of labour service in rotten conditions stationed away from home; good, in so far as some factories offered enlightened conditions and there was always the chance of a cheap KdF holiday. The precise balance of experience would have varied from case to case. Taking the German workers as a whole, while this was not a situation tailormade for the sort of total loyalty Hitler would have wanted ideally, nor was it ever likely to provoke widespread open rebellion. Frequent complaint and dissatisfaction, yes; individual protests when things got too bad, yes; the growth of wholesale, class-based opposition, no.

So certainly there were brave Communists and Socialists at work in the Third Reich who, at various times, took great risks in trying to oppose it. Although not always drawn from the working class (for example, the members of Red Orchestra) and although always more isolated within it than orthodox Marxist readings of history have implied, these were this chapter's real resisters of the Third Reich. By far the majority of the workers faced a complicated political leviathan both representing and conflicting with their interests, but which in any case could always draw on the police to enforce itself. The situation elicited all manner of responses from individuals. This fact alone shows the flaw in the argument that the working class provided a broad-based opposition to the Third Reich. German working people as a whole did not really oppose the Third Reich; relatively few dedicated individuals did this in their name.

3 The churches
opposition born of belief?

Hitler always knew he needed a workforce, but was his attitude so clear-cut towards the Protestant and Catholic churches? In *Mein Kampf* he said that he was not interested in 'a religious reformation' but in a 'political reorganisation' of Germany **(quoted in Zipfel, 1965, pp. 1–2)**. In a speech to the Reichstag on 1 February 1933, he specified that the churches were to be integral parts of national life. Just a month later, however, talking in private in the Reich Chancellery, he contradicted himself.

Document 3.1 Hitler's Private View

All of the confessions [i.e., all of the churches] are the same. Which ever one you choose, it will not have a future. Not for the Germans anyway. [Italian] fascism may, in the name of God, make its peace with the Church. I will do that too. Why not! It won't stop me eradicating Christianity from Germany root and branch. You are either a Christian or a German. You can't be both.

Source: F. Zipfel, Kirchenkampf in Deutschland 1933–45, *1965, p. 9*

Historians J.S. Conway and F. Zipfel have both concluded that even though Hitler may have been fundamentally hostile to the Christian churches by 1933, he had no definite idea of how to proceed against them **(Zipfel, 1965, p. 8; Conway, 1968, p. 1)**. In 1933, 62.7 per cent of the population (i.e., over 40 million people) belonged to one of the country's twenty-eight independent Protestant churches, and 32.4 per cent of Germans (almost 22 million people) were Catholic **(Hehl, 1980, p. 63)**. If anything, Catholicism was the better organised. While 700,000 individuals were affiliated to a multitude of Protestant youth groups, Catholic Youth alone had 1.5 million members. Catholic sentiment was expressed politically through both the Centre Party and the Bavarian People's Party. Together they accounted for about a third of the votes cast in Reichstag elections. Even though these parties were dissolved in early July 1933, the Catholic Church itself remained the largest single social institution in the Third Reich independent of direct Nazi control.

If Hitler was unsure of how to deal with such well-established institutions, from even the earliest days of the Third Reich there was no shortage of National Socialist acolytes willing to take up the challenge. The first significant Nazi crusade in this connection was led by the German Christians against Protestantism. In general terms, German Christians believed they could unify Germany's various Protestant churches and, in so doing, merge Protestantism with National Socialism to create a new, racially attuned brand of Christianity. A new post of Reich Bishop was created, behind which all Protestant churches were to be unified. On 27 September 1933 the German Christian Ludwig Müller was elected to the post. From then on there was a concerted effort to raise the profile of racism in religion. The German Christians of Bremen met and demanded that the Bible be expunged of all Jewish elements.

Naturally there were objections. In response to this growing 'Nazification' of Protestantism, on 21 September, pastor Martin Niemöller set up the *Pastornotbund* (the Emergency Association for Pastors). A total of 1,300 clergymen joined at once; 6,000 had done so by the end of the year. This organisation later formed the basis for the Confessing Church – an outspokenly anti-Nazi organisation. There was no doubting the bravery of at least Niemöller when he, together with a number of sympathisers, met to discuss religious affairs with Hitler and Müller in January 1934. An extract from Niemöller's biography captures the drama of the event.

Document 3.2 Niemöller meets Hitler

The clergy were ushered into Hitler's study where they found him seated at his desk, behind him, motionless as an idol, the Reich Bishop, Ludwig Müller. One by one, Frick, the Minister of the Interior, introduced the visitors and Hitler went forward to greet them. He had resumed his seat and was about to open the discussion, when Goering burst into the room, clicked his heels, gave a Nazi salute and said excitedly:

'Herr Reichskanzler! An hour ago Pastor Niemöller held a conversation closely connected with the subject of this conference. I ask leave to read out to you what he said.'

Hitler nodded assent. It was impossible to tell from his expression whether this interlude had been planned or not, and in any case, Niemöller was at a loss at first to place the conversation that Goering recited. Then he remembered. Of course! The telephone call of that morning! [During the call Niemöller had made a light hearted comment about Hitler's government]. . . .

'Mein Führer!' he [Goering] declaimed. 'These people are trying to drive a wedge between yourself and the Reich President!' This touched Hitler on a sensitive spot, as Goering knew it would, and immediately he flushed with anger and started loading his guests with reproaches, treating them more like an unruly mob of children than responsible leaders of the Church. They misunderstood him, said Hitler, and misrepresented his intentions. Peace, that was what he wanted – peace between Church and State! Yet they obstructed him, sabotaged his efforts to achieve it!

During this outburst Niemöller had come forward so as to be ready to speak as soon as he got a chance. He now tried to explain the incident, telling Hitler that the telephone conversation had been a private one and that the expressions used should not be given undue weight. . . . Finally, said Niemöller, his own work had no other object than the welfare of the Church, the State and the German people.

Hitler had been listening in silence. Now he said brusquely: 'You confine yourself to the Church. I'll take care of the German people!' . . .

When it was all over, Hitler once more shook hands with the clergy. When it came to his turn, Niemöller realized that this was a chance for plain speaking which might never return. Carefully choosing his words, he said:

'Herr Reichskanzler, you said just now: ' I will take care of the German people.' But we too, as Christians and churchmen, have a responsibility towards the German people. That responsibility was entrusted to us by God, and neither you nor anyone in the world has the power to take it from us.'

For a moment Hitler stared. Then as he realized the implications of Niemöller's warning, he turned his back on him without another word.

Source: D. Schmidt, Pastor Niemöller, *1959, pp. 90–5*

The breach between the two men was as irreparable as it was personal. When Niemöller was finally arrested in 1937, it was on Hitler's specific orders. Meanwhile, representatives of the Emergency Association met at Barmen between 29 and 31 May 1934 to discuss where they stood in the Third Reich. The result was the Barmen Declaration.

Document 3.3   Barmen Declaration

In view of the destructive errors of the German Christians and the present national church government, we pledge ourselves to the following evangelical truths:

1 'I am the way and the truth and the life: no man cometh unto the Father but by me' (John 14.6). . . .

Jesus Christ, as he testified to us in the Holy Scripture, is the one Word of God, which we are to hear, which we are to trust and obey in life and in death.

We repudiate the false teaching that the Church can and must recognise yet other happenings and powers, personalities and truths as divine revelation alongside this one Word of God, as a source of her preaching.
2 'But of him are ye in Christ Jesus, who of God is made unto us wisdom, and righteousness, and sanctification, and redemption' (I Corinthians 1.30).

Just as Jesus Christ is the pledge of the forgiveness of all our sins, just so – and with the same earnestness – is he also God's mighty claim on our whole life; in him we encounter a joyous liberation from the godless claims of this world to free and thankful service to his creatures.

We repudiate the false teaching that there are areas of our life in which we belong not to Jesus Christ but another lord, areas in which we do not need justification and sanctification through him.

3 'But speaking the truth in love, may grow up into him in all things, which is the head, even Christ: from whom the whole body (is) fitly joined together and compacted . . . ' (Ephesians 4.15–16).

The Christian Church is the community of brethren, in which Jesus Christ presently works in the word and sacraments through the Holy Spirit. With her faith as well as her obedience, with her message as well as her ordinances, she has to witness in the midst of the world of sin as the Church of forgiven sinners that she is his alone, that she lives and wishes to live only by his comfort and his counsel in expectation of his appearance.

We repudiate the false teaching that the Church can turn over the form of the message and ordinances at will or according to some dominant ideological and political convictions.

4 'Ye know that the princes of the Gentiles exercise dominion over them, and they that are great exercise authority upon them. But it shall not be so among you: but whosoever will be great among you, let him be your minister' (Matthew 20.25–6).

The various offices in the Church establish no rule of one over the other but the exercise of the service entrusted and commanded to the whole congregation.

We repudiate the false teaching that the Church can and may, apart from this ministry, set up or accept special leaders (Führer) equipped with powers to rule.

5 'Fear God, honour the king!' (I Peter 2.17). . . .

We repudiate the false teaching that the State can and should expand beyond its special responsibility to become the single and total order of human life, and also thereby fulfil the commission of the Church.

We repudiate the false teaching that the Church can and should expand beyond its special responsibility to take on the characteristics, functions and dignities of the State, and thereby become itself an organ of the State.

6 'Lo, I am with you always, even unto the end of the world' (Matthew 28.20). 'The word of God is not bound' (II Timothy 2.9). . . .

We repudiate the false teaching that the Church, in human self-esteem, can put the word and work of the Lord in the service of some wishes, purposes and plans or other, chosen according to desire.

Source: E.H. Robertson, Christians against Hitler, *1962, pp. 48–52*

If the language was tortuous the message was not. Taking a text from the Bible to substantiate each point, these churchmen stated openly that no matter what Reich Bishop Müller might say, no matter what Hitler might demand, no matter what social position the Third Reich might accord to Protestantism, they remained completely loyal to the scriptures and to their one true leader, Jesus Christ.

The scene was set for a showdown between Protestants and German Christians. Later in the summer of 1934 Reich Bishop Müller's 'second in command', August Jäger, tried to shore up control of Protestant churches by introducing an oath for all pastors that included a statement of loyalty to Adolf Hitler. The contradiction to the Barmen Declaration was obvious. Many Protestants, especially in Hannover, Bavaria and Württemberg, were outraged. Bishops Würm of Württemberg and Meiser of Bavaria opposed the statement publicly and were placed under house arrest. Popular unrest accelerated to such an extent that both had to be released and, together with Bishop Marahrens of Hannover, were granted a personal interview with Hitler. As a result of the débâcle, Jäger lost his job.

The position of Catholicism during the early years of the Third Reich was more problematic than that of Protestantism. On 20 July 1933 the Pope had agreed the Concordat with Hitler. In return for guarantees of complete religious freedom for Catholics in Germany, the Pope ordered his bishops to swear loyalty to the state, agreed to the dismantling of the Catholic trades unions, accepted the dissolution of the Centre Party and agreed to prohibit the clergy from political activity. In practice Hitler's promises proved worthless and, for example, Hitler Youth groups were soon pressing their Catholic Youth counterparts to close down. Inevitably signs emerged that many Catholics were trying to safeguard their right to independent religious expression. For example, the Good Friday procession in Cologne in 1934 drew 25 per cent more participants than the previous year and was described in a section of a police report.

Document 3.4 Catholic Procession

During the night of 17 March, as in the previous year, the night-time procession of the Catholic men of Cologne took place in that city to the holy statue of the Mother of God in Cologne-Kalk. Pilgrims from the Cologne diocese and parishes flocked together from both near and far to the meeting point at the Hay Market. When the last participant on the pilgrimage had reached the meeting point, at 22.50 the departure from the Hay Market began and went on until shortly after midnight. The procession made its way through the streets of Cologne in groups of up to about a quarter of its size. It is estimated that 25,000 men and young men participated in the pilgrimage. The number of 38,000 participants which has appeared in the daily press may be a considerable over-estimate.

Each parish group carried a large cross in front of it. Flags and banners were not carried in the procession. From the Holy picture of the Mother of God, the pilgrimage made its way back to the cathedral, where after a short prayer and final devotion made by Archbishop Schulte, [the procession] was concluded.

A member of the SA and of the Hitler Youth took part in the pilgrimage wearing their uniforms. An intelligence officer of the NSDAP established who they were.

There were no cases of unrest during the pilgrimage which took place in the most perfect order and discipline. Politically it is noteworthy and illuminating that the Catholic population of Cologne, especially the men, in recent times have banded together strongly. They are taking part in church celebrations and events in numbers of such a size that have hardly been seen in previous years. Even the night-time pilgrimage to Cologne-Kalk showed an extraordinarily increased number of participants relative to previous years. The reason is that people who disapprove of the measures taken against Catholic organisations want to make a show in public that they are loyal to the Catholic Church. Seen from this point of view, the pilgrimage to Cologne-Kalk comes under the character of a political demonstration. . . .

Source: Extract from a police report from Cologne dated 27 March 1934, Federal Archive, Koblenz, 403/16844

The sentiment expressed in Cologne was not unique. In 1937, 60,000 people participated in Bamberg's 700-year-old *Domweihe* festival, and 800,000 Catholics from around the Reich travelled to Aachen for the *Heiligturmfest* **(Hehl, 1980, p. 75)**. What is more, the following extract from an official report concerning the Saarland shows what could happen when local Nazi authorities tried to remove crucifixes from schools.

Document 3.5 The Crucifix

The fact is that 30 to 40 villagers got into the unlocked school on the night of 6 January 1937 to hang the crucifix back in its old place. Against the explicit advice of the witness R. that the crucifix had been taken down by order of the government and that the break in would constitute a breach of the peace if they contravened this order, the accused BA (with the help of a ladder which he fetched), hung the crucifix right up beside the picture of the Führer, which had been put in this newly assigned place. Everyone then left the school.

The court of Rhaunen, on 9 January 1937, ordered a custodial sentence against BA.

Source: Report of an Oberstaatsanwalt from Trier, January 1937, quoted in H. Focke and U. Reimer, Alltag unterm Hakenkreuz, 1989, pp. 111–12

Similar scenes, together with more public protests, accompanied the removal of crucifixes in other Catholic areas. In Bavaria, especially, local Catholic priests led their congregations in minor expressions of dissent over this and related matters. They often greeted people using the traditional, southern German 'Grüß Gott!' rather than the officially approved 'Heil Hitler!' On feast days, they flew the regional flag of blue and white as opposed to the swastika.

By 1937 the anti-Catholic character of Hitler's government had become as plain to Pope Pius XI as to any German. He wrote a statement of his worries called 'Mit brennender Sorge' ('With burning anxiety'). It was issued from the Vatican on 14 March 1937 and read by priests to their congregations throughout Germany on 21 March, Palm Sunday.

Document 3.6 'Mit brennender Sorge'

With burning anxiety and mounting unease We have observed for some time the way of suffering of the Church, the growing harassment of the confessors who stay true to it in spirit and act in the midst of the land and of the people to whom St Boniface first brought the offer of light and peace from Christ and from the Kingdom of God. . . .

He who singles out race, the people of the state, the form of state, the bearers of state power or another basic element of human social organisa-tion – elements that hold an essential place in the worldly order which is worthy of respect – he who singles out such elements from this worldly scale of values and sets them up as the highest norm over all, including over religious values, and reverences them with idolatry, he distorts and falsifies the God-created, God-demanded order of things. Such a person is far from real belief in God and from a conception of life that corresponds to such a belief. Only superficial spirits can fall victim to the false doctrine of a national God, or a national religion.

Source: 'Mit brennender Sorge', issued from Rome 14 March 1937, reproduced in G. Denzler and V. Fabricus, Christen und Nationalsozialisten, 1993

The language was almost as awkward as that of the Barmen Declaration. Just as unmistakably, however, the Pope was taking issue with the way National Socialism was both persecuting the Catholic Church and placing political ideology ahead of Christian doctrine.

Would it be justified to conclude that both the Protestant and Catholic churches, as institutions and from a relatively early point in the Third Reich, were actually taking up deep-seated opposition to Hitler's government? Unfortunately, the Emergency Association and the Confessing Church which grew from it, even the popular support accorded to this movement in Hannover, Württemberg and Bavaria, do not tell the story of German Protestantism as a whole. By tradition, many Protestants were nationalistic and had sympathised with 'right of centre' parties such as the German National People's Party during the Weimar years. It was the predominantly Protestant areas such as eastern Prussia which actually turned into the backbone of Hitler's electoral successes. No small number of educated Protestants found at least the idea of the Third Reich worthy **(Erickson, 1990, p. 119)**. What is more, the ranks of the Protestants actually gave rise to the very German Christianity movement which later tried to absorb their churches. As early as 1932, one-third of all members of the Prussian synod (which included both churchmen and laity) were supporters of that movement. In August 1933, two-thirds of the members turned up to its meeting wearing National Socialist uniforms **(Zipfel, 1965, pp. 36–7)**. It was not by pure chance that no pastors denounced the Reichstag Fire Law, the Enabling Law or even the violent persecution of the Communists. Throughout the life of the Third Reich, and notwithstanding the initial expansion of the Emergency Association, out of 17,000 pastors across Germany, just fifty actually received substantial prison sentences for opposing the government **(Conway, 1968, p. 175)**.

Even Martin Niemöller was not a completely clear-cut protest figure. This First World War U-boat commander had himself at first sympathised with National Socialism. His own church was decorated with swastikas and the Nazi salute was often given there **(Conway, 1968, p. 85)**. Later he personally recognised that the bases of his opposition to the Third Reich had been strictly limited. In prison, with reference to the persecution of Germany's Jews, he showed how little he had appreciated the true character of what was happening in his country.

Document 3.7 Hindsight

At the time I did not realise that we [Christians] would have to pay for these restrictions [on the Jews] with our own liberty. I did not fully take into account that equality had been given to the Jews during our own epoch of political liberalism, and that any restriction imposed on them now would mean the end of that epoch and possibly the end of individual liberty, including the right of worship. In other words, to deprive Jews of political equality would mean turning back the wheel of history.

Source: Quoted in S. Baranowski, 'Consent and Dissent', 1987, pp. 53–78

Interested first and foremost in the spiritual rather than earthly realm, Niemöller had drawn back from exploring the full oppositional consequences of Christian beliefs. As he also admitted after the Second World War, the Confessing Church never, 'neither in the Hitler Reich nor later, placed value on being a "resistance movement"'. It wanted 'to testify to the word of God in our world and time' **(Niemöller, 1946, p. 396)**. Obviously there was a basic failure of understanding here. Niemöller and his followers believed that an accommodation between an independent church and the state was actually possible, that religious freedom could be squared with commitment to the Third Reich, that Hitler ultimately could accept loyalty to two masters – to himself and Christ. Hitler knew that there was no such possibility; Niemöller and those who relied on him realised it too late.

Accepting that between one-third and one-half of all Catholic clergy were persecuted in some way during the Third Reich, we must still acknowledge that the record of the Catholic Church, and in particular of its senior clergy, was far from beyond reproach. The Concordat was the very first international treaty signed by Hitler's government and conferred a certain respectability upon it. The Pope's purpose was to protect Catholics in Germany, but the agreement imposed obligations – especially on churchmen who held positions of responsibility. One result is expressed in a circular from Bishop Gröber of Freiberg to his junior clergy:

'I ask and warn the clergy time and time again . . . [to] . . . adapt and not damage the affairs of the Church through a lack of personal wisdom' **(quoted in Denzler and Fabricus, 1993, p. 87)**. If the Pope would not criticise Hitler, it made it difficult for other, and especially senior, churchmen to do so. During the whole of the Third Reich, only one Catholic bishop was expelled from his diocese and only one was sentenced to a lengthy period of imprisonment for opposing the government **(Conway, 1968, p. 175)**.

Our understanding of the Catholic congregations, including those who participated in the mass processions and crucifix protests, must also be fully rounded, as historian Ulrich Hehl explains.

Document 3.8 The Catholic Dilemma

Even though the believers wanted to identify unequivocally with the demands of the Church, they were indeed at the same time loyal citizens of the state and as such were influenced 'by the great national currents' and feelings of the time. In this respect even the specifically Catholic solidarity effect which had been let loose sixty years beforehand as a result of the *Kulturkampf* [persecution of the Catholics by Bismarck], did not apply. . . .

No one understood how to use this dilemma for his own purposes better than Adolf Hitler. He could suppose that, in spite of all the discontent with church policy as carried out by the regime, the mass of the people still stood behind him, even if not behind National Socialism. The cult of the leader which prevailed generally, of course, had its essential origins in Hitler's great [foreign] policy successes. The reincorporation of say the Saarland, or the '*Anschluß*' of Austria secured for the 'Führer' a popularity that could hardly be surpassed even among the Catholic section of the population.

Source: U. Hehl, 'Das Kirchenvolk im Dritten Reich', 1980, pp. 78–9

Just as the average German worker had a mixed experience of National Socialism, so did the average German Catholic. Some aspects of the Third Reich appealed, others did not. Senior clergy themselves were aware of the related dilemmas and avoided pushing their congregations to make a fundamental choice between church and state for fear of losing members **(Gotto et al., 1983, pp. 662–3)**.

Given the ambiguity of the situation, when National Socialist authorities made their minds up to enforce anti-church policies, more often than not they proved successful. For example, from 1936 National Socialist offices began a persecution of denominational, which meant mostly Catholic, schools. People employed by the state began to be harassed, as the following letter between local National Socialist leaders shows.

Document 3.9 Schools Initiative

Please find enclosed a list of those children who attend the Order of Ursula School [a Catholic order named after Holy Ursula – it was founded in 1535 and was exclusively female]. As you will see from the list, there is a whole series of civil servants among the parents. You should circulate to the civil servant parents a questionnaire that says the following:

'We have established that your daughter Elfriede attends the local Order of Ursula School. Since a state school for girls still exists here in Trier, we would like you to tell us why your daughter is not attending the state school.'

This questionnaire should mean that at least the civil servants send their children to the state schools since at least they get their pay from state funds. If quite a few civil servants do not reply to the letter, after eight days send them a reminder.

Source: Letter of the Kreisleiter of Trier to the Ortsgruppenleiter of the NSDAP, 6 February 1936, quoted in A. Doll (ed.), Nationalsozialismus im Alltag, *1983, pp. 216–17*

The pressure proved catastrophic for church schools. Whereas in 1935 65 per cent of children attended them, by 1937 only 5 per cent did so. By the end of 1939, just about all denominational schools had vanished **(Conway, 1968, p. 182)**.

At the most general level, between 1933 and 1939 the attitudes of both Protestants and Catholics were simply too ambiguous to provide the sort of popular mobilisation to trouble the regime even when it was in a potentially vulnerable position. Popular fear of war was genuine during the Sudeten Crisis of September 1938. The following police report highlights the profound short-comings of the churches' activism at this time.

Document 3.10 Conformity in a Crisis

In the fatefully difficult days of September, when the Führer and the German *Volk* fought over the rights of the Sudeten Germans, the Church of Rome and the Confessing Church were silent. They have left unexploited a rarely favourable opportunity to help 'the justice of God' to victory. . . .

After the end of negotiations in Munich, the Führer received the following from Cardinal Bertram, in the form of an almost smug telegram:

'The great act of securing international peace gives the German episcopacy cause to offer the most worthy congratulations and thanks and to order the celebratory ringing of church bells on Sunday. In commission of the Archbishop Cardinal Bertram.'

The council of the Evangelical–Lutheran Churches of Germany sent the following telegram to the Führer:

'Thanks be to God, who, through the Führer has guaranteed honourable peace for our people. Along with our brothers who have been freed we beg holy victory for the auspicious work of peace. Heil to the Führer.'

Source: Police report of 15 October 1938, reproduced in K. Zipfel, Kirchenkampf in Deutschland 1933–45, *1965, pp. 452–5*

In 1939, 95 per cent of Germans still said they were Protestant or Catholic. Whether laymen or senior clergy, we may wonder what precisely they understood by their belief.

With the outbreak of war, there was a quantum leap in the nature of the attacks by National Socialism on the churches. In his territory of Wartheland, newly constituted from part of what used to be Poland, Gauleiter Greiser introduced the following rules governing the churches and defining their social position.

Document 3.11 Greiser and the Churches

1 There are no longer any churches in the [traditional] state sense, only religious church societies in the sense of clubs.
2 The leadership does not lie in the hands of authorities, but rather there are only club committees.
3 For this reason, there are no longer any laws, orders or decrees in this area.
4 There are no longer any connections to groups outside of the Gau [party organisational area], not even any legal, financial or official connections to the Reich Church.
5 Adults can only become members through an explanatory written application. They are no longer born into [the church] but must explain their entry only when they become adults. There are no regional, national or territorial churches. Whoever comes to the Warthegau from the Reich for the first time must also initially apply in writing.
6 All religious sub-groups just like organisations (youth groups) are cancelled and banned.
7 Germans and Poles may no longer be together in one church (Nationality principle). This comes into power for National Socialism for the first time.
8 No confirmation lessons can be held in schools any longer.
9 Apart from the club fee, no financial allowances may be supplied. . . .
10 The clubs may have no property such as buildings, houses, fields, cemeteries, apart from their cult room.
11 Furthermore they may not be active in welfare work. This is the job of the NSV [National Socialist welfare organisation] and of that alone.
12 All charities and monasteries are dissolved, since these do not correspond to German morality and to the politics of the population.
13 Only priests from the Warthegau may be active in the clubs. These are not full-time priests, but must also have a profession.

Source: Ordinance of Gauleiter Walther Greiser for the churches in Warthegau, 14 March 1940, quoted in G. Denzler and V. Fabricus, Christen und Nationalsozialisten, *1993, pp. 311–12*

In Wartheland, the churches had become member-only clubs which could neither own property nor take collections. In June 1941, on the eve of Germany's attack on the USSR, Reichsleiter Martin Bormann issued a circular stating with renewed clarity the incompatibility of National Socialist and Christian views. The former were characterised as produced through scientific knowledge (which inevitably involved race), the latter as originating in soothsaying and Judaism. Only when the power of the churches would be broken once and for all could the National Socialist leadership of Germany be ensured and the nation's future guaranteed **(Zipfel, 1965, pp. 512–16)**.

This radically anti-Christian mood was associated with a variety of policy initiatives offensive to Catholics in particular. A policy of euthanasia, the compulsory killing of mentally ill and handicapped Germans, began on Hitler's personal order in the days immediately following the attack on Poland. Between October 1939 and August 1941 (when the action ceased) around 80,000 people were killed. It was supposed to have remained a secret. In reality, so many people could not be killed without some repercussions. The religious and moral outrage which accompanied popular suspicions is reflected in the following extract from a letter sent by Bishop Hilfrich of Limburg to Reich Justice Minister Gürtner on 13 August 1941.

Document 3.12 Murder in Hadamar

Perhaps 8 km from Limburg, on a hill directly above the little town of Hadamar, there is an institution which used to serve a variety of purposes. Most recently it was a religious and nursing institution. It has been converted and kitted out as a place in which (according to popular opinion) . . . euthanasia has been carried out systematically for months – since around February 1941. The fact is well known throughout the government district of Wiesbaden, because death certificates are sent from a registry in Hadamar–Mönchberg to the home districts concerned. (This institution is called Mönchberg because until its secularisation in 1803 it was a Franciscan monastery.)

Buses with an increasing number of victims arrive in Hadamar several times per week. School children in the area know these vehicles and say: 'Here comes the murder-box again.' After the vehicles have arrived, the people of Hadamar watch the smoke rising from the chimney and are upset by the constant thought of the poor victims. This is especially so whenever they are troubled by the unpleasant smells after the wind changes direction.

The effect of the principles being carried out here [are as follows]: children taunt each other with the words – 'You're not very clever, you'll end up in the Hadamar baking ovens'; those who don't want to get married or don't have the chance [say] – 'Get married, never! Bring children into the world just to be put down!' You hear from old people – 'I won't go into any state hospital! After the weak-minded, the old will be the next into the ranks of the useless eaters!'

All God-fearing people feel this extermination of the helpless is an almighty crime. And if this is the same as saying that Germany cannot win the war if there is still a just God, then these statements are not caused by a lack of love for the Fatherland, but rather from a deeply concerned frame of mind about our *Volk*. The population just cannot understand that systematic actions are being carried out which, according to section 211 of the statutory law book, are punishable by death. The authority of the government as a moral concept is suffering a dreadful trauma because of these events. The official news that N.N. has died from an infectious disease and that as a result the corpse has had to be burned is no longer credible [a reference to the official 'cover story']. The ethical value of the concept of authority is still more adversely affected by such official reports which are no longer believed.

Officials of the Gestapo are trying, as one hears, to suppress talk about what is going on at Hadamar with severe threats. It might be with good intention for the benefit of public peace, but it doesn't alter the knowledge, conviction and indignation of the population. The conviction is multiplied by the bitter knowledge that talk is banned by threat, but that the actions themselves are not prosecuted under the law.

The facts speak for themselves.

Source: Trial of the Major War Criminals, *1947, document 615–PS*

Ten days earlier Bishop von Galen of Münster had preached a public sermon in which he identified specific victims of euthanasia and prophesied doom if the German people tolerated the transgression of the commandment 'Thou shalt not kill'. In the same month, the euthanasia action was stopped, apparently just as it had been started – on Hitler's personal command.

Although euthanasia drew the most obvious attention of senior Catholic churchmen, there were other, even other *racial*, themes which had an impact at the local level. The spectacular defeat of Poland in autumn 1939 led to the introduction of millions of Poles, most of whom were Catholic, into Germany as industrial and agricultural slave labour. While the government expected the labourers to remain as separate as possible from the German population, some local Catholic churchmen tried to place common religion above nationality. The following example shows what happened when one local Nazi official found out about this Christian charity.

Document 3.13 The Poles

On Sunday 18 Feb 1940 in his church the Catholic priest of Schall-odenbach, Chaplain Seitz, told the parents of the village to stop their children doing things to these *Volksdeutsche*!! [ethnic Germans] from Poland – that is to say swearing at them. The mother of the priest after the service gathered these Poles around her in front of the church and chatted with them – as much as was possible. They then took the Poles into the priest's house where they served the Poles coffee according to their own admission. Only in the evening did the Poles return to their bosses. . . .

I request that this matter be followed up.

Source: Ortsgruppenleiter *of Schallodenbach to the* Kreisleiter *of Kaiserslautern, 23 February 1940, quoted in A. Doll (ed.),* Nationalsozialismus im Alltag, *1983, pp. 194ff.*

The result was a Gestapo interrogation in which the priest continued to maintain he had believed the workers had been ethnic Germans from Poland. With this, Himmler himself entered the affair.

Document 3.14 Arrest

Concerning locum priest Friedrich Seitz, born 28 January 1905 in Mayen.

The Reichsführer-SS [Himmler] has ordered that locum priest Friedrich Seitz be taken into protective custody. I request that . . . [illegible] . . . news of the internment be relayed.

Source: Gestapo telex to Gestapo office, Neustadt, from Berlin, 19 April 1940, quoted in A. Doll (ed.), Nationalsozialismus im Alltag, *1983, p. 199*

Whatever local churchmen may have felt, and irrespective of whether a genuine misunderstanding underlay the case, the Nazi authorities were resolute that nothing would undermine their racial stereotyping.

By the war years, then, the issue was the very survival of Christianity in Germany. Under the circumstances, any concerted action aiming at a reassertion of Christian identity amounted to opposition. In the context of a society which experienced a total war effort against the USSR and the buckling of the military front in the East, Catholicism tried to exploit for its own purposes the nation's inevitable anxieties and losses. The following police report from March 1943 shows how religious services were tailored to the popular psychology of the time.

Document 3.15 Religion and Ritual

The Catholic Church. . . . is developing an extraordinary phantasy in the way funerals are arranged – so say the reports from the Catholic areas unanimously. Consequently it is exercising a deep and lasting influence on the relatives [of the dead] and the local population.

The focus of these events in honour of the dead are memorial services or masses for the fallen soldier:

1 The memorial sarcophagus [*Tumba*] is decked in black and decorated with flowers. Numerous candles burn at its side, a steel helmet and crossed side arms lie on it.

2 Or instead of this, a symbolic soldier's grave is set up in the church and is richly covered with flowers, a birch cross and a steel helmet or an Iron Cross.

3 The cultish proceedings make special use of choirs and orchestral pieces, processions of children and poetry readings.

4 Occasionally a side altar is transformed into an altar to the fallen soldier. Under flowers and burning candles, pictures of the fallen together with their names and their military decorations are set up. Relatives and the population [in general] can bury themselves in the memory of the fallen at any hour of the day.

Source: Police report, 1 March 1943, Federal Archive, Koblenz, R 58/181

The Catholic message received a welcome reception among the population. Police reports from August 1942 and April 1943 give the following anecdotes: civil servants and SA men who had left the church for careerist reasons were returning in numbers, there were stories of soldiers who had left the church returning for Communion before going to fight and during home leave, there were tales of dying SA men requesting absolution, and rumours of escapes from death on the battlefield which could only be explained by divine intervention **(Boberach, 1971, pp. 718–20 and 810–19)**. This trade on human vulnerability did enable Catholicism to fight National Socialism effectively in people's minds.

By comparison to Catholicism, Protestantism was remarkably silent. Certainly individuals did act against the government. For example, pastor Dietrich Bonhoeffer was actively associated with the group which tried to blow up Hitler in July 1944. None the less, it took until October 1943 for the Old Prussian Union to speak out against what had long been going on.

Document 3.16 Words That Came Too Late

14 The sword is not given to the state to be used for killing beyond that of the criminal and the enemy in war. Whatever else it does, is done arbitrarily and to [the state's] own detriment. If life is taken for any reasons other than the appointed ones, then the trust between people is subverted and then the community of the nation is destroyed. Concepts such as 'elimination', 'liquidation' and 'worthless life' are not known to God's order. The annihilation of people, just because they are relatives of a criminal, old or sick, or because

races? He could see no sense in it; he was depressed, and his light-hearted manner disappeared. . . .

Finally the open break came.

Some time before, Hans had been promoted to the rank of *Fähnlein-führer* – troop leader. He and his boys had sewn a handsome banner, bearing in its design a great mythical beast. This flag was something special; it was dedicated to the Führer, and the boys had pledged their loyalty to the banner because it was the symbol of their fellowship. One evening, however, when they had come into formation with their banner and stood in review before a higher-echelon leader, the unheard-of happened. The leader suddenly and without warning ordered the little flagbearer, a cheerful twelve-year-old, to hand over the banner.

'You don't need a banner of your own. Use the one prescribed for everyone.'

Hans was deeply disturbed. Since when was this a rule? Didn't the cadre leader know what this particular flag meant to the troops? After all, it was not just another piece of cloth that could be changed at will.

The order to hand over the banner was repeated. The boy stood rigid, and Hans knew how he felt and that he would refuse. When the order was given for the third time, in a threatening voice, Hans noticed that the flag was trembling. At that he lost control. He quietly stepped from his place in the ranks and slapped the cadre leader.

That put an end to Hans' career as a *Fähnleinführer*.

Source: I. Scholl, The White Rose, *1983, pp. 7–8*

Just as the Nazi ethos could excite and attract, so it could alienate. As a result, it is hardly surprising that groups of youths did develop in opposition to the Third Reich.

One anti-Nazi youth movement was based mainly in the Ruhr and Rheinland and comprised about 90 per cent working-class members. Generally known as the Edelweiß Pirates, these were a loose amalgamation of subgroups with a variety of names. As early as 1934 the Düsseldorf Gestapo came across youths calling themselves Kittelbach Pirates. In 1937 a court in Cologne identified constellations of teenagers calling themselves Navajos. In autumn 1939 the Essen Gestapo found still more calling themselves Edelweiß Pirates **(Kenkmann, 1991, p. 140)**. Historian Detlev Peukert believed that this movement was motivated less by deliberate political or ideological anti-Nazi beliefs (for example, they were not all Communists) than by a spontaneous and emotional rejection of repressive conditions of everyday life found in the Third Reich.

Typically these groups organised hiking weekends in the countryside where they evaded Nazi control. They developed their own greetings instead of 'Heil Hitler!', had their own campfire songs, wore their own type of uniform and took on English or American nicknames. In the Hitler Youth, the sexes were supposed to be kept separate (even though this was not always the reality, since, for example, the

League of German Maidens was nicknamed the League of German Mattresses). In the Edelweiß Pirates, boys and girls mixed more easily. Of course, Nazi authorities saw these groups as a threat and described them in the most degenerate of terms. As the following newspaper report implies, action just had to be taken to stop the corruption of the nation's youth.

Document 4.17 Pirates

'Dangerous Pirate Games'

On 6 October of last year the police authorities from Krefeld and Mörs staged a mass raid on the so-called Wolfsberg near Hüls. It had become known that a great number of 'Kittelbach pirates' had undertaken a special trip to the Wolfsberg. . . . In order to put a stop to their games once and for all, the police patrol of 6 October was made ready. The 80 or so young chaps aged from 16 to 25 who were on the journey were dressed in the typical 'uniform' of the Kittelbach pirates (short summer trousers, white shirt, belt with death's head, death's head ring, lump of porcelain on the trouser buckle, tin whistle in the leg of the boot). They had taken along with them strips of canvas for spending a night in the open, alcohol galore and . . . girls. They greeted each other with 'Ahoi', 'Horridoh' or 'Hummel, Hummel' and then hiked off to the Wolfsberg near Hüls, where they 'made camp'.

When the police arrived, they found most of the 'pirates' completely drunk, and the girls in an indescribable state. The whole group (apparently overcome by a false romantic idea of what it is to be an outlaw) was picked up by the police. Perhaps 70 of these wayward young chaps were taken to the law court in Krefeld where they were found guilty of offences against section 4 of the ordinance of 28 February 1933 [Reichstag Fire law] – wearing a banned uniform. Ten additional ones, among them two 'group leaders', had to appear before the Düsseldorf special court today facing the additional charge of offences against the Reich President's Order for the Protection of the State and Party of 30.12.1934.

In the main trial, which was conducted 'in camera', all of the accused (who used [English and American] nicknames like 'Bobby', 'Jumbo', 'Sonny Boy', 'Black Hand' and the like) admitted their guilt. They all had been thoroughly warned by the police before and some had even been punished by the police already on account of membership of or activity in association with the banned Kittelbach pirates. 'Bobby' and 'Black Hand' were 'troop leaders'. They had enthusiastically recruited for the group and persuaded many impressionable youths to join the banned group. 'Black Hand' was sentenced to two months in prison, 'Bobby' to one month. The other pirates each got a 75 Mark fine instead of three weeks in prison. The chairman of the court explained that quite different penalties would have been on the cards if the accused had been older and had displayed activity which amounted to subversion. Under such circumstances the senior state lawyer would have taken action for high treason on account of a prior criminal record. The death penalty, life imprisonment or a long prison sentence would have been expected. The chairman of the special court concluded that this may serve as warning to any other 'members of other special groups'.

Source: Rheinische Landeszeitung, *15 February 1936*

Wartime actually increased the opportunities available to groups such as this to win freedom from National Socialist control. A one-time Edelweiß Pirate confirms how easy it became for groups to meet.

Document 4.18 Free Time

You just didn't have to go into the bunker. You had to stay outside until the public was inside, along with the most over-anxious air-raid wardens. That was the rule. I can remember no occasion on which there weren't at least 30 youths outside, say from 5 PM until 5 or 6 AM. We were not always together in one group. Often we sat or lay around somewhere in separate groups. It all simply happened in the darkness, in the wasteland which was rather difficult [for the authorities] to supervise. If you wanted, you just joined a group and were accepted. Then we did the following things: chatted, sang, smoked, had sex – the latter not very often. For that you could separate off beforehand or do it some other time. On very odd occasions there was something to drink. Mostly we chatted. About something personal, on the fringes about politics – the sum of our knowledge about that and the flow of information were not very great. We cooked up common plans. Spoke about work and school. . . . [T]ime passed quickly, above all because time and again people had to go away, were drafted into the military or the flak [air defence]. As a result, contact with each other was not continuous. Now and again people vanished for two to three months. The circle was always changing a little.

Source: Quoted in D. Peukert, Die Edelweiß Piraten, *1988, p. 16*

A great deal of what we take for granted as normal teenage life was outside the realms of 'acceptable' behaviour in the Third Reich.

There had always been violent confrontations between the Edelweiß Pirates and the Hitler Youth, but these increased dramatically during wartime. By April 1942, the Düsseldorf Hitler Youth was complaining that parts of the city had become 'no-go' areas **(Peukert, 1988, pp. 95–6)**. As the end of the war approached, supplemented by deserters from the military and run-away forced workers from Eastern Europe, the Edelweiß Pirate groups in some cities developed into bandit units. By January 1945, the authorities in Cologne were reporting twenty such groups up to 128 members strong. They stole food, terrorised local party officials and committed a number of murders **(Peukert, 1988, p. 106)**.

Rumours of contact between the Pirates and known Communists only compounded the authorities' anxiety. There were a number of police crack-downs. In March 1940, 130 Navajos were arrested by the Cologne Gestapo **(Boberach, 1971, p. 435)**. In December 1942, the Düsseldorf Gestapo arrested 739 Edelweiß Pirates **(Peukert, 1988, pp. 35–6)**. In the final months of the war, a number of Pirates were hanged. One of them, Bartholomaus Schink, was only 16 years old **(Goeb, 1981)**.

A rather different type of counter-culture was called the 'Swing' group. This comprised mainly upper middle-class teenagers who could afford the trappings of its identity. While the working-class Edelweiß Pirates met on wasteland or on outings, Swings had the money, clothes and status to meet in bourgeois inner-city nightclubs. In place of the Hitler Youth's emphasis on militarism, sport and Germanic ideals, Swings favoured American jazz culture and the sleazy lifestyle they felt had to accompany it. A comparison of documents 4.19 and 4.20 shows how different the images of the two groups were.

Document 4.19 Hitler Youth Drummers

[See illustration on facing page]

Document 4.20 Swings

[See illustration on p. 88]

The following is an official report of a Swing festival which was attended by 400–600 teenagers in Hamburg in 1940.

Document 4.21 Swing It

The dance music was all English and American. Only Swing dancing and jitterbugging took place. At the entrance to the hall stood a notice on which the words 'Swing prohibited' had been altered to 'Swing requested'. The participants accompanied the dances and songs, without exception, by singing the English words. Indeed, throughout the evening they attempted only to speak English; at some tables even French.

The dancers were an appalling sight. None of the couples danced normally; there was only swing of the worst sort. Sometimes two boys danced with one girl; sometimes several couples formed a circle, linking arms and jumping, slapping hands, even rubbing the backs of their heads together; and then, bent double, with the top half of the body hanging down, long hair flopping into the face, they dragged themselves round practically on their knees. When the band played a rumba, the dancers went into wild ecstasy. They all leaped around and joined in the chorus in broken English. The band played wilder and wilder items; none of the players was sitting down any longer, they all 'jitterbugged' on the stage like

Source: Ullstein Bilderdienst, Berlin

wild creatures. Several boys could be observed dancing together, always with two cigarettes in the mouth, one in each corner. . . .

Source: Quoted in D. Peukert, Inside Nazi Germany, *1993, pp. 166–7*

During the hardships of wartime, police authorities were supposed to put a stop to scenes like this.

With the Third Reich locked in a bitter conflict for survival, the relatively large numbers of Edelweiß Pirates and Swings seemed to be subverting its fundamental values. They were proving that National Socialism did not control German society completely. But this does not mean that the dividing lines between con-

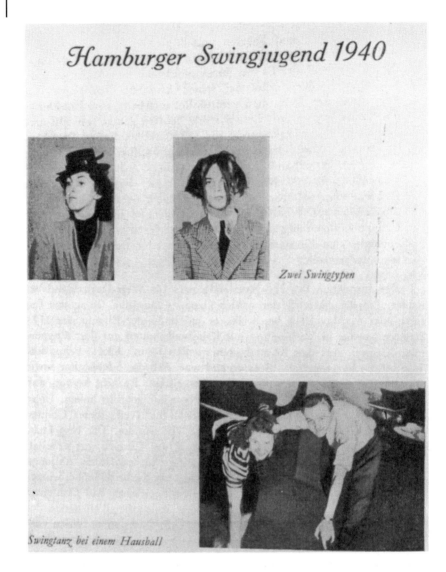

Hamburger Swingjugend 1940

Zwei Swingtypen

Swingtanz bei einem Hausball

Source: Federal Archive, Koblenz

formity and opposition to the regime were always clear-cut. A confidential report into the Hamburg Swing festival acknowledged that of those arrested, 102 belonged to the Hitler Youth in the narrow sense (i.e., the group for boys aged 14 to 18) and eighty-seven belonged to the League of German Maidens. There were even members of the SS, SA and NSDAP present **(Ebbinghaus (ed.), 1987, p. 201)**. Nearly half those arrested actually belonged to Nazi organisations! These were youngsters prepared both to conform to and oppose the regulations of the Third Reich.

Nor was the relationship between Edelweiß Pirates and the Hitler Youth always straightforward. According to historian A. Kenkmann, teenagers often were prepared to give the Hitler Youth a chance and only became Pirates when it was clear that Nazism would not actually satisfy their needs **(Kenkmann, 1991, p. 155)**. The move was often for very personal reasons. At issue might have been the cost of uniforms, arguments with leaders or failure to be promoted. The case of Cologne Edelweiß Pirate Hans Steinbrück underlines some of the ambiguities here **(Rusinek, 1991, p. 286)**. He had been a Hitler Youth leader and even applied to join the Düsseldorf Gestapo, but was imprisoned when he began passing himself off as a secret policeman before his appointment had been authorised. From then on he embarked on a career of opposition which culminated in him being hanged in November 1944. But what would have happened had the Gestapo reached a more speedy original decision (see also document 8.7, p. 170)?

More intriguingly still, during the years immediately after the Second World War, a number of Edelweiß Pirate groups began changing the words of their favourite songs. Now they sang, for instance:

> When the knives flash,
> And the Polish coffins whizz past,
> And the Edelweiß Pirates attack.
> **(Kenkmann, 1991, p. 157)**

Even the Werewolves would have approved of the new ending. Having rebelled against the Third Reich, these Edelweiß Pirates were now out to shock Allied-dominated society. Apparently part of what motivated them was a type of youthful protest common to just about any time and any place; had this not also been part of what drew Melita Maschmann towards the Party (document 4.3, pp. 70–1)? In a sense, Maschmann and the Pirates were united in being the rebels of their particular social worlds.

Such ambiguities only emphasise the truly remarkable nature of the White Rose group which grew up during 1942 and 1943 in National Socialism's city of origin – Munich. At its centre were Hans and Sophie Scholl. Certainly Hans had had unfortunate personal experiences while a member of the Hitler Youth (document 4.16, pp. 82–3), but still his actions were born of deliberate moral choices rather than personal resentments. As a medical student, in 1942 Hans undertook hospital service on the Eastern Front. He was horrified by the carnage he found there. The euthanasia action shocked Sophie in a comparable way. In autumn 1942, together with friends and a philosophy professor at Munich University called Kurt Huber, they began writing what turned into a series of five leaflets. These were distributed around Germany packed in suitcases. Stating openly some of the government's worst crimes in ways guaranteed to strike at the consciences of all decent Germans, extremely perceptive arguments called for popular mobilisation against Hitler. Here are brief extracts from the first three leaflets.

Document 4.22 The White Rose

FIRST LEAFLET

It is certain that today every honest German is ashamed of his government. Who among us has any conception of the dimensions of shame that will befall us and our children when one day the veil has fallen from our eyes and the most horrible of crimes – crimes that infinitely outdistance every human measure – reach the light of day? If the German people are already so corrupted and spiritually crushed that they do not raise a hand frivolously trusting in a questionable faith in lawful order in history; if they surrender man's highest principle, that which raises him above all other of God's creatures, his free will; if they abandon the will to take decisive action and turn the wheel of history and thus subject it to their own rational decision; if they are so devoid of individuality, have already gone so far along the road toward turning into a spiritless and cowardly mass – then, yes, they deserve their downfall. . . . Offer passive resistance – resistance – wherever you may be, forestall the spread of this atheistic war machine before it is too late. . . . Do not forget that every people deserves the regime it is willing to endure.

SECOND LEAFLET

[S]ince the conquest of Poland three hundred thousand Jews have been murdered in this country in the most bestial way. Here we see the most frightful crime against human dignity, a crime that is unparalleled in the whole of history. For Jews too are human beings – no matter what position we take with respect to the Jewish question – and a crime of this dimension has been perpetrated against human beings. . . . Why do the German people behave so apathetically in the face of these abominable crimes, crimes so unworthy of the human race? Hardly anyone thinks about that. It is accepted as a fact and put out of mind. The German people slumber on in their stupid sleep and encourage these fascist criminals. . . . Each man wants to be exonerated of a guilt of this kind, each one continues on his way with the most placid, the calmest conscience. But he cannot be exonerated; he is guilty, guilty, guilty!

THIRD LEAFLET

SABOTAGE in armaments plants and war industries, SABOTAGE at all gatherings, rallies, public ceremonies, and organizations of the National Socialist Party. Obstruction of the smooth functioning of the war machine . . . SABOTAGE in all the areas of science and scholarship which further the continuation of the war – whether in universities, technical schools, laboratories, research institutes, or technical bureaus. SABOTAGE in all cultural institutions which could have potentially enhanced the 'prestige' of the fascists among the people. SABOTAGE in all branches of the arts which have even the slightest dependence on National Socialism or render it service. SABOTAGE in all publications, all newspapers, that are in the pay of the 'government' and that defend its ideology and aid in disseminating the brown lie. Do not give a penny to public drives. . . . Do not contribute to the collections of metal, textiles and the like. Try to convince all your acquaintances . . . of the senselessness of continuing, of the hopelessness of this war.

Source: I. Scholl, The White Rose, *1983, pp. 73–6, 78–9, 82*

On 18 February 1943 Hans and Sophie Scholl threw between 1,500 and 1,800 leaflets down the main staircase in the entrance hall of Munich University. The building superintendent saw them and all the doors were locked. They were arrested, tried by a People's Court and sentenced to death. Hans (aged 24) and Sophie (aged 22), together with some of their friends, were hanged.

After the war, the Federal Republic of Germany (West Germany) treated the Scholls with a respect comparable to the treatment of Communist resisters in the former East Germany **(Kershaw, 1993, ch. 8)**. Today the institute of politics at Munich University is named after them. An analysis of the aftermath of the execution provided by historian J.P. Stern, however, underlines the extent to which the White Rose group was out of step with no small number of their fellow students.

Document 4.23 Aftermath

[T]hey [Hans and Sophie Scholl] seemed sure that their action would be supported by their fellow students. 'What does our death matter', Sophie Scholl said to a fellow prisoner on the morning of her execution, 22 November 1943, 'if thousands will be stirred and awakened by what we have done? The students are bound to revolt!' The opposite was the case. The same evening a demonstration organized by the official students' union was attended by more than 3,000 students eager to express their loyalty to the government. (The majority were medics on study leave from the Russian front, and they had reason to wish to be in good standing with the party officials.) The figure of 3,000 is mentioned by the *Reichsstudentenführer* in charge of the union and may well be exaggerated. His report as a whole, however, is fully borne out by the account of one of the students present: 'That demonstration in the *auditorium maximum* is one of the most terrible memories I have of those days', she writes. 'Hundreds of students shouted and stamped their feet to greet the beadle of the University who had denounced [Hans and Sophie Scholl]. He received their ovations standing and with open arms.'

Source: J.P. Stern, Hitler, *1975, p. 137*

Resistance and conformity

Of those who actually grew up in the Third Reich, there were very few indeed who were sufficiently independent minded and brave enough to take unequivocally and on selfless grounds the moral decision to reject what that society stood for and then to take action against it.

5

Conservative élites

successful opposition from the men of 20 July?

Document 5.1 The Briefing Room

[See illustration on p. 94]

Hitler staggered from the wreckage of the prefabricated building. His hair was alight, his trouser legs were torn off at the belt and his tunic had been ripped by something falling from the roof. It had hit him on the back and he had, to use his own words, 'a backside like a baboon' **(Wheeler-Bennett, 1964, p. 641)**. The Führer's legs were badly burned, both eardrums were damaged and his right arm was partially paralysed. It was 20 July 1944. At just after 12.50 the main briefing room in the so-called 'Wolf's Lair' military headquarters in Eastern Prussia had been ripped apart by an explosion (document 5.1). Initially Hitler assumed he had been bombed from the air. Of course, this was not the case, as he said in his radio announcement to the German people that same night.

Document 5.2 Criminal Officers

German racial comrades! I do not know how many times an assassination attempt against me has been planned and carried out. If I speak to you today, I do so for two reasons: first, so that you may hear my voice and know that I myself am uninjured and well. Secondly, so that you may also learn the details about a crime that has not its likes in German history.

A very small clique of ambitious, wicked and stupidly criminal officers forged a plot to eliminate me and virtually the entire staff of the German leadership of the armed forces. The bomb which was planted by Colonel Count von Stauffenberg burst two metres to my right. It very seriously injured a number of associates dear to me; one of them has died. I myself am completely uninjured except for some very small scrapes, bruises or burns. I regard it as a confirmation of my assignment from Providence to continue to pursue my life's goal as I have done hitherto. . . .

The group represented by these usurpers is ridiculously small. It has nothing to do with the German armed forces, and above all with the German army. It is a very small coterie of criminal elements which is now being mercilessly extirpated. . . . We will settle accounts the way we National Socialists are accustomed to settle them.

Source: Hitler's public announcement of the night of 20–21 July 1944, quoted in J. Fest, Hitler, *1974, p. 710*

Hitler was lucky to be alive. The bomb had been placed near the leg of a very solid oak table which shielded him from most of the blast.

The actual assassination attempt was only the most obvious side of an ambitious effort to stage a *coup d'état*. The following document is the text of a telegram sent out by von Stauffenberg and one of his accomplices, Field Marshal von Witzleben, from their headquarters in the military offices at the Bendlerstrasse in Berlin. Assuming incorrectly that Hitler was dead, they were trying to orchestrate the seizure of Germany's political system. The telegram shows how this was to be done.

Document 5.3 Coup

1 An unscrupulous clique of non-combat party leaders has tried to exploit the situation to stab the deeply-committed front in the back, and to seize power for selfish purposes.

2 In this hour of highest danger, the Reich government has proclaimed a state of martial law, and has at the same time delegated supreme executive power of the armed forces to me.

3 Accordingly I order the following:

(a) I delegate the executive power . . . in the Zone of the Interior to the commander of the replacement army [General Fromm], appointing him at the same time commander in chief of the Zone of the Interior. . . . [Goes on to identify the others delegated in the various army groups.]

(b) To the holders of executive power [i.e., von Stauffenberg and his associates] are subordinated:

(i) All officers and units of the armed forces, including the *Waffen-SS*, the Reich Labour Service and the Organization Todt. . . .

(ii) All public authorities . . . in particular the entire police forces, including forces for keeping order, for security and for administration.

(iii) All office holders and formations of the National Socialist Party and its affiliated units.

(iv) Traffic and supply units.

(c) The entire *Waffen-SS* is incorporated into the army, with this order to take effect immediately.

(d) The holders of executive power are responsible for the maintenance of order and public safety. In particular they are charged with:

(i) The security of signals installations.

(ii) The elimination of the SD [the security service]. Any resistance to the military executive supremacy must be broken regardless of the consequences.

(e) In this hour of highest danger for the Fatherland, solidarity of the armed forces and maintenance of full discipline is of the highest order.

. . . The German soldier is facing an historic task. On his determination and bearing will depend whether Germany is to be saved. . . .

The Commander-in-Chief of the Armed Forces.

signed: v. Witzleben, Field Marshal.

Source: H.A. Jacobsen (ed.), Germans Against Hitler, 1969, pp. 131–2

The plan was to trick the army and key party institutions into believing that elements of the Nazi movement themselves were trying to implement a coup against Hitler's government. Using this as a cover story, senior party men were to be arrested, key party organisations (such as the security service) were to be closed down, others (for instance the *Waffen-SS*) were to be incorporated into the military command system or subordinated to regional governors appointed by von Stauffenberg and his collaborators. In other words, von Stauffenberg and his closest associates were trying to carry out a coup by accusing party men of doing the same! Of course the plan failed. Within twelve hours its key instigators were either dead or under arrest. But still its nature tells us a lot. Although the coup did have some influential sympathisers, such as Field Marshal Rommel (the hero of the North African campaign), its basis in deception emphasised that the conspirators were far from confident of rallying the necessary support from senior military men. By this stage of the war Hitler was expending considerable resources on ensuring that his generals remained loyal. According to historian G.L. Weinberg, they were being bribed with gifts of large, landed estates and regular monthly payments of 2,000 to 4,000 RM **(Weinberg, 1995, pp. 308–9)**. So in a sense Hitler was right. The attempted assassination and coup are best understood as the province of a relatively small group of hard-core conspirators.

And yet these events did not just come out of the blue. In the previous eighteen months, a variety of army officers had made a number of assassination attempts (including a possible bombing at a military 'fashion show' and the placing of explosives packed like a bottle of French brandy on the Führer's aeroplane). But the clique responsible for 20 July has to be put into a wider historical context still. The officers immediately responsible for the events of that day represented just one of a number of associations in Germany's military and government circles which became ever more opponents of National Socialism in the face of first the possibility and then the reality of war. These people generally had conservative political ideas and, by virtue of their social and political positions, were among the nation's élites. Historian Joachim Fest highlights the main characteristics of their opposition 'movement'.

Document 5.4 Three Groups

To treat it as if it were a single concept is inaccurate; it was a loose assemblage of many groups objectively and personally antagonistic and united only in antipathy for the regime. Three of these groups emerge with somewhat sharper contours: (1) The Kreisau Circle, called after Count Helmuth James von Moltke's Silesian estate. This was chiefly a discussion group of high-minded friends imbued with ideas of both Christianity and socialist reform. As a civilian group its opportunities were limited, and it practiced revolt only in the sense of intellectual encouragement. 'We are being hanged because we thought together,' von Moltke wrote in one of his last letters from prison, with a note of almost happy pride at the power of the spirit thus attested by his death sentence. (2) Then there was the group of conservative and nationalist notables gathered around Carl Goerdeler, the former mayor of Leipzig, and General Ludwig Beck, the former army chief of staff. These men, not yet cognizant of the meaning of Hitler's policies, were still claiming a leading role for a Greater Germany within Europe. It has seriously been questioned whether they even offered any real alternative to Hitler's imperialistic expansionism. So strong was their leaning toward an authoritarian state that they have been called a continuation of the anti-democratic opposition in the Weimar Republic. Moltke spoke tersely of the 'Goerdeler trash'. (3) Finally there was the group of younger military men such as von Stauffenberg, von Tresckow, and Olbricht, with no pronounced ideological affiliations, although for the most part they sought ties with the Left and in contrast to Beck and Goerdeler did not look to a rapprochement with the Western powers, but with the Soviet Union. [This last sentence is very debatable. Bear it in mind when you read document 5.20, p. 113.]

In terms of background, a strikingly large number of the conspirators belonged to the Old Prussian nobility. There were also members of the clergy, the academic professions, and high-ranking civil servants. . . . [In addition they developed links with a number of labour leaders.]

Source: J. Fest, Hitler, *1974, pp. 701–2*

Fest is quite right that contact between these groups did not automatically mean agreement. In addition to the tension between von Moltke and Goerdeler, von Moltke and von Stauffenberg found it hard to get along. What is more, Goerdeler described von Stauffenberg as 'a cranky, obstinate fellow who wanted to play politics' **(Steffahn, 1994, pp. 99–100; Hoffmann, 1977, p. 366)**. The sort of person sufficiently strong-willed to oppose the Hitler state was not well suited to cooperation, even with other opponents!

This insight contributes to our understanding of why members of the conservative élites did not get organised sufficiently to take wholesale action against the Third Reich until summer 1944. But what was the full explanation? Did they really oppose Hitler and all he stood for, or, as Fest suggests, did at least some of them have much common ground with him? Would these men have been happy to go along with the Third Reich indefinitely so long as it was successful? We need to analyse the attitudes of the three conservative élite groups (the Kreisau Circle, the older Goerdeler–Beck group and von Stauffenberg's band) as they developed throughout the 1920s, 1930s and 1940s.

It is logical to start with the older men led by Goerdeler and Beck. They enjoyed relatively senior positions in government during both the Weimar Republic and the earlier years of the Third Reich. Under Hitler's rule Carl Goerdeler was first a Lord Mayor and then a Price Commissioner. Only later did he become a courier carrying messages from would-be conservative resisters to Britain and the USA. The case of General Ludwig Beck is more intriguing still. Eventually he would become the conspirators' choice as head of state in a post-Hitler Germany and he committed suicide at their headquarters on 20 July 1944. None the less he was a soldier who had been 'steeped in the Prussian tradition of service' typical of the nineteenth century. The heritage hardly prepared him to carry out a coup **(von Klemperer, 1992, p. 19; Brandt, 1991, p. 15)**. As he once said, 'Mutiny and revolution are words not to be found in a German officer's dictionary' **(Hoffmann, 1977, p. 46)**. Nor had his background fitted him to support a Weimar Republic hamstrung by the Treaty of Versailles. When, during the years 1929–30, some junior officers in Beck's command were accused of pro-Nazi activity (something banned for members of the military), he actually tried to hinder the investigation against them. The case came to court and Hitler appeared as a witness. Historian Nicholas Reynolds explains the situation.

Document 5.5 The Trial

Hitler understood the army's mood, and when he came to Leipzig [where the trial of the junior officers was being held] to testify on the nature of his party, he shrewdly combined his attacks on the [political] leaders of the Reichswehr [the Reich's armed forces] with pledges to seek power only by legal means. . . .

Beck was clearly impressed by Hitler and his ideas. The testimony at the trial suggested to him that National Socialism was in tune with his politics. But of course he saw in National Socialism only what he wanted to see, which was all that was on exhibit during the trial. Beck was instinctively attracted to National Socialism as the creed that promised to make Germany great again, to bring back some measure of glory to imperial Germany and, especially, of the Imperial Army. In 1943, he told a friend how happy he had been when he had first seen the black-white-red on a National Socialist poster: he had missed the old imperial colours. It was, similarly, a good sign for him that the Kaiser's son, Prince August Wilhelm, had joined the Party.

After the Reichswehrprozess [the trial of the junior military officers], Beck was openly numbered among the enemies of the Republic. Young officers throughout the Reichswehr praised him for his defence of Ludin and Scheringer [two of the junior officers in question], and their elders were impressed by his courageous stand for their ideals. So was Hitler. After listening to Beck's testimony, he had asked his companion, Otto Wagener, to note Beck's name. He wanted to be reminded of that fine officer once he had come to power.

Source: N. Reynolds, Treason was no Crime, *1976, pp. 42–3*

Beck's support for National Socialism crossed the threshold of 30 January 1933. He showed himself ready to take on board racialism by authorising a series of lectures on racial hygiene for the War Academy in August 1934 **(Reynolds, 1976, pp. 73–4)**. He was also sympathetic to aspects of Hitler's aggressive foreign policy. On one occasion he wrote, 'It is correct . . . that Germany needs a larger living space both in Europe and in the colonial sphere. The first of these can only be acquired through war.' He agreed that Czechoslovakia was a threat to Germany which needed to be removed, 'if necessary by war' **(Reynolds, 1976, pp. 42–3)**. The same historian responsible for document 5.5 explains Beck's activities on behalf of the Third Reich as follows.

Document 5.6 Misguided

From 1933 to 1938 Beck had conformed to the overall pattern set by the officer corps. He had worked with great care to lay the foundations for German rearmament, to create an army of exceptionally high quality, and since his work had been governed by the hope of attaining German hegemony in Central Europe, he had made preparations for war against Czechoslovakia and, if necessary, France.

Beck's apolitical attitude had had a similar effect in the sphere of domestic politics. The *Primat der Aussenpolitik* [primacy of foreign policy] had led him to ignore many of the regime's crimes and misdeeds within Germany, even though they were abhorrent to him. Thus Beck had contributed to the process whereby Hitler had been able to increase his strength and consolidate his control over Germany and her Wehrmacht [armed forces].

Source: N. Reynolds, Treason was no Crime, *1976, pp. 42–3*

Beck was a professional soldier and a patriot. So long as National Socialism was strengthening his country in the international forum, he could accept those racial lectures and a great deal of whatever else went with them.

The older generation was not alone in being compromised by the overlap of traditional conservative and National Socialist values. Claus von Stauffenberg was born into a family of minor nobility in Schwabia. Even National Socialists would have been impressed by the aggressive patriotism displayed in a school essay written in 1923 when he was 15.

Document 5.7 Patriot

Despite everything which the Fatherland and the new Reich [Weimar Germany] has made available, there is only the one noble profession which the great Greeks and Romans showed us and which the knights exemplified in its supreme form: to become worthy of the Fatherland, to fight for the Fatherland and then to sacrifice yourself in the supreme battle for the nation;

to lead a life which is conscious of reality and of battle. This calling must be put into effect, must be turned into reality, must be pursued with this as its leading idea.

Source: Extract from a school essay by Claus von Stauffenberg, quoted from H. Steffahn, Stauffenberg, *1994, p. 21*

It was no great surprise that by 1930, now aged 22 and a junior army officer, von Stauffenberg favoured the NSDAP as the best political force in Germany. Comments written in *Mein Kampf* and used as themes by local Nazi speakers, for example, that the army was the 'things of greatest value . . . in the body of the German people' and 'the most powerful school of the German nation', coincided entirely with his way of thinking **(Steffahn, 1994, p. 34)**.

But there was more to von Stauffenberg than traditional patriotism. As a teenager he had been friendly with and deeply influenced by the Romantic poet Stefan George. Some of the latter's visionary character rubbed off on the budding officer and seems to have pushed him into a type of politics which overlapped in some ways with National Socialism (document 5.20, p. 113). Accordingly von Stauffenberg's sympathy with Hitler's government lasted longer than that of Beck and the older generation. While they had been retired or had resigned before the outbreak of war, the younger man participated in the Polish campaign of autumn 1939. A letter sent to his wife at this time shows little indication of the way his life would develop later.

Document 5.8 Poland

The population [here in Poland] is an unbelievable rabble, there are a lot of Jews and a lot of cross-breeds. It is a people which only feels good when it is under the whip. The thousands of prisoners will do our agricultural economy good. They are certain to be put to good use in Germany [and will be] industrious, willing and easily satisfied.

Source: H. Steffahn, Stauffenberg, *1994, p. 57*

He was endorsing both the tyrannical occupation of Poland and the use of its people as slave labourers. When von Stauffenberg was sounded out on behalf of the leader of the Kreisau Circle, Helmuth von Moltke, in spring 1942, he rejected any association with opponents of the regime. Whether his first loyalty was to the Nazi movement or to his nation at war, von Stauffenberg was still conforming to the demands of Hitler's government.

What of the Kreisau Circle? A descendant of the famous nineteenth-century Field Marshal, Helmuth von Moltke was unique among those discussed here. A confirmed supporter of the Weimar Republic, he never looked favourably on National Socialism. In the early months of the Third Reich, he condemned both its government without the endorsement of the Reichstag and its anti-Semitism **(Roon, 1971, p. 25)**. Throughout the 1930s von Moltke visited England at different times, and was friendly with a number of people at Oxford University – including individuals attached to the Foreign and Commonwealth Office. He passed English law examinations. With the outbreak of war von Moltke was recruited into the *Abwehr* (German military intelligence) to work in the section for international law. This was, in fact, a remarkable organisation in which the chief, Admiral Canaris, knowingly provided cover for a variety of anti-Nazi conspiracies. During a trip by Mussolini to Berlin, von Moltke showed his own dissent by refusing to stick pro-Fascist and pro-Nazi posters in his office windows.

More seriously, von Moltke tried to use his post to counteract a variety of criminal orders which were issued by the Nazi leadership during wartime. At issue here were the rules of naval engagement, the treatment of prisoners of war and that of Jews in the occupied territories. As the following letter from von Moltke to his wife shows, a depressing majority of military men was prepared to go along unquestioningly with whatever the political leadership demanded.

Document 5.9 Man of Principle

What war breeds is cowardice, cant and mass psychosis. To give you an example, yesterday I was at a meeting in the [German] Foreign Office about the Jewish persecutions. It was the first time that I had been involved with this question officially. Single-handed against twenty-four other people I attacked an ordinance and for the time being held it up after it already had the approval of all ministers and of the chief of the OKW [Supreme Military Command]. And then I came back and the responsible official in the OKW asked me, 'Why have you done that? You can't change anything about it now; naturally all these measures lead to catastrophe.' I am not insensitive to the charm and qualities of people like that but their actions are determined by expediency and have no moral basis. Like chameleons they make a good impression in a healthy society, a bad one in a depraved society. In reality they are neither one thing nor the other. They are stuffed shirts. True they have to be stuffed shirts. But what is intolerable is when a stuffed shirt, who has sat by and let the depravity spread, acts as though he had a moral justification for doing so. Yes, I know I am being extremely severe. But it is necessary if one isn't to slide into hypocrisy without noticing it.

Source: Letter of November 1941 from Moltke to his wife, quoted in M. Balfour and J. Frisby, Helmuth von Moltke, *1972, p. 173*

His post in the *Abwehr* and offices in central Berlin exposed von Moltke on a daily basis to information and experiences which were formative, as the following letter, once again to his wife, shows.

Document 5.10 Knowledge

The day has been so full of horrible news that I can't write collectedly although I came back at 5 and have had tea. What cuts me to the quick at the moment is the inadequacy of the soldiers' reaction. Falkenhausen [General Officer Commanding Belgium] and Stülpnagel [General Officer Commanding France] have returned to their posts instead of resigning after the latest incidents, dreadful new orders are going out and nobody seems to find them remarkable. [Again the letter shows that a readiness to conform to Hitler's orders was the usual response.] How can one bear one's share of guilt?

In one part of Serbia two villages have been reduced to ashes, 1,700 men and 240 women of the inhabitants have been executed. That is the punishment for an attack on three German soldiers. In Greece 240 men were shot in one village. The village was burnt down, the women and children left on the spot to mourn their husbands and fathers and homes. In France extensive shootings are going on as I write. In this way more than a thousand men are being murdered for a certainty every day and thousands more Germans are being habituated to murder. And all that is child's play compared to what is happening in Poland and Russia. How can I bear this and sit just the same in my warm room and drink tea? Don't I make myself into an accomplice by doing so? What shall I say when someone asks me, 'And what did you do during this time?'

They have been collecting the Berlin Jews since Saturday. They are taken away at 9.15 in the evening and shut for the night into a synagogue. They go off with what they can carry in their hands to Litzmannstadt and Smolensk. The authorities want to spare us the sight of how they are left to perish in hunger and cold and so arrange this in Litzmannstadt and Smolensk. A friend of Kiep's saw a Jew collapse in the street: when she wanted to help him, a policeman intervened, prevented her and kicked the body as it lay on the ground so that it rolled into the gutter. Then he turned to the lady with a last vestige of shame and said, 'Those are our orders.'

How can one know things like this and yet walk about a free man? What right has one to do so?

Source: Letter from Moltke to his wife Freya, 21 October 1941, quoted in M. Balfour and J. Frisby, Helmuth von Moltke, *1972, pp. 171–2*

Von Moltke was moved deeply by the fundamental dignity of every human being and this determined his opposition to the Third Reich. He was so much of a moral idealist that he never actually accepted the need to assassinate the Führer. Imprisoned several months before von Stauffenberg's attempt was made, he once commented that had he been free, the bombing would never have happened. Von Moltke's convictions pushed him into contact with all manner of resistance-minded groups. Most famously, he brought together their representatives at three conferences on his estate at Kreisau, Silesia, which were held during 1942 and 1943. Participants discussed the way in which they wanted a postwar Germany to be organised.

So why did Goerdeler, Beck and von Stauffenberg have changes of heart and become opponents as dedicated as von Moltke? Certainly the escalation of anti-Semitic persecutions played its part. Goerdeler resigned as mayor of Leipzig in 1937 when a local Party man removed a statue of the German–Jewish composer Mendelssohn from the city's square. But the decisions of these men were rooted in more than one cause. For example, the revolutionary irresponsibility of National Socialism was also important. They became aware that the movement was actually threatening their country.

Taking the case of Beck first, the nineteenth-century traditions of the Prussian officer corps which he valued so highly had always brought with them notions of honour and responsibility which were more important than a strict duty to obey **(Whalen, 1993, pp. 90–1)**. Beck himself stated in the early 1930s that there had to be 'no doubt whatsoever about' the 'integrity' of a senior military man, and that if there was then he should resign **(Whalen, 1993, p. 81)**. It was in character that when, in February 1938, Generals Blomberg (Reich Minister for War) and Fritsch (Supreme Commander of the Army) were ousted from the General Staff by a National Socialist smear campaign, Beck was outraged.

If this began the process of his disillusionment, it was Hitler's actions over the Sudetenland later that same year which forced Beck into outright opposition. Although Beck favoured the ultimate incorporation of at least parts of Czechoslovakia into Germany, he was alienated by the totally irresponsible way Hitler was prepared to go about their acquisition. As Chief of Staff, Beck was involved in the military planning which Hitler commissioned in summer 1938 for possible military action against Czechoslovakia. He believed Hitler was genuinely prepared to put the plans into effect regardless of the consequences. That July Beck began a campaign of writing memos to the Commander of the Army, General von Brauchitsch. Using arguments typical of a military man, he called for a change of policy.

Document 5.11 Memo of 16 July 1938 (1)

[A] forcible military advance by Germany against Czechoslovakia would lead to an immediate military intervention against us by France and thereupon also by England. . . .

Thus we are facing the fact that a military advance by Germany against Czechoslovakia will lead automatically to a European or a World War. That such a war by all human probability will end not only with a military but also a general catastrophe for Germany will surely not need any further belabouring on my part. . . .

1 The prospect of smashing Czechoslovakia by a military action within a foreseeable time without immediately involving France and England is non-existent. . . .
2 Today it seems less sure than one and a half months ago that a speedy intervention by Hungary against Czechoslovakia can be reckoned with – or

even intervention at all. Furthermore, the intervention by Poland against Czechoslovakia need by no means come about in a way which supports Germany [i.e., Germany cannot count on Hungary and Poland as automatic allies against Czechoslovakia]. . . .

3 Even in declaring war on France, Italy will not be in a position to keep France from interfering in favour of Czechoslovakia.

4 A sufficient rearguard cover in the West cannot be attained. . . .

5 The Danzig area can give a new impulse to Polish greediness if Germany is entangled in a war on several fronts [i.e., with Germany at war, Poland might try to capture the free city of Danzig. Germany wanted this for herself]. . . .

6 The effect of the contemplated propaganda war would hardly be able to bear the whole weight of the military facts.

Based on my above arguments I consider myself obliged today . . . to express the urgent request that the Supreme Commander of the Armed Forces be induced to shelve the war preparations ordered by him and to postpone the plan for a forcible solution of the Czech question until the military prerequisites for it have basically changed. . . .

Furthermore, it seems to me urgently necessary to listen soon personally to the commanding generals about the spirit, mood and inner stability of the troops in view of potential eventualities and to remain in touch with them. . . .

A conference with the Commander-in-Chief of the Army with all the above mentioned gentlemen is also necessary so that all questions can be cleared up before the conference which is intended by the Führer with the commanding generals and so that a clear and uniform opinion can be presented to him.

Source: Memo from General Beck dated 16 July 1938, quoted in H.A. Jacobsen (ed.), Germans Against Hitler, *1969, pp. 45–6*

Beck felt that Germany was weaker, relatively speaking, than she had been in 1914 and so should not be risking war under any circumstances. He wanted the generals to form a united front to persuade Hitler of the same. Nor was he averse to expressing himself in more emotive terms.

Document 5.12 Memo of 16 July 1938 (2)

It seems that the Führer considers as inevitable a forceful solution of the Sudeten German questions by marching into Czechoslovakia [the Sudeten-land was an area of Czechoslovakia bordering the German Reich and inhabited by large numbers of ethnic Germans]. . . .

The highest leaders of the armed forces are directly involved and primarily concerned in this situation, for the armed forces are the state's executive powers in the carrying through of a war.

Final decisions about the continuity of the nation are at stake here. History will burden these leaders with a blood guilt if they fail to act according to their knowledge and conscience both as experts and as members of the state. Their soldierly obedience has its limit at that point where their knowledge, their conscience and their responsibility forbid the execution of an order.

If in such a situation their advice and warnings fail to find a hearing, then they have the right and duty to the people and to history to resign from their offices. If they act with a united will, execution of an action of war is impossible. Thereby they will have saved their Fatherland from the worst, from ruin.

. . . Exceptional times demand exceptional actions.

Other upright men in responsible positions of state outside the armed forces will join the military men on their course. If one keeps one's eyes and ears open, if one doesn't cheat oneself by false figures, if one doesn't live in the intoxication of an ideology, then one can only come to the recognition that at present we are not prepared for war either politico-strategically (leadership, training and equipment), politico-economically, or as far as the political atmosphere [of the nation] is concerned.

Source: Memo by Beck dated 16 July 1938 for Commander-in-Chief of the Army von Brauchitsch, quoted in H.A. Jacobsen (ed.), Germans Against Hitler, *1969, pp. 23–4*

If the worst should happen, Beck was advocating a mass refusal by Germany's generals to follow Hitler's orders.

Unfortunately, when it came to the crunch Beck did not receive the support of senior military men around him. Under mounting political pressure, he was forced from office in August. As luck had it, the Führer managed to annex the Sudetenland 'peacefully' after the so-called Munich meeting of that September, at which Britain and France refused to support Czechoslovakia's borders. But Beck had become a determined opponent of Hitler.

Some explanations of von Stauffenberg's change of heart have emphasised his poetic, utopian side **(Schlabrendorff, 1994, pp. 245–6)**. Historian Hans Mommsen is right that idealism can motivate people to outstanding actions, but in coming to terms with this man we also have to understand the impact which the military realities of the eastern campaign had on him **(Mommsen, 1985, p. 14)**. The following extract from a biography explains the dilemma he encountered during the winter of 1942–3.

Document 5.13 Crisis

In October 1942 Stauffenberg attended a conference at Vinnitsa [a town in the Ukraine] with Schmidt von Altenstadt in the chair and some forty staff officers present. According to Otto Schiller, who was there, Stauffenberg got up and made a half-hour extempore speech amounting to a passionate condemnation of German policy in the east. Germany was in the process, he said, of sowing such hatred in the east that 'our children will reap the reward of it one day'. The war could only be won if it was possible to win over the eastern peoples to Germany's side. At present Germany's eastern policy was calculated to turn this mass of humanity into enemies. It was a scandal that, at a time when millions of German soldiers were risking their lives daily, no one was to be found among the senior commanders with the courage to put on his steel helmet and go and tell the Führer quite openly about these things, even at the risk of losing his life as a result.

Source: J. Kramarz, Stauffenberg, *1967, pp. 102–4*

At a time when German forces were under growing pressure from Russian troops, the German occupation authorities were treating the Slavic peoples as little more than slaves. To von Stauffenberg's mind, this amounted to the same sort of criminal negligence by the national leadership as that which alienated Beck four years previously.

Von Stauffenberg saw the capitulation of the Sixth Army at Stalingrad in January 1943 as a turning-point. From then on German forces were perpetually in retreat. With a major Russian offensive launched on 22 June 1944 (soon after the D-Day landings), the very borders of the Fatherland came under direct threat. Horrific casualties and a Nazi government incapable of dealing with the threat tipped von Stauffenberg and his closest associates into the desperate acts of 20 July 1944. The following comments were made by the man himself during summer 1944 and indicate how a life without action had become intolerable for this idealist and patriot.

Document 5.14 Moral Imperatives

Claus von Stauffenberg: I could never look the wives and children of the fallen in the eye if I did not do something to stop this senseless slaughter.

Source: R.W. Whalen, Assassinating Hitler, *1993, p.63*

Claus von Stauffenberg, June 1944: Now it is not the Führer or the country or my wife and children which are at stake; it is the entire German people.

Claus von Stauffenberg, just before 20 July: It is now time that something was done. But who has the courage to do something must do so in the knowledge that he will go down in German history as a traitor. If he does not do it, however, he will be a traitor to his conscience.

Source: quoted in P.Hoffmann, The History of the German Resistance 1933–45, *1977, pp. 373–5*

Bearing these comments in mind, consider document 5.15. It shows Hitler arriving at the 'Wolf's Lair' on 15 July 1944. The tall officer on the left is von Stauffenberg. The drama of the scene becomes ever more apparent as we try to think ourselves into it; it lies in the juxtaposition of appearance and deep reality. Von Stauffenberg is standing strictly to attention, betraying no outward emotions, but confronted with the man whom he knew he had to kill. What must have been going on inside his mind?

Document 5.15 Assassin

Source: Ullstein Bilderdienst, Berlin

Von Stauffenberg's decision to act, then, reflected a dual motive. As a military man he was responding to the practical effects of a flawed political ideology and the catastrophic military situation it had brought about. As a patriotic idealist he was prepared to sacrifice himself to show the world that 'Nazi' was not the same as 'German'.

So how have these conservatives been judged? Winston Churchill's reaction was given in the House of Commons on 2 August 1944. He dismissed events by saying that 'the highest personalities of the German Reich are murdering one another, or trying to'. The conclusion of course was hardly justified. Everyone associated with 20 July had come to stand firmly in opposition to the Third Reich. Yet the Western Allies had been making comparable judgements to Churchill's throughout the preceding years. For example, having been contacted through the Bishop of Chichester by some of the resisters in July 1942, Britain's Foreign Minister Anthony Eden stated in a letter that it 'would be contrary to the interest of our nation' even to send them a reply **(Jacobsen (ed.), 1969, p. 64)**. At the Casablanca conference of January 1943 Churchill and Roosevelt agreed that they would only accept 'unconditional surrender' from the German army. Thereafter it became a concerted policy to ignore all peace proposals emanating from Germany. Why was there this hostility? Why were the men who eventually tried to blow up Hitler counted as his acolytes?

Part of the answer lies in the character of the peace plans transmitted. Consider the proposal from Goerdeler to the British government sent in May 1941.

Document 5.16 1914 Borders

A group of Germans, among them personages from every sphere of public life, are prepared to take upon themselves the responsibility of setting up a government that would in due time invite confirmation by free elections of the German people. All measures taken in this connection would be entirely domestic. Meanwhile, however, the group's leaders wish to clarify whether, in accordance with earlier assurances on the part of the British government, it will be possible to initiate negotiations for a peace treaty immediately after the establishment of a German government that rejects National Socialism. The following are the objectives that the German group would wish to pursue as a basis for negotiations:

1 Re-establishment of full national sovereignty for all neutral countries occupied by the combating parties during the war.
2 Confirmation of the pre-war annexations of Austria, the Sudetenland and Memel by Germany.
3 Re-establishment of Germany's 1914 boundaries with Belgium, France and Poland.
4 Settlement of European national boundary lines by a peace conference of all countries concerned, on the basis of national self-determination.
5 Restoration to Germany of her colonies, or of equivalent colonial areas,

together with the establishment of an international mandatory system for all colonies.

6 No reparations; joint reconstruction.

7 Gradual elimination of customs barriers.

8 Establishment of an authorized, international economic council.

9 International control of currencies.

10 Renewal of the activities of the International Labor Office.

11 Enlargement of the scope of international arbitral jurisdiction.

12 Introduction of an institution for a regular conference of European countries, and appropriate integration on a regional basis.

13 General limitation and reduction of armaments.

14 General international control of armaments and armament industries.

Source: Goerdeler's peace plan, 30 May 1941, quoted in H.A. Jacobsen (ed.), Germans Against Hitler, *1969, pp. 54–5*

Individual measures, for example, concerning regular European conferences and arms limitation, were worthy of applause, but in section three Goerdeler was asking Britain to accept the German military conquest of Alsace from France and of the most sensitive parts of Poland. True, by spring 1941 Germany had won a great deal more land than that. Likewise Goerdeler's proposals were modest in comparison to the Führer's ultimate foreign policy goals. A restoration of the nation's borders of 1914 would have added 70,000 square kilometres to Germany's pre-1939 size. In his *Second Book*, Hitler had talked of the need to acquire 500,000 square kilometres **(Weinberg, 1961 and 1995, p. 35)**. But Britain had gone to war specifically over the Polish corridor (a key area that Goerdeler wanted to retain) and France had been her ally. The proposals could not have been agreed.

Even worse flaws were evident in the preconditions laid down for negotiations by von Stauffenberg in early summer 1944.

Document 5.17 Little Change

1 Immediate abandonment of aerial warfare [by the Allies].

2 Abandonment of invasion plans.

3 Avoidance of further bloodshed.

4 Continuing function of [German] defence strength in the East. Evacuation [by Germany] of all occupied regions in the North, West and South.

5 Renunciation of any occupation [of Germany by the Allies].

6 Free government, independent, self-chosen constitution [by Germany].

7 Full co-operation in the carrying out of truce conditions and in peace preparations.

8 Reich borders of 1914 in the east.

Retention of Austria and the Sudetenland within the Reich.

Autonomy of Alsace-Lorraine.

Acquisition of the Tyrol as far as Bozen, Meran.
9 Vigorous reconstruction with joint efforts for European reconstruction.
10 Nations to deal with own criminals.
11 Restoration of honour, self-respect and respect for others.

Source: Gestapo report on von Stauffenberg's conditions for negotiating with the Allies, early summer 1944, quoted in H.A. Jabobsen (ed.), Germans Against Hitler, *1969, pp. 95–6*

At a time when the Western Allies were preparing for Operation Overlord and pursuing a crushing aerial campaign, with the Red Army pressing ever closer towards Germany's borders in the East, proposals 1, 4 and 5 were totally out of the question. Given the war crimes committed against Allied soldiers and the population of France, let alone what had happened in the occupied East, point 10 was equally unrealistic. By this stage the Allies were hardly likely to discuss the *Anschluß* or the retention of the Sudetenland, never mind the Polish corridor!

One of von Moltke's contacts with an American representative in Turkey in 1943 gives at least an initial impression that he might have been a more promising source of cooperation with the Allies.

Document 5.18 Mixed Signals

CONDITIONS OF COLLABORATION WITH THE ALLIES

The following are the future material factors and present political arguments which form the logical prerequisites of a successful collaboration between this Western Group of the German democratic opposition and the Allies.

1 Unequivocal military defeat and occupation of Germany is regarded by the members of the group as a moral and political necessity for the future of the nation.
2 The Group is convinced of the justification of the Allied demand for unconditional surrender, and realizes the untimeliness of any discussion of peace terms before this surrender has been accomplished. . . .
3 An important condition for the success of the plan outlined in the following points is the continuance of an unbroken Eastern front, and simultaneously its approach to within a menacing proximity of the German borders, such as at the line from TILSIT to LEMBERG. Such a situation would justify before the national consciousness radical decisions in the West as the only means of forestalling the overpowering threat from the East.
4 The Group is ready to realize a planned military co-operation with the Allies on the largest possible scale, provided that exploitation of the military information, resources, and authority at the Group's disposal is combined with an all-out military effort by the Allies in such a manner as to make prompt and decisive success on a broad front a practical certainty.

The victory over Hitler, followed by Allied occupation of all Germany in the shortest possible time, would at one stroke so transform the political situation as to set free the real voice of Germany, which would acclaim the action of the Group as a bold act of true patriotism. . . .

5 Should, however, the invasion of Western Europe be embarked upon in the same style as the attack upon the Italian mainland [which had begun in July 1943], any assistance by the Group would not only fail to settle the issue of the War, but would in addition help to create a new 'stab-in-the-back legend'. . . .

Source: Notes on a conversation with von Moltke kept by the American contact, quoted in G. van Roon, German Resistance to Hitler, *1971, pp. 373–4*

Neither Goerdeler nor von Stauffenberg would ever have wished for Germany's total defeat. But what did von Moltke mean by this? Clearly not occupation by the USSR. Stalin's reaction, should he have heard even the merest hint of negotiations along these lines, is easy to guess. And if the Western Allies were themselves to defeat and occupy Germany, how exactly was this to be achieved? What, in fact, could Britain and the USA have thought of von Moltke's attempt to put conditions on the provision of military information? An interesting additional insight here is that on one occasion von Moltke refused an invitation to undertake espionage on behalf of the USA **(von Klemperer, 1992, pp. 331–2)**. He saw himself as a principled politician, not a spy. While much about von Moltke was very worthy indeed, the price of even his cooperation was far too high for Britain and the USA.

We can see that a mixture of patriotism and pride on the part of these members of the conservative élites crystallised in unrealistic expectations of how the Allies would treat their country even after Hitler was deposed. Germany could not, in fact, escape losing the lands acquired by Hitler (whether before or during the Second World War) or occupation by the Allies, including the Soviet Union. Viewed objectively, these men were in no position to place conditions on their cooperation. Under the very dangerous conditions of total war, and because they were not ready to go along completely with the Allied cause, the only option for London and Washington was to leave the members of the conservative opposition at arm's length. Since their hopes did not conform to the goals of the Allies, even if they were not conforming to the demands of the Third Reich, they had to be treated *as if* that was the case.

More surprising than the judgement of the Allies under the pressures of war is that of modern social theorist Ralf Dahrendorf.

Document 5.19 Reaction

[T]he [conservative] German resistance must indeed be understood as largely a reaction. . . . If it is true that, in order to establish its total rule, the Nazi regime had to bring about a social revolution, then resistance against the regime may be described as counterrevolutionary. Given the premise, the substance of resistance is the attempt to resurrect the prerevolutionary state. Where the National Socialist revolution promoted, however reluctantly, modernity, the counterrevolution aimed at the conservation of traditional ties to family and to class, region and religion. While the social revolution of National Socialism was an instrument in the establishment of totalitarian forms, by the same token it had to create the basis of liberal modernity; the counterrevolution on the other hand can be understood only as a revolt of tradition, and thus of illiberalism and of the authoritarianism of a surviving past.

. . . German resistance against Hitler is a leaf of fame in German history; but it is not a step on the path of German society toward the constitution of liberty.

Source: R. Dahrendorf, Society and Democracy in Germany, 1967, pp. 412–15

To this way of thinking, the conservative opponents of Hitler were backward looking and had little to offer the modern world. Historian Hans Mommsen's assessment is not much more encouraging. He says the men of 20 July exemplified 'the narrowness of German political thinking' and that their failure 'spelt the end of "the German way"' **(Mommsen, 1970, p. 147)**. So what ideas did these men have about the future reconstruction of Germany's domestic political order?

The constitutional drafts prepared by the Beck–Goerdeler group are long and complicated. None the less, today's reader is struck by important omissions. Despite occasional talk of the need for national elections (document 5.16, p. 107), typically their planned state had no really significant place for a sovereign parliament based on direct national suffrage. Rather, national representative bodies were either to be appointed or to be elected indirectly. In any event, they were to have strictly limited powers. Real authority would lie with the head of state, the Chancellor and the German government. In a sense, then, these men did favour an authoritarian government and politics. While they also embraced Christianity, proposed the abolition of concentration camps and wanted the dissolution of the secret police, as historian Krüger-Charlé puts it, their plans bore 'a striking resemblance to the Bismarckian constitution' **(Krüger-Charlé, 1991, p. 77)**. They were this chapter's real reactionaries.

Relatively little hard evidence survives about von Stauffenberg's views of domestic politics. We do, however, have the text of an oath he wanted all of his fellow resisters to take.

Document 5.20 The Oath

We wish there to be a new order of society, which will make all Germans supporters of the state, guaranteeing them justice and right, but we despise the lie that all men are equal, and accept the natural ranks. We wish to see a people with its roots deep in the soil of its native country, close to the forces of nature, finding happiness and satisfaction in labouring in the status into which it has been called, and proud to overcome the base emotions of envy and ill-will. We wish to see leaders from all classes of society, bound to the divine forces, taking the lead on the grounds of their highmindedness, virtue and spirit of self-sacrifice.

Source: P. Hoffmann, The History of the German Resistance 1933–45, *1977, p. 321*

In line with his own upbringing in Schwabia and the influence of the poet Stefan George, von Stauffenberg was thinking of a regenerated society based on the principles of an aristocratic and idealised medieval Germany. Although such ideas clearly have a reactionary ring about them, they also bear comparison with aspects of National Socialism. At least some of Hitler's supporters, most notably the agrarian ideologist Walther Darré, hoped for the creation of a rurally idyllic Germany. National Socialists also would have agreed with the emphasis on natural inequalities between men. In the context of the Third Reich, von Stauffenberg was more than just a reactionary.

Greater evidence exists about von Moltke's thinking. Following opposition conferences at his Kreisau estate, in August 1943 he wrote 'The Basic Principles of Reconstruction', a plan of how Germany's political system could be rebuilt once Hitler was overthrown. As we might expect given his character, and bearing some comparison to the Goerdeler–Beck group, he emphasised Christian principles, human freedom, the inviolability of law, the sanctity of the family and anti-racism. More unexpected for the modern reader was his description of how Germany's prospective electoral system should work.

Document 5.21 Alternative Democracy

I THE PARISH

The representative institutions of the parish are to be elected by all who are qualified to vote in secret and direct ballots. Everybody who is over 21 or who has fought in the war has the right to vote; heads of family have an additional vote for each child not entitled to vote; anybody can be elected who is over 27 and whose candidature is agreed upon by a number of voters – the number depending on the local community; members of the Armed Forces cannot be elected.

II THE COUNTY

The representative institutions in the counties and in the towns that are independent of the counties are to be elected in accordance with the same principle as those that govern the representative institutions of the parishes. The same applies to the subordinate divisions of the towns that are independent of the counties. Electoral districts that are too large for the individual voter to survey are to be subdivided.

III THE LAND [REGION]

1 The Landtag [regional assembly] in the *Länder* and the city assembly in the cities outside the counties are to be chosen by the representative bodies of the counties and cities or, in the case of the cities outside the counties, by the representative assemblies in the political sub-divisions. Any male citizen who has completed his 27th year can be elected. Political civil servants and members of the armed forces cannot be elected. . . .

2 The Landtag government consists of the chief minister and the requisite number of privy councillors. The chief minister is to be chosen by the Landtag. . . .

The Land government is responsible for the government of the Land and the execution of the Reich's functions within the territory of the Land. . . .

IV THE REICH

1 The Reichstag [national assembly] is to be elected by the Landtags. Any male citizen of the Reich over 27 can be elected. Political civil servants and members of the Armed Forces cannot be elected. For the time being the electoral arrangements should ensure that at least half of those elected do not belong to one of the electoral bodies.

Source: 'Basic Principles of Reconstruction', draft of 9 August 1943 by Helmuth von Moltke, quoted in G. van Roon, German Resistance to Hitler, *1971, pp. 347–54*

Local elections would determine local assemblies. These assemblies would choose their own representatives to progress to the next level of government. In turn these would then elect representatives for the Reichstag. Clearly the ideas bear little relation to the way today's democracies actually work, but does this mean they were reactionary? To understand von Moltke's ideas properly, we need to put them into their historical context. He was trying to learn from the collapse of the Weimar constitution. At a time of national crisis, Hitler the demagogue had proved able to subvert the whole country by exploiting nationwide elections. By replacing these with numerous local ones, von Moltke was trying to develop a system which would never allow the same mistake again. In this light, even if von Moltke's ideas do not bear much relationship to the way Germany's political system actually developed after 1945, they were forward looking nevertheless.

These, then, were the men and the ideas at the heart of the conservative opposition to Hitler. Each individual became an opponent by his own route and from a different starting-point. Goerdeler and Beck were patriots, traditionalists and reactionaries who conformed to National Socialism's demands until the movement showed its crudest, most warlike character. Equally patriotic was von Stauffenberg who went along with the Third Reich until it became clear that National Socialism's ideological fixity was destroying the war effort. A rural utopian, it is ironic that the man who came nearest to killing Hitler conformed to the greatest extent with the politics of his movement in ideological terms at least. By contrast von Moltke was always at odds with National Socialism's inhumanity. A democrat of sorts, he tried to come up with a forward looking alternative political model for Germany. It was a genuine tragedy that these men could never bridge the gap completely to bring about cooperation with Britain and the USA. Unwilling to conform to the standards of either the Third Reich or the Allies, they were, and had to remain, a German opposition.

So were the conservative élites one of the great failures of history? Such a verdict has been flatly contradicted by the Chancellor of the Federal Republic of Germany, Helmut Kohl, who is also an historian. The following views are drawn from a speech delivered in the early 1980s and have to be read against the background of a Germany at the time still divided between East and West.

Document 5.22 West German Verdict

The attempt to assassinate Adolf Hitler on July 20 1944 is one of the great events in our country's history. . . .

It is a reminder that Hitler did not succeed in pulling the German nation as a whole into an abyss of immorality and cynicism. It helps us to save German history in the face of the perversion it suffered at the hands of this dictator. It imposes on us the obligation of combining our shame at what happened with the appeal to resist any totalitarian tendencies in the political sphere. . . .

[It has] . . . become a symbol of that 'other Germany', i.e. of all those Germans who stood up for their democratic, religious, political and ethical values under a totalitarian regime and fought against the criminal National Socialist system . . . !

We are thankful for the fact that our freedom was reborn in the death chambers of Plötzensee [the prison where many of those involved in 20 July were executed]. The members of the resistance movement proved themselves to be free individuals who, in the face of evil and overwhelming odds, claimed for themselves the dignity of responsibility and, on the basis of their courageous actions, expressed for their people the hope of freedom. At a time when lies abounded in Germany, they again brought truthfulness and responsible action to the fore. In doing so, they brought about Germany's rescue from moral despair. . . .

Our commemoration of July 20th is an appeal to distinguish between our free democratic society and the dictatorship imposed by a totalitarian regime. . . . [The Chancellor was implying a similarity between Nazi and Soviet totalitarianism.]

Source: T. Heuss et al., Reflections on July 20 1944, 1984, pp. 11–21

Certainly the Chancellor of what was then West Germany emphasised the democratic credentials of Hitler's conservative opponents to excess. In a world affected by the Cold War, his purpose was political: to criticise all types of non-democratic government, both National Socialist and Communist. Likewise just as the old East Germany used the Communist opposition as a means to create a valid link between postwar and prewar society (see document 2.2, p. 24), so Helmut Kohl was doing the same for the Federal Republic through the conservative opposition. History used for political ends always has to be treated with care. None the less the Federal Chancellor was correct that all the members of the conservative opposition, whether or not implicated directly in the events of 20 July, were involved in acts of moral testimony.

This reality is readily apparent in the sense of responsibility which underlay both Beck's memos of 1938 (especially document 5.12, pp. 104–5) and von Stauffenberg's comments of summer 1944 (document 5.14, p. 106). It alone gave meaning to von Moltke's life. Although these men neither killed Hitler nor seized power, they did provide future generations of Germans with a symbol to combat any resurgence of interest in National Socialism. From this perspective, their story is not just that of fundamental opponents of the Third Reich, it is of a real success.

6

Germany's Jewish citizens
like lambs to the slaughter?

Within weeks of Hitler becoming Chancellor, the train of anti-Semitic persecutions synonymous with the history of the Third Reich began. In April 1933, boycotts of Jewish shops were organised and legislation was passed removing Jews from public employment. After a summer of popular anti-Semitic agitation, in September 1935 the Führer personally proclaimed the Nuremberg Laws which defined as Jewish anyone 'descended from at least three grandparents who were racially full Jews' and which deprived these individuals of protection before the law. From this time on, Jews and 'Aryans' could no longer marry. A dramatic escalation in discrimination occurred in November 1938 when, across the nation, Jewish homes and synagogues were ransacked in a string of pogroms called 'Crystal Night'. Over the following days, Germany's Jews were stripped of their financial assets. During wartime, they were deported to Eastern Europe where their fate became inter-twined with that of every Jewish community in Nazi occupied territory. Some 'fortunate' individuals initially were used as slave labour. Nevertheless, sooner or later the vast majority of Europe's Jews (altogether some 6 million people) fell victim to the attempted genocide known as 'the Final Solution to the Jewish Question' or 'the Holocaust'.

Jews held a place in the Third Reich fundamentally different to that of most other Germans. Whether workers, churchgoers, youths or members of the conservative élites, non-Jews could claim a chance to survive by conforming to Hitler's demands. For a 'Jew', conformity led to certain death. So why did history develop in that way? We have already seen evidence both of Hitler's long-standing, deeply felt anti-Semitism and of the intrinsically radical nature of National Socialism (documents 1.2 and 1.12, pp. 2–4 and 12). But historian Raul Hilberg believes that the way the victims reacted to their persecution also played a part. In his monumental study of the Holocaust, Hilberg discusses how so many people could have been killed so quickly.

Document 6.1 Inaction and Compliance

The reaction pattern of the Jews [to the gradual escalation of Nazi persecutions] is characterized by almost complete lack of resistance. . . . On a European-wide scale the Jews had no resistance organization, no blue-print for armed action, no plan even for psychological warfare. They were completely unprepared. . . . They took up resistance only in a few cases, locally, and at the last moment.

If, therefore, we look at the whole Jewish reaction pattern, we notice that its two salient features are an attempt to avert action and, failing that, automatic compliance with [German] orders. Why is this so? Why did the Jews act in this way? The Jews attempted to tame the Germans as one would attempt to tame a wild beast. They avoided 'provocations' and complied instantly with decrees and orders. They hoped that somehow the German drive would spend itself.

This hope was founded on a two-thousand-year-old experience. In exile [after leaving the Holy Land in biblical times] the Jews had always been a minority; they had always been in danger; but they had learned that they could avert danger and survive destruction by placating and appeasing their enemies. . . . Time and again they were attacked, they endured the Crusades, the Cossack uprisings, and the Czarist persecution. There were many casualties in these times of stress, but always the Jewish community emerged once again like a rock from a receding tidal wave. The Jews had never really been annihilated. . . . Only in 1941, 1942, and 1943 did the Jewish leadership realize that, unlike the pogroms of past centuries, the modern machine-like destruction process would engulf European Jewry. But the realization came too late. A two-thousand-year-old lesson could not be unlearned; the Jews could not make the switch. They were helpless.

Source: R. Hilberg, The Destruction of the European Jews, *1985, pp. 662–8*

To Hilberg's mind, over the centuries Jewish communities had learned to survive persecution by conforming to the demands of their host society. This lesson helped seal their fate. Although the following source does not tell us the precise nationality of the Jews concerned, it does provide a most poignant example of how some did go along quietly with Nazi orders right to the end. The event took place in German occupied Eastern Europe during the war years.

Document 6.2 Lambs to the Slaughter

The father was holding the hand of a boy about ten years old and was speaking to him softly; the boy was fighting his tears. The father pointed to the sky, stroked his head, and seemed to explain something to him. . . . I remember a girl, slim and with black hair, who passed close to me, pointed to herself, and said, 'Twenty-three' . . . . The people, completely naked, went down some steps which were cut in the clay wall of the pit and clambered over the heads of the people lying there, to the place where the SS-man directed them. They then lay down in front of the dead or injured people; some caressed those who were still alive and spoke to them in a low voice. Then I heard a series of shots.

Source: Eyewitness account of killing action, quoted in R. Hilberg, The
Destruction of the European Jews, *1985, p. 669*

Is Hilberg's overall assessment fair? Did Germany's Jews really go 'like lambs to the
slaughter'? We have to start by identifying the position they had held in German
society before Hitler came to power. According to a census carried out in 1933,
about half a million people living in Germany called themselves Jewish. They made
up less than 0.8 per cent of the national population. With 70 per cent of their
number living in towns of over 100,000 inhabitants, and 33 per cent of all German
Jews living in Berlin, they were disproportionately urban **(Kaplan, 1990,
pp. 580–1)**. Correspondingly Jews were underrepresented in agricultural trades,
but overrepresented in commerce and the free professions, such as law and
medicine. These patterns were also in part 'hang-overs' from the days before Jews
enjoyed full social emancipation, when they were allowed neither to own land nor
to work in the civil service. In accordance with their commercial and professional
status, by and large Germany's Jews felt they belonged to the nation's thoroughly
respectable urban middle classes.

About 80 per cent of Jewish families had lived in Germany for many centuries.
While they were anxious to retain their own Jewish identity, still they had assimilated into unobtrusive, important components of 'their' country. The other 20 per
cent were so-called *Ostjuden* (Eastern Jews) **(Kaplan, 1990, p. 581)**. During the
First World War, Germany's assimilated Jews had been as shocked as anyone
to discover large communities of very poor and very distinctive Orthodox Jews in
the eastern lands that were occupied temporarily. After 1918 a number of these
people migrated to Germany. As recorded in *Mein Kampf*, when he saw an
Orthodox Jew in Vienna, Hitler had been struck dramatically by 'an apparition in
a black caftan and black hair locks' **(Hitler, 1985, pp. 48–52)**. Many of
Germany's assimilated Jews considered the newcomers just as alien and a source
of humour **(Zuelzer, 1991, p. 156)**.

In other words, by 1933 Germany's well-established Jews were relatively few in
number, enjoyed relatively secure existences and were so well integrated into
urban life that they hardly felt Jewish at all. They certainly felt little in common with
the generally new, even less numerous Orthodox Jews and did not expect
seriously to be categorised alongside them. As a result, at the start of the Third
Reich many German Jews did not appreciate that they were facing much of a
threat. Such misplaced confidence is displayed in historian A.J. Sherman's discussion
of the influential and well-established Jewish banker Max Warburg.

Document 6.3 Warburg and Co.

A senior partner in M.M. Warburg and Co., Max Warburg naturally
attempted to assess the new circumstances, and almost immediately came to
an essentially optimistic conclusion that contrasted sharply with the views of
his family; he was later to confess that he had completely underestimated
the demonic energies Hitler was able to exploit, and the mass support he

enjoyed. Max Warburg wrote: 'I considered it absolutely inconceivable that this man could ever become the ruler of one of the most creative, industrious and powerful of peoples.'

As far as his own personal position was concerned, Max Warburg brushed aside all efforts to warn him of *Gestapo* surveillance or physical danger: after all, he and two other Jewish bankers were among the eight members of the *Generalrat* [general council] of the *Reichsbank* [national bank] who on 17th March 1933, had jointly signed Schacht's formal appointment as President; and signatories included both Hindenburg and Hitler.

Max Warburg overrode his partners' and family's advice, and decided to continue the bank's business, come what may. 'I was determined to defend my firm like a fortress', he wrote, 'I had no doubt that we were at the beginning of one of those many periods of suffering that the Jews in particular have had to undergo; but it was my firm belief that this period would be limited in duration. From this belief I drew the strength that enabled me to carry on.'

Source: A.J. Sherman, 'Eine Jüdische Bank in der Ära Schacht', 1986, pp. 167–8

When persecution began, the responses of Jews reflected their degree of integration into German society. Representing the unassimilated Jews, the Organization of Independent Orthodox Communities wrote to Hitler personally as early as October 1933 stating that they seemed to be 'sentenced to a slow but certain death by starvation' and pleading to be told 'the bitter truth' about their future **(Arad et al. (eds), 1981, pp. 59–63)**. More confidently, believing they could influence Hitler's government, assimilated Jews and the organisations representing especially their interests wrote to the Reich authorities protesting against growing discrimination. The following is the text of a letter sent to the Reich Minister of War.

Document 6.4 The Right to Join the Army

The Government of the German Reich, on March 16, 1935, published the Law for the Reconstruction of the Wehrmacht. 'Service in the Wehrmacht is based on general conscription.' The duty of serving in the Army means the right to be a German soldier. This right and this duty is also claimed by the German Jews. In view of the legislation on Aryans the Reich Association of German Jews [see document 6.6, pp. 122–3] feels called upon to bring this fact to your especial knowledge, Mr Reich Minister of War, as it will be your responsibility to prepare the supplementary regulations to the Law.

Twelve thousand German Jews gave their lives for Germany in the World War. In memory of these dead, as representatives for the living, for ourselves and our children, we declare:

We German Jews are confident that we will not be denied participation in military service on equal terms with other Germans.

Source: Protest of the Reichvertretung sent to the Minister of War against the refusal to include Jews in the Wehrmacht, March 1935, quoted in Y. Arad *et al. (eds),* Documents on the Holocaust, *1981, pp. 71–2*

The demand went unheeded. On 25 July 1935, Jews were excluded completely from the armed services.

In keeping with middle-class notions of respectability and responsibility, Germany's well-established Jewish population also began looking to legal institutions for protection. A remarkable success in this connection was won not through the German legal process, but through the League of Nations. As an accident of the post-First World War peace settlement, the Geneva Convention of 15 May 1922, which stipulated that national minorities be treated fairly, was in force in Upper Silesia during the early years of the Third Reich. When anti-Semitic measures were introduced into the area, some Jewish lawyers protested over the heads of the Reich government. Historian Karol Jonca explains what happened.

Document 6.5 Success in Silesia

The case of Franz Bernheim was made into a pretext. Bernheim had been discharged from the DEFAKA store in Gleiwitz on account of his Jewish descent; he was deprived of his livelihood and emigrated to Czechoslovakia. Several other acts discriminating against the Jewish population and violating the provisions of the Geneva Convention were mentioned in the petition to the Council of the League of Nations by [Arnold] Wiener on 12 May. Among them were the statutes on the 'Reorganisation of the Civil Service' of 7 April 1933 and on admission to the legal profession of the same date, as well as the decree about exercising notarial duties of 1 April, the statute on the introduction of a *numerus clausus* into the educational system of 15 April, and the like.

A report on the situation of the Jewish population in Silesia was delivered to the League by the Irish delegate, Sean Lester. Bernheim's case, presented against the background of new discriminatory statutes applied by the Third Reich, led him to draw the conclusion that the Acts infringed upon the provisions of the third part of the Convention by 'unequal treatment of the Jewish population'. Lester emphasised that the discriminating statutes should not be applied in the part of Silesia that was covered by the Convention of 1922. Arguments put forward during the debates by the German delegate, von Keller, were unconvincing and were rejected. During the debates of 26 May and 6 June, von Keller had to give assurances that the Reich legislation would not break international commitments, and that the Reich government would honour those commitments in the third part of the Geneva Convention. Von Keller declared that offences against the Convention had been taking place until then due to the application of the statutes by the German administrative authorities, and that the damage they had caused would be compensated for. . . . Bernheim was awarded damages on account of his unfounded dismissal from the store. The consequences of the affirmative decision by the League were of much greater significance to the Jewish population of *Regierungsbezirk* [government district] Oppeln. In the part of Silesia coming under the Geneva Convention, the Jewish population was recognised as a minority and protected by the minority statute. Only Jews of non-German citizenship were not guaranteed the status of minority members. . . .

Source: K. Jonca, 'Jewish Resistance to Nazi Racial Legislation in Silesia, 1933–1937', 1990, pp. 80–2

Nor did success end there. As a result of continuing discrimination, in September 1933 the Association of Synagogues in the Province of Upper Silesia informed the German Foreign Office of its intention to send a fresh set of petitions to the League of Nations. Rather than risk another national humiliation, Prussian Minister of the Interior Ludwig Grauert met Jewish representatives at once. Thereafter the Geneva Convention was properly enforced until the League of Nations' supervision expired in 1937. Thereafter Upper Silesia's Jews suffered the same fate as the others.

Organised, 'respectable' Jewish activity was, however, far from limited to petitions and the law courts. All manner of German Jews began to band together to help themselves as best they could. The strategy built on quite extensive ties which existed already. Jewish religious and welfare organisations had been set up before the First World War, and had proliferated during the Weimar years. For example, Zionist organisations had prepared settlers for Palestine, others had helped Jews living in the poorer areas of Berlin. But now the need for self-help was more urgent. Articles appeared in newspapers calling for action. As early as spring 1933, Jewish doctors and artists began to organise **(Barkai, 1989, p. 41)**. Most important, to coordinate all their efforts, an umberella organisation, called the Reich Association of German Jews, was established. In September 1933 it laid out its goals.

Document 6.6 Reich Association of German Jews

At a time that is as hard and difficult as any in Jewish history, but also significant as few times have been, we have been entrusted with the leadership and representation of the German Jews by a joint decision of the State Association of the Jewish Communities (*Landesverbände*), the major Jewish organizations and the large Jewish communities of Germany.

There was no thought of party interests, no separate aims in this decision, but solely and wholly the realization that the lives and future of the German Jews today depend on their unity and cooperation. The first task is to make this unity live. There must be recognition of the vitality and aims of every organization and association, but in all major and decisive tasks there must only be one union, only the totality of the German Jews. Anyone who goes his own way today, who excludes himself today, has committed a wrong against the vital need of the German Jews. . . .

There is only one area in which we are permitted to carry out our own ideas, our own aims, but it is a decisive area, that of our Jewish life and Jewish future. This is where the most clearly defined tasks exist.

There are new duties in Jewish education, new areas of Jewish schooling must be created, and existing ones must be nurtured and protected, in order that the rising generation may find spiritual strength, inner resistance, and physical competence. There must be thoughtful selection in order to develop and redirect our youth towards professions which offer them a place in life and prospects of a future.

All there is now, all that has been begun, all that has been attempted must be joined together here to give aid and support. All that is destructive must be opposed, and all our strength devoted to reconstruction on the religious base of Judaism.

Much of our former economic security has been taken from us German Jews, or at least reduced. Within the area that remains open to us the individual must be drawn away from his isolation. Occupational connections and associations, where permissible, can increase existing strength and give support to the weak, can make experience and contacts useful for all. There will be not a few who will be refused a place of work or the exercise of their profession on German soil. We are faced by the fact which can no longer be questioned or opposed, of a clear, historic necessity to give our youth new [living] space. It has become a great task to discover places and open roads, as on the sacred soil of Palestine [the state of Israel as we know it today did not exist at this time], for which Providence has decreed a new era, as everywhere where the character, industry and ability of the German Jews can prove themselves, robbing none of their bread, but creating a livelihood for others.

For this and all else we hope for the understanding assistance of the authorities, and the respect of our gentile fellow citizens, whom we join in love and loyalty to Germany.

We place our faith in the active sense of community and of responsibility of the German Jews, as also in the willingness to sacrifice of our brothers everywhere.

We will stand united and, in confidence in our God, labour for the honour of the Jewish Name. May the nature of the German Jews arise anew from the tribulations of this time!

Reich Association of German Jews
Leo Baeck. . . .

Source: Jüdische Rundschau no. 78, 29 September 1933, reproduced in Y. Arad et al. (eds), Documents on the Holocaust, *1981, pp. 57–9*

If Germany's Jews had been too diverse and, in part, too unaware of their Jewishness to form a nationwide community before 1933, the aim of the Reich Association was to forge this now for the common good. Germany's Jews had to re-experience their culture, redirect their education, sponsor their own businesses, maybe some of them even had to look to Palestine for their future.

Self-help organisations tried to offer aid wherever it was needed. From early 1933, twenty-five small Jewish organisations had been arranging loans of 100 to 200 RM. Originally set up to help *Ostjuden*, they quickly took on a more general purpose. As discrimination increased, by 1935 a third of all German Jews needed some sort of financial assistance. Jewish community funds were used to supply it. In the same year, a Jewish 'Winter Help' campaign was launched. It was supported by 83 per cent of salaried Jews. The project raised 4 million RM (out of a total of 25 million RM donated to communal aid that year) and was used to help 85,000 people, or 20 per cent of the German–Jewish population at that time. In 1934, Jewish welfare organisations provided 11,200 food packages and 66,350 warm meals to Jewish families. By 1937 the figures were 26,400 and 78,700 **(Barkai, 1989, p. 95)**. As document 6.6 recommended, extensive retraining schemes were instituted. By the end of 1933, 6,000 Jews were participating in these. All in all, by the end of 1938, 30,000 people had been through one of the different programmes on offer – that is to say 55 per cent of German–Jewish youth.

But did this mixture of semi-official complaint, recourse to law and self-help constitute a valid Jewish response? Did it amount to opposition to the Third Reich? Arguing from one particular angle, the views of historian H. Winterfeld put us in mind of Hilberg's initial line.

Document 6.7 Misguided?

Nothing was done, at least in the provinces, by those Jews who had recognized the Nazis' true intentions, to make clear to their uneducated co-religionists . . . that there was no future in Hitler's Germany for Jews and 'non-Aryans'. . . . . Instead of trying to make life for Jews under Nazi tyranny as pleasant as possible, everything, and every possible Pfennig [penny or cent], should have been invested in attempting to get Jews out of the country. . . . People were far too concerned with trying to give life under Nazi rule some content and meaning and to make it as pleasant as possible. The efforts undertaken by Jewish organizations were also in this direction – instead of forcing people, possibly with Nazi assistance, to emigrate.

Source: H. Winterfelt, quoted in A. Barkai, From Boycott to Annihilation, *1989, p. 141*

Since it was impossible to change the government's clear and mounting anti-Semitism, did anything short of a dedicated policy of escape amount to conformity to the government's desire to victimise Jews?

Jewish emigration from Germany could indeed have been greater. Until 1939, for example, the USA's immigration quota of 25,000 people per year from that country was never actually filled **(Koonz, 1987, p. 363)**. What is more, of the 35,000 people who emigrated in 1933, 2,000 had returned by 1935 believing that the threat was over! But the decision to emigrate was never an easy one. Typically, while Jewish women were quite prepared to leave, Jewish men, with their business interests rooted in Germany, were not **(Koonz, 1986, pp. 285ff.)**. Nazi emigration policies imposed penal levels of taxation of would-be emigrants. Financial losses for Jewish emigrants were 60 per cent in 1934, rising to 96 per cent in 1939 **(Kwiet, 1991a, p. 143)**. Under the circumstances, there is a case for being impressed that German Jews showed as much interest as they did in emigration. For example, the Jewish leadership did not ignore it (as Winterfelt suggests). The initial declaration of the Reich Association of German Jews (document 6.6, p. 122) had raised the prospect of a future in Palestine. What is more, of those training for new jobs in 1933, 1,300 people were active on farms run by Zionists, and so by definition were orientated to lands beyond Germany **(Barkai, 1989, p. 46)**. Eighty per cent of those who retrained in agriculture eventually emigrated. In all, 130,000 German Jews, or almost 20 per cent of the 1933 population, left Germany between 1933 and 1937. Another 118,000 left in the wake of the 'Crystal Night' pogroms **(Barkai, 1989, p. 142)**. As a result of continuing emigration, by October 1941 only 164,000 Jews remained. Of these, over 50 per cent were aged over 50 and only 13 per cent under 18 **(Kwiet, 1991a, p. 147)**. If emigration amounted to opposition through escape, the vast majority of German Jews did oppose the Third Reich.

This is not such a bad record for a group which started out as far from coherent, numbered less than 1 per cent of the population and many of whom never believed they could become targets. Naturally, ignoring their respectable, middle-class heritage, individuals also took direct action against the government in their own way. Here are the memories of Edith Wolff, a half-Jew. Although there was a limit to what one person could do, she did her best to undermine anti-Semitism wherever she found it.

Document 6.8 'Danger – Poison!'

There was nothing left for me but to proceed against the hated Third Reich through individual actions – naturally I could only limit myself to occasional 'pin pricks' – with trivial efforts that lacked real significance, that were really only for my personal satisfaction.

So I got into the habit of sticking written slips of paper in catalogues and indexes of public libraries (which still admitted Jews and non-Aryans until the Nuremberg Laws), at those places where Hitler's *Kampf*-book and other National Socialist literature (Rosenberg's *Myth of the Twentieth Century*) were referred to. I'd got stickers for medicine bottles from a pharmacist with the printed slogan 'Danger – Poison!' I stuck them to the top or bottom of the classification and description of this political trash. Now and again I even borrowed such books and returned them with critical comments in the margin and polemical notes added.

When the Nazis started special actions against the Jews, I typed a note and sent it to National Socialist central offices and authorities – for instance to the secretariat of the Propaganda Ministry, to the editors of leading Nazi newspapers or to the management of German radio stations. Often I just put cards or pieces of paper I had written on (with the simple address 'to the German People') in various postboxes. It was always just one-line comments or quite short pieces of writing which I sent like that.

After the boycott of 1 April 1933 I sent several postcards – at that time from abroad – just addressed 'Germany' and reading as follows: 'You say: the Jews are your misfortune? – We say: Let's hope so!'

After the burning of the synagogues and arson attacks of 9.11.1938 I wrote: 'National Socialism is the greatest cultural disgrace of world history' – signed 'the Eternal Jew'.

After the obligatory introduction of the Jewish star for the Jewish population in September 1941 my text read: 'Now Germany means *Braunschweig* [Brunswick]: One half is '*Braun*' ['brown' – i.e., National Socialist], the other half '*schweigt*' [is silent].'

Source: Quoted in F. Kroh, David kämpft, 1988, p. 104

Individual Jews also participated in opposition groups involving 'Aryan' Germans. Police reports from the Nuremberg area in 1934 indicated that Jews were disproportionately active in Communist and Socialist organisations. For example, seventy-nine Jews were identified as left-wing activists and thirteen were said to be guilty of treason **(Eschwege, 1989, p. 438)**.

During the period 1933–9, Jews opposed the Third Reich by a whole host of strategies. How did their activities develop in wartime? We will look at evidence relating to three main themes: the deportations of Jews from Germany to Eastern Europe, the nature of self-government of Jewish communities in the East and life in extermination camps.

Of 134,000 German Jews who were transported from Germany eastwards, only 8,000 survived the war **(Kwiet, 1991a, p. 140)**. In her diary, Else Behrend-Rosenfeld described the way Jewish welfare organisations were tasked by German authorities to organise 'resettlement'.

Document 6.9 Resettlement

Now I have been sitting a long time at my writing desk with my diary in front of me, deeply shaken by the experiences of the last ten days, and wondering how to put them into words. But often words are not enough. So I want to describe to you as well as I can what has stirred me up (and indeed all of us) to such an extent. On 5 November [1941] a resident in our [welfare] home came to me in my daily afternoon consultation session and asked me if I knew that a deportation was being planned and prepared at the moment right here in Munich. I replied to him truthfully that I didn't know anything about it and added rather angrily, because I was shocked, that people shouldn't see ghosts everywhere because we had enough to do in dealing with our real problems. I asked him to calm down and above all not to spread this dreadful rumour around – something which he promised. On the very next day, the head teacher reported to me that he had been asked anxiously by another resident what this rumour was all about. On 7 November, the office of the Jewish community asked head teacher Heilbronner and I to a discussion about affairs to do with the home at midday on 8 November in the office of the Jewish community in Lindwurmstraße. . . .

All of the managers of the homes and welfare organisations were at the meeting, and the two chairmen of the Jewish community appeared. Director Stahl explained to us in brief and very earnestly – I can still feel my deep shock – that actually around a thousand Jewish people were to be deported from Munich in the coming week. The final selection of these poor people had not yet been carried out. . . . Head teacher Heilbronner and I exchanged a horrified glance when the number of 85 people from our home was mentioned. We knew that our board of directors had succeeded in ensuring that younger children would not be separated from their parents and women would not be separated from their husbands. But it was impossible for siblings to stay together. . . .

We went home together in silence. . . . In the long hall on the ground floor there was a confused crowd, just as whenever the workers were at home. And today everyone was expecting our return tensely, they were hoping to learn something about the meeting . . . to get comforting news about the lack of foundation for the rumours that were flying around. Each of us was surrounded immediately by a thick circle of a lot of people. We warded off all of the penetrating questions, saying that the meeting had only been about administrative affairs. I saw the disbelief, indeed the disappointment written clearly on most faces when I gave my unsatisfactorily short reply [i.e., she did not tell the people at the home either that deportations were about to begin or whom they would affect]. . . .

As early as midday on the next day, a Sunday, a message arrived from the community with the deportation order for each individual.

Source: Diary entry of 16 November 1941, in E. Behrend-Rosenfeld, Ich stand nicht allein, *1988, pp. 121–4*

Involvement obviously was never easy. We can even attribute noble motives to it. Behrend-Rosenfeld provided aid packages and money for deportees in an effort to make the whole process at least minimally tolerable. It was felt that if German authorities carried out the measures on their own, things would be worse still. But once again we have to ask whether the response was justified. As early as spring

1940 Behrend-Rosenfeld had read in letters from Poland that conditions there were truly dreadful. It was said that twenty-five Jews in every thousand died during the journey alone **(Behrend-Rosenfeld, 1988, pp. 82–5)**. Should the only relation-ship between Jewish organisations and deportation have been one of protest?

Once in the East, German Jews found communities (or better 'ghettos') run by committees of well-respected co-religionists, including representatives from their own country. The committees were called *Judenräte* and had been set up by the German occupation authorities in accordance with an order given out by chief of the security police, Reinhard Heydrich, on 21 September 1939 **(Arad et al. (eds), 1981, pp. 173–5)**. They were expected to administer the ghettos. The job involved registering everyone who was there, providing any reports that were required and supplying lists of names for forced labour **(Hilberg, 1977, p. 33)**. The *Judenräte* were supposed to stop smuggling, confiscate property and round up people for further 'resettlement' (a 'cover' term for extermination). In fulfilling these tasks, just like Behrend-Rosenfeld's organisation, the *Judenräte* felt that some-how they could avoid the worst that the German authorities might hand out to them. But historian Raul Hilberg argues that whatever their precise motives, it was the effects of the *Judenräte* that mattered most.

Document 6.10 *Judenrat* (1)

The Jewish Councils [*Judenräte*], West and East, tried to postpone disaster or, failing in that attempt, to reduce its extent. They cautioned against provoking the Germans and sought out ways to create work projects that would make as many Jews as possible indispensable to the war economy. The effort played into German hands. The perpetrators too had a minimization strategy. They wanted to reduce their costs to a minimum, keeping guard forces small, and exploiting scarce Jewish labour until the last moment. The Jewish and German policies, at first glance opposites, were in reality pointed in the same direction.

If we look at the Councils as Nazi Germany saw them, they were clearly tools created for the purpose of maintaining law and order and mobilizing the Jewish community for German ends. They were all the more effective to the extent that they were authentic, concerned, and compliant. We might add that often enough the Councils were necessary tools, that they relieved a burden on an overtaxed German apparatus, that in supplying information, money, police, and labour they performed tasks for which the Germans themselves did not have sufficient means. By and large, the Gestapo and the civil administration did not finance ghetto walls, did not keep order in ghetto streets, did not make up deportation lists. They availed themselves of the intermediary structure of the Jewish Councils and offices. We can see the syndrome now, but was it observable then?

Source: R. Hilberg, 'The Judenrat: Conscious or Unconscious Tool?', 1977, p. 38

Hilberg asks how members of the *Judenräte* understood their actions. A particularly terrible example, once again with echoes of the Behrend-Rosenfeld case, is provided by Leo Baeck. Formerly the chairman of the Reich Association of German Jews (document 6.6, pp. 122–3), he became a member of the *Judenrat* in Theresienstadt (a ghetto in Czechoslovakia). One day he met an engineer who had escaped from Auschwitz camp. He was told that Jews were being gassed there. Baeck had to decide what to do with the information. After the war, this is how he looked back on his decision.

Document 6.11 The Terrible Secret

If the Council of Elders [in effect the rest of the *Judenrat*] were informed, the whole camp would know within a few hours. Living in the expectation of death by gassing would only be the harder. And this death was not certain for all – there was selection for slave labor; perhaps not all transports went to Auschwitz. So came the grave decision to tell no one. Rumors of all sorts were constantly spreading through the ghetto, and before long rumors of Auschwitz spread too. But at least no one knew for certain.

Source: L. Baeck, quoted in L. Baker, Days of Sorrow, 1978, p. 137

Baeck opted for total secrecy to stop people worrying. The motive may have been pure, but as historian Jacob Robinson has pointed out, to some minds the policy amounted to deliberate deception, even 'collaboration' **(Robinson, 1972, p. xxxi)**.

It is hardly surprising that many accounts portray Jews as thoroughly dejected by the time they faced extermination camps and death. The years of experience of growing discrimination coupled with the processes of self-organised deportation and self-government must have gone a long way towards wearing down the will to oppose the system. Referring to unpublished reports, in the following document an historian summarises the views of two internees in Auschwitz about the attitudes of Jews by the time they reached the camp.

Document 6.12 Dejection

Erich Hoffmann [an internee of Auschwitz], who was in external camp Jawischowitz [at Auschwitz] from August 1942, writes that of the 1,500 Jews interned there, only a few were motivated to join the resistance group which was created by about 30 Jewish Communists. Later perhaps 80 and then 140 youths came on the scene, in whose block Hoffmann had become superintendent. Hoffmann refers in . . . [his] . . . report to the 'many difficulties' which the Communist Party group in Jawischowitz had with 'the Jews who for the most part were indifferent', since they had lost hope, had resigned themselves to their fate and were of the opinion that they couldn't do anything other than wait. *Heribert Kreuzmann* [another internee], who also signed this report, later emphasised the particularly difficult situation of the Jews, who he characterised as lacking in will. There was only 'anything to be done' with those who had had contact with the workers' movement.

Source: H. Langbein, ... nicht wie die Schafe zur Schlachtenbank, 1994, p. 196

But dejection was not the only reason why people did not summon up the courage to resist in the face of death. The following memory of a Jew who was attached to a 'special work detail' at the gas chambers of Auschwitz shows us how the total cynicism of the National Socialist system militated against action.

Document 6.13 Deception

One night an SS man came from the political section. It was around 4 AM. The whole camp was still asleep. There wasn't a sound in the camp. We were again taken out of our cell, and led to the crematorium. There for the first time I saw the procedure used with those who came in alive. We were lined up against a wall and told: 'No one may talk to those people.' Suddenly, the wooden door to the crematorium courtyard opened, and two hundred and fifty to three hundred people filed in – old people and women. They carried bundles, wore the Star of David. Even from a distance I could tell they were Polish Jews [comparable experiences would have befallen German Jews too], probably from Upper Silesia, from the Sosnowitz ghetto, some twenty miles from Auschwitz. I caught some of the things they said. I heard fachowitz, meaning 'skilled worker'. And Malach-ha-Mawis, which means 'the Angel of Death' in Yiddish. Also, Harginnen: 'They're going to kill us.' From what I could hear, I clearly understood the struggle going on inside them. Sometimes they spoke of work, probably hoping that they'd be put to work. Or they spoke of Malach-ha-Mawis, The Angel of Death. The conflicting words echoed the conflict in their feelings. Then a sudden silence fell over those gathered in the crematorium courtyard. All eyes converged on the flat roof of the crematorium. Who was standing there? Aumeyer, the SS man, Grabner, the head of the political section, and Hössler, the SS officer. Aumeyer addressed the crowd: 'You're here to work for our soldiers fighting at the front. Those who can work will be alright.'

It was obvious that hope flared in those people. You could feel it clearly. The executioners had gotten past the first obstacle. He saw it was succeeding. Then Grabner spoke up: 'We need masons, electricians, all the trades.' Next, Hössler took over. He pointed to a short man in the crowd. I can still see him. 'What's your trade?' The man said: 'Mr. Officer, I'm a tailor.' 'A tailor? What kind of a tailor?' 'A man's. . . . No, for both men and women.' 'Wonderful: We need people like you in our workshops.' Then he questioned a woman: 'What's your trade?' 'Nurse,' she replied. 'Splendid! We need nurses in our hospitals, for our soldiers. We need all of you! But first, undress. You must be disinfected. We want you healthy.' I could see the people were calmer, reassured by what they'd heard, and they began to undress. Even if they still had their doubts, if you want to live, you must hope. Their clothing remained in the courtyard, scattered everywhere. Aumeyer was beaming, very proud of how he'd handled things. He turned to some of the SS men and told them: 'You see? That's the way to do it!' By this device a great leap forward had been made! Now the clothing could be used.

Source: C.Lanzmann, Shoah, *1985, pp. 68–70*

In fact the people were about to be 'disinfected' in the gas chambers. On some occasions barbers gave women haircuts and there were notices telling people to hand their valuables to the guards and collect them after their 'shower'. Postcards were to be sent home. The mass of lies distracting people from the reality of their impending murder was just too great to be untangled in the time allowed. As a result, many people did conform with Nazi orders right up to the end.

And yet a picture which omits all signs of hope is fundamentally flawed. Between 10,000 and 12,000 Jews tried to evade deportation from Germany by going into hiding. In 1943, an estimated 5,000 Jews were living illegally in Berlin alone, that is to say 7 per cent of the Jewish population which had been registered there in 1941, and 1,402 Jews survived the war in Germany's capital alone **(Kwiet, 1991a, p. 150)**. Ironically, having helped organise the deportation of other Jews, Else Behrend-Rosenfeld went into hiding herself. What is more, elaborate schemes were developed to help those living illegally. Frank Kaufmann lived in Berlin and was a baptised Jew. He used his Christian connections to encourage churchgoing Germans to put food coupons rather than money into collection boxes. He bought coupons on the black market and became friendly with a forger who produced whatever identity papers he needed. Edith Wolff (see also document 6.8, p. 125) was a half-Jewish factory worker. Here she remembers what she did during the war.

Document 6.14 Forgery

One of my jobs was to make passports and identity documents. For this basically I had to produce suitable documents which Günther Rogoff [the forger] then worked on. My identity document for the postal service had already been falsified in this way for Eva Fleischmann, [a Jew in hiding who was] the cousin of von Schwersenz. I had an old student identity document from University too. I even still had English and French identity papers from my earlier trips abroad. I handed these papers over for Rogoff to work on. Through Dr Kaufmann and Hallermann they were used for the benefit of other escapees.

In the end I found a source for foreign documents in my workplace too

– the address book publisher's *Diederich*. They had letter headings for the most different firms there, stored for advertising sheets and circulars. To produce any work certificate you wanted, you only needed to get hold of a couple of blank sheets of paper with the names of what were for the most part very average firms, write on them with a typewriter and then somehow give them an official stamp.

Source: Quoted in F. Kroh, David kämpft, *1988, p. 112*

No small number of German Jews did organise, some in quite sophisticated ways, to avoid deportation. In the end, and with the right sort of help, Else Behrend-Rosenfeld escaped to Switzerland.

What of the *Judenräte*? Certainly some of these organisations went a very long way indeed in cooperating with what the German authorities demanded. For example, in ghettos in Upper Silesia there were cases of *Judenräte* using ghetto police to stamp out popular opposition to Nazi orders. In at least one case, the ghetto police handed over would-be resisters to the Gestapo **(Trunk, 1971, pp. 202ff.)**. But how should we understand these actions really? Historian Isaiah Trunk offers a more charitable interpretation.

Document 6.15 *Judenrat* (2)

Those opposed to active resistance [in the *Judenräte*] argued as follows: any attempt of physical resistance can only bring disaster upon the ghetto and speed its liquidation as a nest of rebellion. Under the system of collective responsibility, any act of a single person could lead to collective punishment of the whole ghetto community, whose doom would then be sealed. Even young people, eager as they were to escape to the forests and join in the partisan forces, began to have grave doubts as to their moral right to endanger the lives of the remaining ghetto population, among whom were their families.

Source: I. Trunk, 'The Attitude of the Judenrats', 1971, p. 205

The principle of collective responsibility meant that if an individual was found committing an anti-German act, German authorities exacted revenge not just against the individual but against the collective community. The members of the *Judenräte* always knew that the slightest provocation could bring disaster on the heads of everyone in their ghetto. They knew that while independent, resistance-minded young people might be able to flee German wrath to a nearby forest or swamp, children and older people were in a different situation. Would-be resisters and *Judenräte* alike faced genuine moral dilemmas which were only compounded by the reality that ghetto-dwellers did not have ready supplies of arms and often faced hostility from the surrounding Polish populations and partisan groups. To make matters worse, there were indications that Jewish communities really were dealt with more swiftly and brutally where no *Judenrat* existed **(Krakowski, 1977, p. 198)**.

We also have to bear in mind that a readiness to work with occupation authorities could bring at least some tangible benefits. One *Judenrat* bribed German officials to prevent twenty Jewish girls being taken to a brothel. In exchange for cash, others obtained the release of a few Jewish forced labourers and had the death penalty rescinded in connection with a variety of laws **(Trunk, 1972, pp. 396–7)**. By this stage, could the *Judenräte* have expected much more? Under the circumstances we have to give serious consideration to Yehuda Bauer's argument that 'the *Judenräte* as a whole . . . tried to act for the good of the community . . . to the best of their understanding and under impossible conditions' **(Bauer, 1977, p. 393)**.

And what of those Jews interned in the Third Reich's system of camps? Sachsenhausen was located in Germany and, admittedly, was more of a concentration than an extermination camp. On 22 October 1942, upon finding out that they were to be deported East, during roll-call eighteen Jewish prisoners rioted in front of the other 12,000 inmates. They were returned to their huts. This was the only recorded riot in a camp in Germany throughout the twelve years of the Third Reich **(Steinberg, 1970, p. 53)**. During the next year, as it became clear that the extermination camps on formerly Polish territory were about to be closed down (which meant death for the inmates), a number of remarkable uprisings broke out. On 2 August 1943, just 850 prisoners were left in Treblinka extermination camp. Fearing imminent death, most participated in a riot which resulted in 750 of them escaping. One hundred or so were never recaptured **(Arad, 1989, pp. 263–5)**. In October of the same year an uprising at Sobibor extermination camp resulted in 300 of 600 prisoners escaping. Two hundred were never recaptured **(Arad, 1989, pp. 278–9)**. One of the Sobibor organisers was a Russian Jew who had been a soldier. His memories of the break out, recorded after the war, show that on that day Jews of every nationality cooperated in the quest for freedom.

Document 6.16 Sobibor, 14 October 1943

[A]s though in response to an order, several axes that had been hidden under coats appeared and were brought down on his [the German guard's] head. At that moment the convoy from the second camp approached. A few women who were frightened by what they saw began to scream, some even fainted. Some began to run crazily, without thinking and without purpose. In that situation there was no question of organizing or maintaining order, and therefore I shouted at the top of my voice: 'Forward Comrades!'

'Forward!' someone echoed behind me on the right.

'For the Fatherland, for Stalin, forward!'

The proud cries came like thunder from clear skies in the death camp. In one moment these slogans united the Jews of Russia, Poland, Holland, Czechoslovakia, Germany. Six hundred men who had been abused and exhausted broke into cries of 'Hurrah!' for life and freedom.

The assault on the arms store failed. Machine-gun fire barred our way.

Most of the people who were escaping turned in the direction of the main gate. There, after they finished off the guards, under cover of fire from the rifles that a few of them had, they threw stones and scattered sand in the eyes of the Fascists who stood in their way, broke through the gate and hurried in the direction of the forest. One group of prisoners turned left. I saw how they attacked the barbed-wire fence. But after they had cleared away this obstacle, they still had to cross a minefield that was about 15 metres wide. Many of them surely fell here. I turned towards the Officer's House with a group of prisoners; we cut the barbed wire there and so made an opening. The assumption that the area near the Officer's House would not be mined proved correct. Three of our comrades fell near the barbed wire, but it was not clear whether they stepped on mines or were wounded by bullets, as salvoes were fired on us from various directions. We are already on the far side of the fence, and the minefield is behind us. We have already gone 100 metres, then another 100 . . . fast, still faster . . . we must cross the bare open area where we are exposed to the bullets of the murderers . . . fast, still faster, we must get to the forest, get among the trees, get into shelter . . . and already we are in the shade of the trees.

I stopped for a moment to catch my breath and cast a glance backwards. Exhausted, with their last strength, running bent over, forwards . . . we were near the forest. Where is Loka? Where is Shlomo?

Source: A. Peczorski, 'Ha-Mered be-Sobibor', 1981, pp. 356–8

Germany's Jews did help bring about the process of deportation, did help govern themselves when relocated to Eastern Europe, and sometimes did go to their deaths too dejected and deceived to object; but this is not the whole story. Thousands tried to avoid deportation; hundreds succeeded. There were cases of people resisting in the very face of death. And still we have not mentioned the most famous case of German–Jewish opposition to the Third Reich during wartime. The group led by Herbert Baum carried out 'one of the most successful operations mounted by the resistance movement in Germany' **(Eschwege, 1989, p. 423)**. Only four of its thirty-two active members were aged 19 or more in 1933 and most of them were committed Communists. After 1939 they worked in special departments for Jews in the Siemens factory in Berlin. Initially Baum and his close colleagues set up a secret organisation to raise the morale of Jewish workers and campaigned to have factory conditions improved. After the attack on the USSR, they began to put up anti-Nazi posters around the city and developed contacts with surrounding opposition groups. Baum and his friends even dressed up in Gestapo uniforms to confiscate goods from wealthy Berlin homes. It was when Propaganda Minister Josef Goebbels set up an anti-Soviet exhibition that the group was moved to carry out its real *pièce de résistance*. Historian Ber Mark takes up the story.

Document 6.17 The Herbert Baum Group

At the beginning of May 1942, Goebbels organised an anti-Soviet exhibition, the theme of which was *Das Soviet Paradis* (The Soviet Paradise) in the Lustgarten in Berlin. The exhibition was opened with great pomp. In the opinion of the German anti-Fascist group, its purpose was to distract the population's attention from the defeat suffered by the German army at the Moscow front, the food shortages, and other difficulties resulting from the drawn-out war. The Berlin anti-Fascist circles considered taking some steps against it. The Schulze–Boysen–Harnak group [Red Orchestra, see document 2.13, pp. 33–4] showed great initiative in this respect by issuing special leaflets and posting them on the walls at night. In these leaflets the group unmasked the exhibition's real aim.

The Baum Group also discussed ways and means of acting against it. They decided to begin with the distribution of leaflets among the Berlin population and to start at the exhibition. Baum and Kochmann then went there to study the possibilities of leaflet distribution. They returned with a negative decision. Baum proposed the plan to set the exhibition on fire. After an exchange of opinions in which Kochmann expressed certain reservations about the plan, it was adopted by all sections of the group. (In the end Kochmann also agreed.)

The plan was co-ordinated with the Franke Group, a German anti-Fascist Group, through the intermediary Steinbrink. The collaboration of the Franke Group for the realization of the concrete plan was both welcome and necessary, because both Franke and Steinbrink worked in the Chemical Institute and were in a position to supply the needed explosives. On May 15 Steinbrink handed over to Baum explosive and inflammable substances. The date for the action was set for May 17, Sunday at noon.

On the morning of the appointed day several members of the group met at Kochmann's home. A discussion developed about the plan. Practically every member of the group wanted to take part in the action, but for security and technical reasons the number of the participants was limited [group members who looked stereotypically Jewish were not allowed to participate]. The group chosen to carry out the plan left for the Lustgarten, but because of the large number of viewers (it was on a Sunday) the plan could not be carried out and had to be postponed until the following day.

On Monday evening, May 18, 1942, the group, consisting of Herbert and Marianne Baum, Hans Joachim, Sala Kochmann, Gerd Meyer, Suzanne Wesse, and Irene Walter, went to the exhibition and distributed the explosives and inflammable material in various places. In no time flames shot up. The group left without mishap. Part of the exhibition was destroyed by the fire. Firemen called out by a fire alarm saved the rest. This demonstration did not have any wide repercussions, because the newspapers, probably acting on superior orders, suppressed the entire affair.

But the attack on the exhibition evoked recognition and enthusiasm in the underground circles, though there were some who expressed misgivings. One of the German Communist groups wrote: 'Naturally, from an apolitical standpoint the attack of the Baum Group was a mistake, because it could provide the Hitlerites with a pretext for increasing the wave of Gestapo terror against the Jews to a degree unheard of until now. Still, the attack should be regarded as an act of breaking the isolation. The failure to evaluate the situation is also the result of this isolation.'

The aim of the Baum Group, which acted on its own responsibility and had the approval only of the Franke Group, was to put on record the activity of the Jewish anti-Fascists. In this respect it achieved its goal.

Four days later, on May 22, Herbert and Marianne Baum, Gerd Meyer, Heinz Rotholz, and Werner Steinbrink were arrested by the Gestapo. The following day Sala Kochmann, Suzanne Wesse, and Irene Walter were arrested. The seventh participant in the attack, Hans Joachim, managed to avoid arrest until June 9. In the meantime other members of the group were rounded up.

These prompt arrests gave rise to the suspicion that a Gestapo agent might have infiltrated into the Baum Group.

Source: B. Mark, 'The Herbert Baum Group', 1968, pp. 89–90

Before he died, Herbert Baum was tortured and dragged around Siemens, but he refused to identify anyone who had helped him.

Germany's Jews were persecuted like no other group in history, deceived by the machinery of an entire modern state, hamstrung by their responsibilities to friends and relatives and, since Israel did not exist as such at this time, and lacked the support and safe haven of a country of their own. It is not really so remarkable that many of this small minority of Germans experienced the saddest of fates with little opposition. In this respect, Raul Hilberg's argument quoted at the outset misses the point. As Polish Jew Elie Wiesel put it: 'The question is not why all the Jews did not fight, but how so many of them did. Tormented, beaten, starved, where did they find the spiritual and physical strength to resist?' **(Suhl, 1968a, pp. 13–16)**. We should hardly say that Germany's Jews went 'like lambs to the slaughter'.

7

Exploring the inexplicable

what was the relationship between ordinary
Germans and racial policy?

The experiences of Germany's Jews naturally raises the question of the relationship of the German population as a whole both to their fate and to the enactment of wider racial goals in the Third Reich. We have already seen the importance of racism both to Hitler 'the person' and for his political movement (documents 1.11, 1.12 and 1.13, pp. 10, 12 and 12–13), but while it was unique for a national leader and his state to accord racism such central importance, racism itself was nothing new. George Mosse, for example, has dated the rise of modern racism to traditions growing out of the eighteenth-century Enlightenment **(Mosse, 1978, p. 1)**. During the mid-nineteenth century, British naturalist Charles Darwin theorised about competition for survival in the animal kingdom, that is to say between both individuals and species. His thinking was epitomised in concepts such as 'the survival of the fittest' and 'natural selection'. As the century wore on, others began to apply his ideas to humans and their ongoing social problems. A place began to be carved out for biologically based, potentially racist thinking among respectable, educated, even trend-setting circles. Historian Detlev Peukert explains the phenomenon with specific reference to Germany.

Document 7.1 Racism as fashion

[During the late nineteenth and early twentieth centuries the] belief that social problems could be finally and scientifically solved by a joint application of educational and social reforms and measures of racial hygiene and improvement of the hereditary stock was especially widely canvassed in the popular scientific literature and was by no means restricted to extreme right-wing circles. The prominent [German] biologist Ernst Haeckel, for example, whose popular-science bestseller *The Riddle of the Universe* was widely read in the labour movement (where it helped to shape the scientific Weltanschauung of a whole generation of Social Democrats), wrote in 1915, in *Eternity: Wartime Thoughts on Life and Death, Religion and Evolution*:

> One single cultivated German warrior – and they are now falling in their masses – has a higher intellectual and moral life-value than hundreds of the raw primitives whom England and France, Russia and Italy are pitting against them.

The social Darwinianism of the National Socialists, then, not only had roots in relatively offbeat nineteenth-century racial theorists (Gobineau, Houston Stewart Chamberlain etc.), but could claim support from well-established academic schools of thought in psychology, medicine, criminology and social welfare. These scholarly disciplines were by no means 'fascist' in character, but they were receptive to arguments, modes of perception and schemes for action which entailed the separation of people into groups according to their social usefulness, defined in terms not only of environmental but of notionally hereditary factors. Wherever health, welfare or educational practitioners came up against limits to their work's effectiveness, academic theorists and practitioners alike were inclined to hold immutable hereditary factors responsible. The implication lay ready to hand: for the sake of future generations, these limits to social and medical intervention should be clearly drawn, and such intervention should be complemented by eugenic measures and selection from the genetic stock on the basis of social usefulness. This optimistic view, that scientific and industrial progress in principle removed the restrictions on the possible application of planning, education and social reform in everyday life, lost its last shreds of innocence when the National Socialists set about engineering their 'brave new world' with compulsory sterilization, concentration camps and gas chambers.

Source: D. Peukert, Inside Nazi Germany, *1993, pp. 222–3*

Race hatred of specifically the Jews reached back even further – to biblical times – but it saw a renaissance during the late nineteenth and early twentieth centuries. For example, both Vienna and Berlin experienced noteworthy anti-Semitic political movements during the period. In the former, Georg Schönerer led first the German National Union and then the Pan-German League, while Karl Lueger headed the Christian Social Party; in the latter, Adolf Stoecker led the Christian Socialist Party and Otto Böckel the Anti-Semitic People's Party. In fact, in 1916 the Ministry of War in Berlin carried out a remarkable census to find out what German Jews were doing during the First World War. It implied they were either dodging the war effort or profiteering from it.

With both post-Darwinian biologism and traditional anti-Semitic prejudice at large, it is hardly surprising that, at least as far as some German families were concerned, anti-Jewish feeling was a background feature of everyday life. This is reflected in the memoirs of Melita Maschmann (who later went on to become an SS officer).

Document 7.2 Mixed Neighbourhood

The house in which my twin brothers and I were born stood in a street off the Kurfürstendamm. As far as I can recall, the majority of the occupants were always Jews. My parents were only on friendly terms with our Gentile neighbours. . . . From odd remarks of theirs I gathered that Jews were 'foreigners': our neighbours pronounced the word with scorn. . . .

Contact with the other Jewish inhabitants of the house was limited to an exchange of greetings if one met them on the stairs.

Whether I had any Jewish classmates at my primary school I no longer remember: but at the secondary school Jewish girls at times made up one third of my class. My parents often complained about this situation. Why it was lamentable I did not understand, but then our parents also complained about the unemployment, although we did not suffer from it ourselves.

I ask myself now how my Jewish school fellows struck me. First, almost without exception, by their physical and mental precociousness. They were 'ladies' already, while I felt I was still a child, and the ostentatious clothes many of them wore annoyed me. Not one of them came from a poor home. Most of them, indeed, were rich and there were some who sought to impress with their fathers' cars in which the chauffeurs sometimes came to fetch them. The fact that these airs particularly upset me may have been connected with my mother's frequent complaints about '*nouveaux riches*'. If this expression refers to the time a family's prosperity dates from – and not to a style of life – then my mother came from a '*nouveau riche*' family herself anyway. Her father was a tradesman who had worked his way to the top. . . .

The first 'political conversations' I can remember having with other girls at school were provoked by a girl in my form whose father had been an officer in the First World War and belonged to the '*Stahlhelm*' [a nationalist paramilitary group]. These consisted of boasting about the 'exploits' of one's brothers and cousins, which were directed against the new German Republic and also, even before 1933, against the Jews. . . . One day Gerda brought me a railway ticket which looked like an ordinary one. It was only on closer examination that I realised this was a 'political joke'. It carried the imprint 'To Jerusalem'. Underneath was written in smaller print: 'And no return'. We gave this ticket to Rachel K. for her father. We chose Rachel because she was a particularly goodnatured girl, somewhat simple in her friendliness. . . . I was then twelve years old.

Source: M. Maschmann, Account Rendered, *1964, pp. 37–9*

Even in an extract written twenty years after the end of the Third Reich, Maschmann's former racial resentments are clear enough to see. Document 1.15 (p. 14) provides additional evidence that *some description* of racism was often taken for granted as a part of German community life.

But of course in the Third Reich anti-Semitism was made into something of much greater significance, something much more threatening. What was the relationship between average Germans and these changes? On one occasion there was a significant public demonstration against the persecution of the Jews. It happened in Berlin on 27 February 1943 when 2,000 German wives supported by 4,000 sympathisers protested against the internment and proposed deportation of their Jewish husbands **(Gordon, 1984, p. 195)**. The men were released two days later. Was this incident an exception which proved that most Germans, weakened by the sort of views outlined already, were willing to conform to the demands of Nazi racial policy? Or was it a rare public indicator of a latent feeling of opposition harboured by many Germans towards what was being done in their name?

The memories of surviving German Jews provide anecdotal evidence. The following, recalled some years after the war, shows the reaction of ordinary commuters when, in 1941, a youngster was obliged for the first time to wear a sign of his religion.

Document 7.3 Star of David

In 1941, when I was 16 years old, I was forced to perform hard labor in a parquet flooring factory. I had to catch the commuter train every morning at 5:20 AM. I always sat in the same part of the train, and pretty soon I knew all of the other commuters. There was a bricklayer, an Italian, an older man who always wore a coat and tie, a chubby-faced blonde woman who rode five station stops with us, and others. We greeted one another every morning. And then came September 18, 1941. That was the first day I had to wear the Star of David. I was terribly embarrassed. All of a sudden everyone could tell what you were. They could spit on you, beat you to death – you were suddenly totally unprotected. I wanted to hold my lunch bag in front of the Star, but I knew if I was caught, I'd be deported. No, I couldn't do that.

I walked to the train station that first morning as inconspicuously as I could. I wanted to get into another train car, but everything happened so quickly. I got on the train and ended up in my old compartment. I stood at the door and almost whispered 'Good morning.' The others looked at me as if they were thinking, 'What's the matter with him today?' Then they noticed what I was wearing: the Star. What followed after that really surprised me. Like a chorus, they all sung out loudly and clearly, 'Morning.' The bricklayer asked, 'Why don't you come in and sit down in your seat.' I told him that I couldn't and that it wasn't allowed. And he said, 'Oh, that's ridiculous! Come on in and sit down!' The person sitting across from me gave me a cigarette, and the old man offered me a light.

Everybody smiled reassuringly at me for a few seconds, then the expression on their faces changed. It was as if they suddenly realized they were betraying the German people. During the last several years, they had been indoctrinated with the idea that the Jews were Public Enemy Number One. They felt like traitors just because they knew a 16-year-old Jewish boy. They never came back to that compartment again. There was so much mistrust, they even avoided one another after that day.

Source: Klaus Scheurenberg, quoted in J. Steinhoff et al., Voices from the Third Reich, *1989, pp. 292–3*

Apparently anti-Semitism in itself was not terribly important to these commuters, but still they felt compelled to go along with the stigmatisation of Jews.

Of course memoirs give us a highly personalised view of life. Was such relatively passive acceptance of racism as far as popular conformity went? Robert Gellately's research into the Gestapo's policing techniques shows otherwise. At the centre of his inquiry are the facts that in 1937 the Gestapo in Essen had just forty-three officers to deal with a population of over 650,000, while Wuppertal and Duisburg, both with populations of over 400,000, had only forty-three and twenty-eight officers respectively **(Gellately, 1990, p. 18)**. How did such small secret police forces manage to administer extensive sets of laws, only some of which involved racial legislation? Apparently most Gestapo offices destroyed their documents in the final stages of the war and so surviving evidence is quite rare, but still Gellately has managed to form a picture. In fact, over half of the cases investigated by the Würzburg Gestapo concerning the relationship between Germans and Jews were initiated by tip-offs from the general population. Since this implies that Germans effectively chose to enforce racial policy on themselves, Gellately has termed the phenomenon 'autopolicing'. In fact we shouldn't be too surprised by this process. Many 'racial crimes' were highly personal affairs, concerning for instance sexual relations, and involved spheres of life generally more likely to be penetrated by neighbourhood gossips than policemen (although see document 1.10, pp. 9–10).

An insight into the truly oppressive character of this 'autopolicing' is expressed well in Gellately's summary of one police case.

Document 7.4 Autopolicing

In her interrogation on 5 September 1941 by the Gestapo in Würzburg, Totzke [a German lady] recalled that she began making friends with Jewish people (women) in 1934–35, that is, almost at the very moment when this behavior was being actively discouraged. Her first brush with the Gestapo had come in 1936 when, for reasons unknown in her file, her mail was watched. Nothing turned up. On 3 April 1939 a more serious denunciation came to the Gestapo via a neighbor, a *Studienrat* (high school teacher), attached to the local university, who said that he 'felt bound by his duty as a reserve officer' to inform on her 'suspicious behavior'. He believed that Totzke was a spy, a point he reiterated in a separate (later) letter (in mid-1940) as well, when he heard that she had been seen near troop movements!

Little could be done about such vague allegations, although in specific interviews her neighbors casually offered the most damaging gossip. Nothing further happened until 29 July 1940, when yet another denouncer appeared at Gestapo headquarters. This time it was a clerical worker, a twenty-two-year-old woman and neighbor whose suspicions were aroused because Totzke had always avoided the 'Heil Hitler!' greeting. Furthermore, Totzke was said to sympathize with Germany's enemies (the French, the

Jews); while she had no job, she always had money, and obviously knew a lot about armies and such things. Totzke went out late at night and stayed home all day. As well, there sometimes appeared in her company a woman (about thirty-six years old) who 'looked Jewish'. Still nothing untoward resulted, even when an additional denunciation, contained in an anonymous letter 'from a close neighbor' in early 1941, alleged similar 'suspicions'. The spelling and grammatical errors in that letter suggests that neither the teacher nor the clerical worker wrote it. Although Totzke had done little or nothing of a 'criminal' nature, she had been questioned by the police, incriminated by neighbors, and denounced on at least five occasions.

Source: R. Gellately, 'Enforcing Racial Policy in Nazi Germany', 1993, pp. 54–5

In other words, no small number of Germans was prepared not just to go along with the Third Reich's racial legislation passively, *they were active in supporting its application.*

Why did people act in these ways? We know about fear of National Socialist terrorism and some measure of popular prejudice. More provocatively still, one analysis of the reasons underlying denunciations of race crime found that almost 40 per cent of cases were not simply motivated by either of these causes, but first and foremost by personal grudges **(Gellately, 1991, pp. 144–7)**. This puts us in mind of the stoker who informed against a prostitute after she had given him a disease (document 1.20, p. 19). With this in mind, consider the following account given by the victim of a racial attack to the police during the period immediately before the Nuremberg Laws were enacted.

Document 7.5 Race or Money?

On 21 August 1935 I was returning from the Landshut cattle market and shortly after 7 PM I got aboard the passenger train to Haßloch in Neustadt. I was very tired from the journey and did not chat with anyone on the train. At Neustadt, Groß and Remle also got into the carriage where I was sitting. I first noticed Groß when he greeted everyone conspicuously loudly with the German greeting [i.e., 'Heil Hitler!']. The railway carriage was a through carriage, and Groß and Remle sat down not far from me. Then Groß began to abuse the Jews without any cause. Among other things he said: 'This evening the Jews in Haßloch will all get their throats cut. They'll be strung up and smoked. You people, now you really will see something. When the train starts, a Jew will be thrown head first through the carriage window, and it will be Heinrich Heene from Langgasse in Haßloch.' Several other people from Haßloch who knew me personally were sitting on the train and now were made aware of my presence by Groß. [We might observe that these people did not try to intervene in what was going on.] Groß insulted me in the most impertinent fashion. I request that I be spared having to repeat what he said, because at my age I do not deserve this. When eventually the train stopped in Haßloch, the people from Haßloch got out and Groß stayed until he was the last one in the carriage. When I was leaving the carriage and was standing on its step, Groß kicked me twice in the back and bottom. At the last moment I managed to keep myself upright by holding on to another traveller, otherwise I would have fallen onto the platform. I was afraid of further outrages by Groß against me and so I stayed standing on the platform. The railway official of Haßloch then called me into the railway building and telephoned my relatives so that I would be picked up from the railway. . . .

Groß has owed me the sum of about 400 RM for several years. I lent the money to Groß honestly, but I have already accepted that the money has been lost and I want nothing more to do with Groß. For this reason I have not supplied him with cattle recently. Groß does not get a single cow from any cattle dealer anymore because he is deeply in debt everywhere and does not pay the suppliers. About three weeks ago he wanted to buy a calf from my nephew Solly Elekan. Even he won't supply him with any more cattle, because he still owes him a large sum of money.

Source: Interrogation of Jewish cattle dealer Heinrich Heene II about repeated mistreatment of himself and his family by party member Heinrich Groß, 12 September 1935, reproduced in J. Simmert (ed.), Die nationalsozialistische Judenverfolgung in Rheinland-Pfalz 1933 bis 1945, *1974, pp. 65–6*

The whole tone of the attack makes it safe to assume that a genuinely anti-Semitic motive was in play here. But we also have to admit that Groß most probably was using racist insults and capitalising on the unique vulnerability of Jews for other reasons too. He attacked specifically this man not just because he was a Jew, but because he was associated with personal financial frustrations. In other words, the racist attack in question was actually quite a complicated event, the causes of which lay in both racism and personal resentments. The message is that when people conformed to racist expectations they need not have been acting simply. For each individual, some or all of an array of motives including fear of National Socialism, racism and more personal resentments would have been mixed together in measures which varied from case to case.

Bearing these issues in mind, we also have to be aware that just as the actual racial policies being pursued changed during the twelve years of the Third Reich, so did the attitudes of Germans to them. Evidence can be found in the public opinion reports compiled by both the German Socialist Party in exile and those of the German administrative and police authorities. Historian Sarah Gordon has summarised what these tell us.

Document 7.6 Trends in anti-Semitism

Between 1933 and 1945 German attitudes toward Jews underwent notable changes. From 1933 to 1935 attitudes toward Jews were fairly favourable compared to later years. A small minority demanded stringent restrictions, but these, even on the limited scale of a four-day boycott in April 1933, were not popular with the public. The public did, however, appear to support exclusion of Jews from the civil service as well as quotas on numbers of Jews allowed in schools and universities. There was a minority that opposed these measures, but by and large such restrictions imposed up until 1935 received much popular support.

Between 1935 and 1938 anti-Semitic propaganda had a noticeable impact. Anti-Semitic policies were accepted when introduced through legal or pseudo-legal decrees and when they involved no violence. A majority of Germans apparently viewed the Nuremberg Laws as a stabilizing influence that would end illegal violence. A minority, particularly party men and the SA, but also some nonparty members, were pleased with their new power to harass Jews. On the other hand, another minority opposed racial persecution and continued to conduct business and have sexual relations with Jews. These two minorities were probably polarized around an acquiescent majority; otherwise one could have expected more definite reports on the attitudes of the public at large toward the Nuremberg Laws, pro or con.

By 1938 anti-Semitism appeared to be taking root among the majority, but the pogrom of November 9 and 10, 1938, quickly shifted its attitude to disapproval of Nazi methods. The peak of opposition to anti-Semitism was reached after *Kristallnacht* ['Crystal Night'], when by almost all accounts the vast majority of Germans rejected violence, destruction of property, and murder. Many Germans felt strongly enough about this to aid Jews; however, large-scale arrests and Nazi harassment of these individuals discouraged opposition to the economic 'Aryanization' that accelerated between 1938 and 1939, as did the blackout about it.

During the war a marked worsening of attitudes toward Jews became apparent. Before 1939 almost no reports on public opinion indicated a genuine desire for forced deportation or physical attacks on Jews; after 1939 this was not the case. Several reports indicated support for draconian measures against Jews, including forced deportation. There is no evidence that labor camps and extermination were welcomed by the general public, but a host of restrictions on the domestic activities of Jews was approved by an increasing minority of hard-core anti-Semites.

At the same time, growing numbers of Germans opposed racial persecution. When rumors of deportations and shootings in the East spread through Germany, criticism of the regime snowballed. A number of reports indicated public opposition to these measures, and extrapolating from these reports, one can probably conclude that labor camps, concentration camps, and extermination camps were opposed by a majority of Germans. [But see below, pp. 152–60.] At the same time, aid for Jews became increasingly more difficult. As the number of Jews was reduced by emigration and deportation, it became easier to root out sympathizers, and penalties for aiding Jews were a very effective deterrent to sympathetic acts. Still, some Germans did aid Jews at considerable personal risk.

Source: S. Gordon, Hitler, Germans and the 'Jewish Question', *1984, pp. 206–8*

The extract implies that the more extreme National Socialist racial policies became, the less popular support they enjoyed. So was there a point past which most people would not conform, whether passively or actively, whether intimidated or not, to National Socialist racism? What is more, assuming such limits existed, how could the Holocaust have been implemented?

The early twentieth century did see dreadful racial atrocities in areas bordering Germany and Austria. During the First World War, the Turkish state carried out an exceptionally severe persecution of the Armenian people. As the war ended, Polish troops committed a number of anti-Semitic pogroms. In 1919 Ukrainian nationalists killed 60,000 Jews near Lvov **(Gilbert, 1987, p. 22)**. But it is true that, notwithstanding the apparent growth of racial awareness in Germany during the nineteenth and early twentieth centuries, violent racial attacks remained foreign there. In keeping with this history, Sarah Gordon seems correct in her assumption that when Nazi Party officials orchestrated the anti-Semitic 'Crystal Night' pogroms across the country, they were rejected very widely indeed.

During the night of 9–10 November 1938, and over the next two nights, 7,500 Jewish shops were ransacked, synagogues across the country were destroyed, 30,000 Jews were interned, there were even cases of people being murdered in their own homes. Although these pogroms were supposed to look like spontaneous racial riots by the German people, most likely they were instigated by the Nazi leadership and coordinated by local party officials **(Graml, 1992, ch. 1)**. Reports compiled by the German Socialist Party in exile noted, for example, that 'the decent public' of Karlsruhe distanced themselves from the destruction of a synagogue as quickly as possible, the people of the Saarpfalz region rejected the way Jews were beaten up and taken away from their local communities, in Hindenburg (in Silesia) a railway official stood up for a Jew who was being attacked by members of the Hitler Youth, and even influential Nazis in the Rheinland were said to have protected Jews whom they knew **(*Sopade 1938*, 1980, pp. 1337–8; *Sopade 1939*, 1980, p. 225)**. An administrative report from Lower Bavaria complained that the pogroms were not understood at all by the vast mass of the population, were condemned in even some party circles and that they were causing unnecessary sympathy for the Jews **(Michalka, 1985, p. 169)**.

One little known story of an individual German taking the side of the local Jewish community during this time comes from the notoriously anti-Semitic region of Franconia. It concerns a local dignitary who was very active in local history circles. A pamphlet published in the early 1980s by a local history society describes what happened.

Document 7.7 'Crystal Night' in Schnaittach

In his records for the local history museum and also in his personal correspondence Gottfried Stammler describes on several occasions the dramatic events during and after 'Crystal Night' in Schnaittach. He reported about it in most detail in a hearing which took place in Schnaittach on 22.6.1948.

Gottfried Stammler emphasises that before Crystal Night he already had good relations with Schnaittach's Jewish population in his capacity as head of the museum. Before they went away [presumably this means before they emigrated] several Jews gave pieces of furniture to his museum and asked him to look after various cultural objects until their eventual return.

On 10 November 1938 Gottfried Stammler was told at about 04.30 in the morning that the synagogue [which dated back to at least 1570] was on fire. He hurried at once to the site of the fire and demanded that the fire chief put it out. The fire chief, however, referred Stammler to *Ortsgruppen-leiter* Gösswein because he was only there to protect neighbouring homes. On the way to the *Ortsgruppenleiter*, it struck Stammler that the synagogue could be totally destroyed before things could be discussed properly. He turned around at once, pretended that he had the authorisation of the *Ortsgruppenleiter*, and the fire was put out. Afterwards, Stammler looked through the burned ashes for cultural objects worth keeping. 12 Thora rolls [Jewish religious scripts] were lying around heavily smudged, and the 16 chandeliers, among them 2 valuable ones, were smashed in the ruins. . . . Apparently the burning of the synagogue had been prompted by *Kreisleiter* Walz and mayor Herzog, both from Lauf.

When Gottfried Stammler was just about to clean up a Thora roll which was very dirty indeed, the *Kreisleiter* appeared, gave Stammler a kick, and threatened to send him to Dachau [a concentration camp near Munich]. Without any fear at all Stammler told him that this building was historically valuable and was officially protected. Mayor Vitzthum from Schnaittach, who had come along at the same time, at once made the building available to Stammler for alteration into a local history museum.

A good acquaintanceship with Bavarian Minister President Siebert and the backing of mayor Vitzthum spared Gottfried Stammler further political persecution.

In the weeks that followed, Stammler travelled around the whole of Middle Franconia collecting every Thora roll and cultural object he could find. . . . He buried them under the floorboards of the museum's vaults and in the cellar. . . . In 1945 Gottfried Stammler returned the Thora rolls to the thankful Jewish communities in Lauf and Nuremberg.

Source: W. Tausendpfund and G.P. Wolf, Die jüdische Gemeinde von Schnaittach, *1981, pp. 45–6*

In light of such an act of bravery, it is particularly sad that the synagogue in question, although today supposed to be Schnaittach's local history museum, has been allowed to fall into a state of disrepair. None the less Gottfried Stammler was determined that Jewish culture should not be 'written out' of Germany's past. In November 1938, while Nazi activists wreaked anti-Semitic havoc across Germany, more ordinary Germans began to find the limits beyond which they could not conform to discrimination carried out right under their noses during peacetime.

How did these patterns develop under conditions of war, during which the threat against the Jews became more acute? There certainly were individuals who tried to help. Industrialist Robert Bosch gave 1.2 million RM to the Association of German Jews to promote emigration between 1938 and 1940 **(Kwiet, 1991b, p. 67)**. After the Second World War, the senate of West Berlin honoured 687 citizens for helping to rescue Jews from persecution. In 1971 Yad Vashem in Jerusalem honoured sixty-nine Germans **(Kwiet, 1989, p. 69)**. Individuals certainly did help Jews go into hiding to avoid deportation, provided food while they were there and gave information about impending police raids. So did the escalating anti-Semitic policies of the war years have very much to do with average Germans?

One controversial source of information suggests not. On two occasions, once immediately after 'Crystal Night' and then in 1942 (by which time Jews in Germany were either having to wear the Star of David or faced the gruesome fate of deportation to the East), Müller-Claudius carried out conversations with a number of members of the National Socialist party to gauge their attitude to Jewish policy. When he brought up the topic in conversation, Müller-Claudius recorded the reaction of the person in question. The following table lays out his findings.

Document 7.8 The Müller-Claudius survey

A SURVEY OF THE REACTION OF NSDAP MEMBERS TO THE
WAY JEWS WERE BEING TREATED IN 1938 AND 1942

| Reaction of individual when Jewish policy was discussed | *Year* | |
	1938	*1942*
Extreme indignation	63 %	26 %
Noncommittal or indifferent	32 %	69 %
Approval	5 %	5 %

Müller-Claudius discussed Jewish policy with forty-one individuals in 1938 and sixty-one people in 1942.

Source: Quoted in S. Gordon, Hitler, Germans and the 'Jewish Question', *1984, pp. 263–4*

Now Müller-Claudius's survey was conducted in a highly impressionistic fashion. Taking the evidence at face value, and given that more than twice as many people reacted to Jewish policy with indignation in 1938 as in 1942, we can see a drift among Nazi Party members towards indifference about what was being done to the Jews. None the less, consistently only 5 per cent of respondents approved. If this was the case with NSDAP members, it leaves the impression that support for anti-Semitic policy must have been much weaker still among the mass of Germans.

From this perspective, how can we make sense of the Holocaust? Consider the following brief extract from a lengthy and detailed report made by SS and police leader Katzmann in 1943 about the fate of the Jews of Galicia, a region which is now in the Ukraine but which at the time had been occupied by Germany.

Document 7.9 Free of Jews

Thanks to the concept 'Galician Jew', Galicia really was the corner of all the world best known in connection with Jewry and which was on everyone's lips. They lived here in great, compact masses, creating their own world, from which time and again the rest of world Jewry renewed its population. You encountered Jews in their hundreds of thousands in every part of Galicia. . . .

All positions of power in the land were in their hands. So it was also understandable that in July 1941, after German troops occupied this area, wherever you went, you bumped into Jews. As a result it had to be our most urgent task to solve this problem as quickly as possible. . . .

When the Senior SS and Police Leader . . . involved himself in the Jewish Question on 10 November 1942, and a police order was issued for the creation of Jewish [living] quarters [i.e., ghettos], 254,989 Jews had already been evacuated or resettled. . . . In the meantime further evacuation was implemented energetically, so that all Jewish living areas could be dissolved with effect from 23.6.43. As a result, apart from the Jews in camps under the control of the SS and Police Leader, the district of Galicia is

FREE OF JEWS.

. . . Altogether, up to 27.6.43, 434,329 Jews had been evacuated. . . .

Despite the extraordinary burden, which every member of the SS and police had to endure during these actions, the attitude and spirit of the men was extraordinarily good and praiseworthy from the first to the last day.

Only through a consciousness of personal duty on the part of each leader and man were we successful in mastering this PLAGUE in the very shortest time.

Source: Brief extracts from the report 'The Final Solution to the Jewish Problem in Galicia', 30 June 1943, Federal Archive, Berlin-Zehlendorf, R 70 Polen/205

The terminology is deceptive. 'Resettled' and 'evacuated' were words concealing reality. SS and Police Leader Katzmann meant that these people had been sent for extermination. Given this information, the whole tone of the report suggests someone completely under the influence of anti-Semitic ideology, a genuine believer that Jews constituted vermin, a man understanding that the killing of 434,329 people had constituted a hard but necessary task. If questioned, presumably Katzmann would have been one of Müller-Claudius's 5 per cent. But does this mean that the most severe, the ultimately murderous aspects of Jewish policy were the isolated province of an ideologically zealous, strictly limited minority (most obviously of the self-styled racial élite, the SS)? Were these dreadful events discussed among even these people in only veiled terms? Was this a secret isolated from ordinary Germans, something they could not oppose and never even had to go along with? Were by far the most people 'indifferent' about Jewish policy during the war years (as Müller-Claudius's report suggests) because they did not know what was going on?

The possibility is reinforced in a report sent by Reinhard Heydrich (who was Head of the Security Police and right-hand man of the Reichsführer-SS, Heinrich Himmler) to Kurt Daluege (head of the more ordinary order police) in the summer of 1940. In one section it discusses cooperation between special police groups and the army while the former pursued racial policies which became ever more severe as first Austria, Czechoslovakia and then Poland were occupied.

Document 7.10 Limits to Cooperation?

In all previous actions [i.e., invasions] (Ostmark [Austria], Sudetenland, Bohemia and Moravia and Poland), by virtue of a special command from the Führer, special police action groups (security police and order police) were acting along with the advancing troops (in Poland with the fighting troops). In accordance with the preparatory work, they carried out significant blows systematically against those elements in the world which were inimical towards the Reich (from the camp of emigration, free masonry, Jewry and political–church opposition as well as that of the Second and Third International [i.e., Communists]) by means of imprisonment, confiscation and securing the most important political material.

Cooperation was generally good with the troops below the staff level and in many cases even with the different staffs of the army; in many cases a fundamentally different view developed with the senior [military commanders] only over basic questions about fighting the enemies of the state. This view, which for the most part developed out of a lack of knowledge of the ideological position of the enemy, caused friction and orders running counter to the political activity which was being carried out by the *Reichsführer-SS* in accordance with the orders of the Führer and of General Field Marshal [Goering].

While until the Polish campaign these difficulties by and large were overcome through personal contact, this possibility did not arise in the Polish action. This was because the directives upon which the police action was being implemented were extraordinarily radical (for example, a liquidation order for numerous Polish leadership circles which ran into thousands). Since the entire leading command positions of the army (and certainly its staff members too) could not be informed of the command, to external appearances the actions of the police and SS appeared to be arbitrary, brutal high-handedness.

Source: Section of a report from Reinhard Heydrich to Kurt Daluege, 2 July 1940, Federal Archive, Berlin-Zehlendorf, R19/395

As racial killing spiralled in Poland, a breach was said to have opened up between the murderous SS and the military onlookers. With orders to the police not to be released to anyone else, cooperation between the two was said to be failing. We are led to conclude that SS men stood alone.

Secrecy may be called on to explain how the killing process was allowed to continue for years. A plausible answer invokes secrecy. One SS action implemented in Poland during 1943 was code-named 'Action Reinhard' (after the now assassinated Reinhard Heydrich). It brought about the death of hundreds of thousands of Jews from all around Europe, although especially from Poland itself. Apparently everyone involved was expected to sign a declaration binding them never to tell a word about their activities **(Arad et al. (eds), 1981, p. 274)**. When 'Action Reinhard' was over, its organiser, SS and Police Leader Globocnik, applied to Himmler for permission to destroy all the documentation associated with it **(Globocnik to Himmler, Nuremberg State Archive, NO–64)**. No one was ever supposed to know what had been done. Eyewitnesses did, however, survive the war. A Polish electrician at Poniatowa camp had got to know the manager of a clothing factory, a man who had tried to help his Jewish workers in a number of ways on a number of occasions. After the war, the electrician remembered the way in which the camp was 'closed' when 'Action Reinhard' was wound up. A passage from what he later recalled reads as follows.

Document 7.11 Secrecy at Poniatowa

On 4 November 1943 all of the Jews present, perhaps 14,000 in number, were shot. I can tell you the following about what happened:

At about 6 o'clock in the morning, when I got up, the camp was surrounded by two battalions of police [Gendarmerie]. When I left my house to go to work like always, I was turned back by an SS officer. Thereupon

I went to the office to find out what I should do. No one there knew anything either. Then we made our way to T. [i.e., the factory manager] to find out there what the whole thing meant. T. was very worked up and was holding his head in his hands. T. said, 'We will go to the factory no matter what happens.' But as soon as we got downstairs in the house we were stopped by an officer and not allowed to go any further. T. was told that he was not allowed to enter the factory and that this was being guarded by the SS. T. nevertheless wanted to go on, but was taken back to his flat. In the flat we found out that we were cut off from the outside world and the telephone line had been cut. T. found this out when he tried to make a 'phone call. At 7.30 the mass murder began. We heard the shooting. When we looked out of the window we were told by an SS officer in a grave tone of voice to leave the window at once. Sometime later we were picked up by the Gestapo and taken down a corridor into the SS office. Here we had to sign a declaration that we would say nothing about what had happened. The form threatened the death penalty if we did not obey. Then we were led back to T.'s flat and not allowed to leave the flat and not even allowed to enter the side of the flat from which we would have been able to watch the Jews being shot.

All of us, especially T., were very depressed. . . .

Source: Passage from statement under oath of Polish electrician J.L. made on 15 January 1946, Federal Archive, Berlin-Zehlendorf, SL 47 A

No one knew the executioners were coming until they arrived. The camp was well guarded and its communications were cut. Everyone present was sworn to secrecy under pain of death. All of this reinforces the impression that the most severe racial atrocities of the war were carried out by a small, dedicated group isolated from wider society and operating under conditions of blanket secrecy. On the very rare occasions their actions became known to other Germans, they were met with abhorrence. The impression is that ordinary people would have opposed what was going on had they been able.

The view is persuasive, but too simple. For a start, secrecy was always less than perfect. The following is how Martin Koller, the son of a Protestant pastor, who served in the German air force, remembered a conversation on a train during the war, most probably during late 1941 or early 1942.

Document 7.12 A Strange Officer

After three weeks' leave I took a train back to the front. Something happened to me *en route* that I still think about to this day: my encounter with injustice. At one point a strange officer came into our compartment. He was amiable and polite, and introduced himself in broken German with a Baltic accent as a lieutenant from Latvia. We talked about all kinds of things, everyday subjects, war and private life. And then he said he'd taken part in shooting Jews somewhere in the Baltic. There had been more than 3,000 of them. They had had to dig their own mass grave 'as big as a soccer field.' He told me this with a certain pride.

I was completely at a loss and asked stupid questions like 'Is that really true? How was it done? Who led this operation?' And I got precise answers to each. It was true, anyone could check it; they did it with 12 men armed with machine pistols and one machine gun. The ammunition had been officially provided by the *Wehrmacht*, and a German SS lieutenant, whose name he didn't remember, had been in command. I became confused and started to sweat. This just didn't fit into the whole picture – of me, of my country, of the world, of the war. It was so monstrous that I couldn't grasp it.

'Can I see your identification?' I asked, and 'Do you mind if I note it down?' He didn't mind, and was just as proud of what he had done as I was of the planes I had shot down. And while I scribbled his strange name down on a cigarette package, my thoughts somersaulted: either what he's told me is true, in which case I can't wear a German uniform any longer, or he's lying, in which case he can't wear a German uniform any longer. What can, what should I do? My military instinct told me, 'Report it!'

Source: Memory of Martin Koller, who served in the Luftwaffe, *in J. Steinhoff* et al., Voices from the Third Reich, *1989, pp. 344–6*

Koller did make a report – which his senior officer quashed. The fact remained, however, that Koller and everyone who saw the report had learned about what was happening to Jews in the Baltic states. Nor was this case unique. Conservative resister Helmuth von Moltke, although based in Berlin, on one occasion spoke to a nurse from a sanatorium for SS men who had broken down while shooting Jewish women and children. At another time he met an SS man who told him of a place where 3,000 Jews were being gassed each day **(Balfour and Frisby, 1972, p. 203)**. Documents 5.9, 5.10 and 5.13 (pp. 101–2 and 105–6) show that racial policies and atrocities were discussed openly in meetings of military and governmental officials. Nor were comparable insights restricted to small, professional circles. The White Rose group consisted of students in Munich (see Chapter 4). Their second protest pamphlet spelled out bluntly that 'since the conquest of Poland three hundred thousand Jews have been murdered . . . in the most bestial way. Here we see the most frightful crime against human dignity, a crime that is unparalleled in the whole of history'. They added that anyone who knew of this but did nothing was 'guilty, guilty, guilty' **(Scholl, 1983, p. 79)**. German Jews were not believed immune to a terrible fate. By summer 1943 there were rumours in Frankfurt and Berlin that deported Jews were being gassed on the outskirts of those cities **(Bankier, 1992, p. 112)**. In other words, even if knowledge was not always perfect, the longer the war went on, the more stories accumulated about racial, and especially anti-Semitic, atrocities to indicate to very many people indeed that *something* was going dreadfully wrong.

Nor was the relationship between the Holocaust and ordinary Germans limited to knowledge. Four special action police units, numbering about 3,000 men in total, followed the Wehrmacht on its invasion of the USSR in June 1941. These police units, together with others, managed to account for about 2 million of the 6 million Jews killed during the war **(Dawidowicz, 1987, pp. 164–8)**. In a space as large as the Soviet Union, how on earth was this possible? SS and Police Leader Bach-Zelewsky was in charge of anti-Partisan activity in the East and after the war was interrogated by Allied authorities. Document 7.13 is a summary of one interrogation session.

Document 7.13 Help from Their Friends

Subject believes that comparatively mild persecution of the Jews at the beginning of the war was due to the resistance of the Army generals. The SD Einsatz Kommandos [special action police groups] were comparatively small at the time and the persecution was carried out by Armed Forces units and all administrative offices, as well as SS units. For the Russian campaign, a definite agreement was made between [security police chief] Heydrich and [General Quarter Master] Wagner, and it was obvious from the indifference of the Armed Forces quarters that they were well informed of the purpose of the Einsatzgruppen. The soldiers, no matter whether Army, Waffen-SS or Police, were, after decades of indoctrination, firmly convinced that the Jew was the German public enemy number one and had to be eliminated. Subject believes that the major amount of anti-Jewish rioting at the beginning of the Russian campaign was not according to a plan but spontaneous action by ideologically well trained troops.

Source: Section from the interrogation summary of 3 September 1947 relating to Bach-Zelewsky, Nuremberg State Archive, Rep 502 VI, B.2

The reality had been complicated, but in the end Bach-Zelewsky was pretty clear that while some generals began by opposing the SS's aims, in the end members of both the armed forces and civilian administrations in the East were complicit in wartime atrocities. His views were not just designed to deflect blame from his own organisation, the SS. Historian Theo Schulte has acknowledged that even during the Polish campaign the German military did not seriously try to stop SS atrocities, and thereafter (especially once the war against the USSR began) moved increasingly towards collaboration **(Schulte, 1989, p. 226)**. A comparative perspective makes a similar point. Historian Jonathan Steinberg has studied the Italian and German occupations of the Balkans. Despite a request to do so, for so long as Italy was an independent country, because Italian officers knew what the result would be, not one of them ever handed over a single Jew to German authorities. By contrast, Steinberg found not one example of a German military officer refusing to transfer a Jew to a concentration camp and hence to certain death **(Steinberg, 1990, p. 8)**. There is a strong case for saying that ordinary soldiers conformed to the demands of racial carnage.

As the process of the Holocaust became more elaborate, so it had to draw on a lot more than military support. Jews had to be rounded up and transported from Germany and everywhere else in Europe to extermination sites in Poland. Consider the following postwar interview with a German official who dealt with railway contracts there.

Document 7.14 Trains

[W]hy were there more special trains during the war than before or after it?

I see what you're getting at. You're referring to the so-called resettlement ['cover word' for extermination] trains.

'Resettlement'. That's it.

That's what they were called. Those trains were ordered by the Ministry of Transport of the Reich. You needed an order from the Ministry.

In Berlin?

Correct. And as for the implementation of those orders, the Head Office of Eastbound Traffic in Berlin dealt with it.

Yes, I understand.

Is that clear?

Perfectly. But mostly, at that time, who was being 'resettled'?

No! We didn't know that. Only when we were fleeing from Warsaw ourselves, did we learn that they could have been Jews, or criminals, or similar people.

Jews, criminals?

Criminals. All kinds.

Special trains for criminals?

No that was just an expression. You couldn't talk about that. Unless you were tired of life, it was best not to mention that.

But you knew that the trains to Treblinka or Auschwitz were –

Of course we knew. I was the last district; without me these trains couldn't reach their destination. For instance, a train that started in Essen had to go through the districts of Wuppertal, Hannover, Magdeburg, Berlin, Frankfurt/Oder, Posen, Warsaw etcetera. So I had to. . . .

Did you know that Treblinka meant extermination?

Of course not!

You didn't know?

Good God, no! How could we know? I never went to Treblinka. I stayed in Krakow, in Warsaw, glued to my desk.

You were a. . . .

I was strictly a bureaucrat!

I see. But it's astonishing that people in the department of special trains never knew about the 'final solution'.

We were at war.

Because there were others who worked for the railroads who knew. Like the train conductors.

Yes, they saw it. They did. But as to what happened, I didn't. . . .

What was Treblinka for you? Treblinka or Auschwitz?

Yes, for us Treblinka, Belzec and all that were concentration camps.

A destination.

Yes, that's all.

But not death?

No, no. . . .

Source: C. Lanzmann, Shoah, *1985, pp. 134–6*

Maybe this man wasn't lying, but his lack of insight needn't have been typical. These trains were taking thousands of people into camps, but never anyone away from them again! Given the information and rumours that were abroad at the time, what could most transport officials (and there were a great many of them) have thought was happening?

What is more, transport officials were not alone among civilians in being compromised by the Holocaust. Sadly other civilian officials had comparable fates. Postal workers often conveyed the initial messages about deportation to the German Jews about to be 'resettled'. Sometimes regular policemen were responsible for local 'round-ups'. As document 7.15 shows (it is a photograph taken in Würzburg), Jews were sometimes moved through the streets for deportation in broad daylight. Anyone could see them.

Doctors and nurses checked the people before departure. Once again we have to ask: what did all of these people believe they were involved in? Even if they didn't know precisely and categorically that genocide was being attempted, still they must have suspected deep down that something was not right. But they still conformed to what was expected and oiled the wheels of the Holocaust. In this respect maybe there is still a valid message behind Müller-Claudius's statistics after all. Had not a considerable number of people (both civilian and military) been so indifferent to the obvious injustices being meted out to the Jews around them, had they not conformed with the demands of noxious policies rather than refuse to implement them, could 6 million people really have been exterminated?

Of course Jewish policy was only the most infamous side of racialism. By the end of the war 7 million foreign workers had been 'press ganged' into working inside Germany **(Herbert, 1990, p. 152)**. Every second worker in agriculture was foreign. In mining, the metal industry and construction it was every third. Twenty-five per cent of the population of large towns in the Ruhr was now foreign. The majority of these people were Slavs taken from the eastern occupied territories. Nazi racial doctrine, reflected in the laws of the Third Reich, defined these as second-class citizens. But did average Germans treat them accordingly?

Historian Ulrich Herbert has participated in an extensive research project into popular memories held by Germans of foreign workers. More or less two-thirds

Document 7.15 Deportation from Würzburg

Source: Centre de Documentation Juivre Contemporaine, Paris

of those interviewed remembered these people. Typically acts of kindness towards them were recalled, for example, donating pieces of bread and butter, helping carry a heavy load, allowing them to share a 'Germans only' air-raid shelter, setting up the occasional illicit visit by a foreigner to a German's home and so on. Is this evidence that Germans were most interested in subverting the official apartheid order? Actually Herbert does not draw this conclusion. As he puts it:

> Behind the formula 'I always got on with forced labourers' lurks the certainty: normally it was different. The foreigners were beaten – but not always by foremen and Nazis – they were starving and had to go begging – but now and again I gave them bread and butter – they were locked in the camp – but one time I invited them over to my place.
> **(Herbert, 1983a, p. 250)**

To Herbert's mind, more genuinely illuminating than memories of good deeds are cases such as that of a lady who originally worked in a menial job. With the introduction of forced labourers, suddenly she became manager of a canteen in charge of thirty Ukrainian trustees and providing meals for 3,000 Russians **(Herbert, 1983a, p. 246)**. Generalising from cases such as this, Herbert argues that by and large working-class Germans actually welcomed the arrival of the foreigners. Their presence opened up new sets of career opportunities, such as being a manager rather than a worker. The previous lower class now had some-one else to look down on! What were the consequences of the new situation? Herbert makes the following comments.

Document 7.16 Racism as Habit

Most Germans evinced little interest in the fate of the foreigners. Their concern for their own survival under National Socialism left them little time or opportunity to view the misery of the foreign workers as anything special or out of the ordinary. The foreigners were simply there, part of the workaday scenery. They belonged as much to the everyday reality of the war as ration cards or air-raid bunkers. The discrimination against workers from Eastern Europe was tolerated as something just as matter-of-fact and given as were the daily work detachments of half-starved labourers marching through the streets of the towns to their jobs in factories. Their own privileged position qua Germans vis-à-vis these workers was nothing exceptional, least-wise nothing that one would wish to expend any extra thought on. Yet this was precisely what constituted the essential ingredients underlying the functioning of the system of National Socialist forced labor for foreigners: the practice of racism here became truly a daily habit, a dimension of everyday life.

Source: U. Herbert, 'Labour as Spoils of Conquest, 1933–45', 1994, pp. 268–9

The longer the Third Reich and its war went on, the more this aspect of racial policy was treated with indifference too.

But it would be wrong for this chapter not to show how racial policy was also applied to the German people as a means to improving its hereditary quality. Euthanasia (see Chapter 3) eradicated genetic weaknesses through killing. Another way was to ensure that undesirable traits were not passed from one generation to the next. As early as 14 July 1933 the Law for the Prevention of Hereditarily Diseased Offspring was introduced to stop the propagation of 'lives unworthy of existence' by sterilisation **(Bock, 1984, p. 276)**. Between 1934 and 1939 320,000 women were sterilised – about 0.5 per cent of the national population! Mental handicap lay at the root of most of the cases. Fifty-three per cent were 'justified' by 'feeble-mindedness' and 20 per cent by 'schizophrenia'. On 24 November 1933, the Law against Dangerous Habitual Criminals allowed for the castration of 'genetically-determined' law-breakers. By 1940, this had been done to 2,006 men.

The raw human anguish which stood behind the statistics is amply expressed in the memories of a girl who suffered from hereditary deafness.

Document 7.17 Deaf from Birth

I have been deaf from birth. My parents can't hear either, but have two other children who are not without hearing. When I was 18 years old I received a letter from the administrative court saying that my mother and I should be sterilised. My mother lodged an appeal with the court and proposed that we should not be sterilised. My mother had two clever children and I too was getting on well at school. But the court had decided I had to be sterilised on account of my heredity. We had a hard battle. In the end my mother was not sterilised but she had to agree not to have any more children because there could be another deaf child.

I was sterilised. It was a gruesome time. I had to put up with a great deal. I was shifted from room to room because I wanted to jump out of the window. I like children a lot, but all of it was no use, I had to let myself be sterilised. After the sterilisation I got no sickness benefit. . . . My mother didn't have much money and I didn't earn much. We had to work day and night.

In 1938, however, I did get pregnant. My mother was not at home. My father was happy that I really had got pregnant. But when my mother came back from holiday she said: 'You are pregnant, that's not on, you've been sterilised, it could be a deformed child'. I had to go to the women's doctor. So I went to the women's doctor and let myself be examined. The women's doctor said that I would have a wonderful, natural birth and that the child was normal. I was happy and the doctor congratulated me. But afterwards my mother told him that I had been sterilised. The doctor was very shocked by that and broke off the treatment and told me: 'You must go to the women's clinic. It is responsible'. I was in despair and did not trust what was meant by the initial congratulations and then the ceasing of the treatment. I swore at my mother for talking to the doctor. . . .

I went to the women's clinic. The professor examined me and said: 'Get dressed again'. I wanted to get dressed again but my stockings and underpants had gone. I asked: 'Where are my stockings and pants?' – 'You stay there!' I asked: 'Why?' – 'Three days urine examination'. I believed him. I didn't realise why my mother was crying. She knew beforehand that I was not allowed to have a child. I went into the clinic and got a room with bars so that I could not run away. I was so worked up because my fiancé hadn't known anything and I hadn't known how to tell him. I was very sad and cried a great deal and was given a lot of injections. The next day I ran out quickly when the nurse opened the door and the other patients looked after me, and I bought a card on which I wanted to write to my fiancé. I gave this card to a friend and she said that she would post the card. But the sister had seen that I had handed over the card. She confiscated the card and I became hysterical.

I waited for three days for my urine to be examined. But no one asked for it. The doctor visited after three days and only said: 'Miss, don't you understand yet?' Because I was still young and not very experienced in life, I asked: 'What is it?' The doctor answered: 'The child may not come into the world'. Then I became hysterical and almost went crazy. They gave me lots of injections and I went to sleep. I woke up in the morning. They had taken me away. I was still not numb. In the operating room I saw the dish with the cloth. With the last strength in my body I screamed, then I was away.

The doctor had told me: 'In ten weeks you must come into the hospital again'. I was to be sterilised again. But when I came home I was in despair. I was really afraid of the next sterilisation. I shook like an animal, that people could treat the deaf like that. At school I had always been the best in the class, had got school prizes, and was good at my job – why did I have to be sterilised? Why was I not allowed to have my child? My mother really was a good mother to her three children, and my two sisters were educated, clever children. My father is also deaf. But his brothers all have good jobs. I often accused my mother for me having to suffer. My mother cried a lot. Previously I did not understand that not everyone was to blame. When the ten weeks were up, I didn't go to the hospital.

When I wanted to marry my fiancé, we had to go to the registry office. The registry official looked up the documents and said: 'Unfortunately, Miss Schwärz, first of all you have to be sterilised. Then you can get married'. Then I was quite stunned. But I asked myself, how did the papers get to the registry office? It's not a matter for the registry office, only the health office. I got up and ran home quickly.

. . . Then with a heavy heart I let myself be sterilised again. It was the most gruesome thing that I ever had to experience. I cannot forget it. Even after this sterilisation I didn't receive any sickness benefit. We had to get through things as best as possible, it was very bad. Then we got married.

Source: A. Ebbinghaus (ed.), Opfer und Täterinnen, *1987, pp. 70–2*

A great many people indeed must have been involved in sterilisation work. There were the doctors and nurses who ensured operations were carried out on unwilling patients. There were the administrators who informed the registrar's office of who should not be allowed to marry. There was the registrar himself. Whether or not everyone in document 7.17 believed in the fairness of what they were doing, they certainly acted as if they did; they all conformed with an inhuman policy to cast a dreadful shadow over a girl's life.

We need to draw together the different strands of this chapter. In the context of a society in which racism formed a background feature of everyday life, very many ordinary Germans indeed played small parts in making a fundamentally flawed system function. Accepting that concrete individual actions always reflect a mixture of motives, during peacetime conformity took the form of both passive acceptance of, and active support for, racial actions and policies which stopped short of the wholesale violence of 'Crystal Night'. With the nation at war, escalating racial policy grew into something people learned to live with; it was for most people a source of indifference. If their job dictated some sort of collaboration in the implementation of racial policy, by and large they conformed to the demand. Naturally there were exceptions to the rule. Eventually genuine public outrage did develop at the euthanasia of the mentally handicapped (see Chapter 3). We know about the demonstration by the wives of Jews in 1943. The names of at least some principled opponents of National Socialist racism merit repeating: Father Lichtenberg (Chapter 3), the Scholls (of the White Rose group, Chapter 4), Helmuth von Moltke (Chapter 5) and Gottfried Stammler (this chapter). But the impression lingers, as Willy Brandt has said (document 1.22, p. 21), that far too few people made conscious choices to oppose this particular form of evil. It became normal to conform to highly abnormal expectations.

Opposition, resistance and German society 8

black and white, or grey?

Notwithstanding the rather disappointing conclusion to the last chapter, Germans did carry out a whole variety of activities against aspects of the Third Reich. They ranged from verbal complaints to assassination attempts, from the distribution of leaflets to an attempted *coup d'état*. The people who participated were suitably heterogeneous. They included aristocrats and workers, rebellious youths and retired civil servants, bishops and Jews. The extent of popular upset caused by different Nazi policies was no less uneven. It extended from the all but universal condemnation of 'Crystal Night' to an extensive conformity to the demands of racial policy during the war years. Fifty years on, and living in societies which are very different to Hitler's Germany, we need to assess critically how we should understand what was happening there.

We can start with the historians' debate about how the word 'resistance' should be used. Originally it was applied more or less solely to highly motivated political activists who organised to overthrow the Third Reich **(Kershaw, 1993, p. 150)**. The men of 20 July are an obvious example. But consider the dictionary definition in document 8.1.

Document 8.1 To Resist

resist Stop course of, successfully oppose, keep off or out, prevent from penetrating, repel, be proof against or unaffected or uninjured by, abstain from . . . strive against, oppose, try to impede, refuse to comply with. . . .
resistance . . . power of resisting, stopping effect (*passive resistance*, refusal to comply . . .). . . .

Source: Pocket Oxford Dictionary, *1969, p. 704*

Someone who 'strived against' the Third Reich (as von Stauffenberg did) certainly resisted it; but so did a person who simply 'refused to comply' with its demands (perhaps a party member who also went to church). Likewise, according to the dictionary definition, someone who 'prevented' Nazi ideas from 'penetrating' his or her mind (maybe a member of an SPD discussion group) was also a resister, and so was a person who just remained 'unaffected' by the new system. The examples could go on, but the immediate issue is this: how narrowly or broadly should historians define 'resistance' activity?

There are arguments for a very broad definition indeed. According to historian H.A. Jacobsen:

> the concept of resistance must comprise all that was done despite the terror of the Third Reich, despite the suffering and martyrdom, for the sake of humanity, for the aid of the persecuted. And the word resistance in some cases applies, too, to certain forms of standing aside in silence.
>
> **(Jacobsen, 1969, p. 11)**

Resistance, as understood by Jacobsen, was not necessarily defined as sensational or even directly subversive action. It was anything at all which showed that 'the German people wanted to dissociate itself from the crimes that were being committed daily and hourly in its name' **(Jacobsen, 1969, pp. 11–13)**.

Another broad approach was offered by the former director of the social historical investigation known as 'the Bavaria project', namely Martin Broszat. While Jacobsen was overwhelmingly concerned with the purposes and moral qualities of historical actions, Broszat tried to identify attributes he felt to be more objectively verifiable. As he put it, 'what counts politically and historically is above all what was *done* and *accomplished*, not just *desired* or *intended*' **(quoted in Kershaw, 1993, p. 160)**. Discussing less dramatic types of activity, such as failures to join party organisations, the maintenance of contacts with non-Nazis and undertaking religious pilgrimages, he explained that these

> forms of resistance, often neglected in traditional histories of *Widerstand* [resistance], in fact were types of subversion more capable of undermining the totalitarian dictatorship than efforts at fundamental opposition, which had little chance of success under the watchful and pervasive system of Nazi control.
>
> **(Broszat, 1991, p. 30)**

At the extreme, the implication is that a housewife who jeered a Nazi demonstration in public was doing something more worthwhile than a Communist trying to arrange a revolutionary cell. The former would have been heard by a whole crowd; the latter may well have been arrested before getting any message across.

Now all actions involving the preservation of humanity and conspicuous shows of independence certainly were in opposition to the Third Reich and are deserving of recognition, but Jacobsen and Broszat leave open the possibility that, to become truly meaningful, such potentially extensive categories of action still need to be subdivided. More particularly historian Ian Kershaw has warned that if we classify every thought and deed directed against the Third Reich as 'resistance', then we risk diluting our understanding of what it really was 'to resist'. He proposes the following distinctions.

Document 8.2 Resistance, Opposition, Dissent

Resistance – active participation in *organized* attempts to work against the regime with the conscious aim of undermining it or planning for the moment of its demise.

Opposition – a wider concept comprising many forms of action with partial and limited aims, not directed against Nazism as a system and in fact sometimes stemming from individuals or groups broadly sympathetic towards the regime and its ideology.

Dissent – the voicing of attitudes frequently spontaneous and often unrelated to any intended action, which in any way whatsoever ran counter to or were critical of Nazism.

Source: I. Kershaw, Popular Opinion and Political Dissent in the Third Reich, *1983, pp. 2–4*

To this way of thinking, when defining 'resistance' it is important to distinguish organised from spontaneous activity, actions directed against the Third Reich as a whole from those with more limited aims and words from deeds. Other historians have agreed broadly with the distinctions. Hans Mommsen has advocated the separation of activity aimed at overthrowing the Third Reich as a totality from that which could run its course within the existing state structure **(Mommsen, 1985, p. 5)**. Richard Löwenthal has differentiated 'politically conscious opposition' (which aimed at the deliberate subversion of the Third Reich), 'social refusal' (whereby people tried to exclude National Socialism from everyday life) and 'ideological dissent' (through which people tried to maintain minds untarnished by Nazi propaganda) **(Löwenthal, 1982, pp. 13–14)**. Roughly speaking, Mommsen's point parallels Kershaw's distinction of 'resistance' from 'opposition'. Löwenthal's concepts highlight the difference between 'resistance' and 'dissent'. They also introduce the perspective of everyday life into discussion.

Detlev Peukert developed his own set of concepts which deal primarily with the concrete experiences of average Germans living in the Third Reich.

Document 8.3 Nonconformity, Refusal, Protest, Resistance

[W]ithin each system, including National Socialism, there are whole areas of behaviour that normally lie below the threshold of police intervention. It was in these areas – usually private ones – that most acts of *nonconformist behaviour* vis-à-vis the Nazi regime were clustered (see diagram). As a rule these were separate individual acts of infringement of the norms [of the state] and did not call into question the system as a whole.

Acts of nonconformist behaviour became one degree more general and hence directed politically against the regime, if they were more than just breaches of particular norms of the system but were undertaken in opposition, say, to orders issued by the authorities. *Refusals* of this sort could, for example, include not sending one's son or daughter to the Hitler Youth or the League of German Girls . . . in contravention of repeated official injunctions, or failing to increase one's personal work output despite recurrent calls by management.

More far-reaching again, because one stage further in the direction of wholesale rejection of the regime, was *protest*, though this might still be a matter of single-issue action, such as the churches' campaign against euthanasia (that is, the murder of disabled people).

On the gamut of dissident behaviour, *resistance* can be taken to denote those forms of behaviour which were rejections of the Nazi regime as a whole and were attempts, varying with the opportunities available to the individuals concerned, to help bring about the regime's overthrow.

FORMS OF DISSIDENT BEHAVIOUR IN THE THIRD REICH

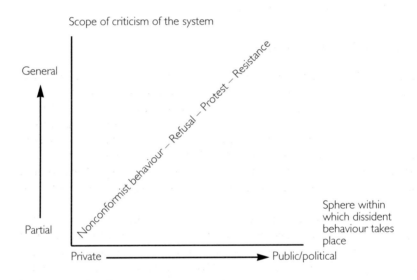

Source: D. Peukert, Inside Nazi Germany, *1993, pp. 83–4*

The benchmarks here reflect whether action was significant enough to worry the police, whether it rejected a direct claim by the government on an individual's life, whether people spoke out publicly against aspects of policy, and finally whether the regime was rejected as a whole.

Obviously Peukert's system has some overlap with Kershaw's (for example, both identify only those who rejected the Third Reich totally as true 'resisters'), but the conceptualisation of 'resistance' is still subtly different. Peukert's concern with everyday life led him to recognise that, dependent on their particular social circumstances, not everyone sensibly could organise to overthrow the regime or plan for the moment of its demise. That is to say, while members of the governmental and military élites (such as Beck and von Moltke, see Chapter 5) relatively speaking did have the expertise and opportunity to plan for a *coup d'état* and a new Germany, it is hard to imagine how an ordinary German worker living in a close-knit community and expected to be in his factory for hours on end could have done anything directly comparable (although one might have tried to assassinate Hitler in November 1939, see documents 8.10 and 8.11, pp. 173–4 and 174–5). It was hard enough for such an individual to hide a Communist or a German Jew 'on-the-run' even temporarily (document 2.14, p. 35). Peukert's introduction of 'opportunity' into our thinking is valid.

Inevitably, however, criticism has been levelled against even Peukert's model. His graph-like depiction of action apparently progressing from stage to stage has been taken to imply that would-be resisters had careers somehow progressing up a hierarchy of increasingly serious action until they reached the pinnacle of 'resistance'. But need careers have been so orderly? Historian W. Breyvogel has put forward the following arguments.

Document 8.4 Spontaneity

On the other hand we can observe that political insights – especially of the young – do not exactly run according to the scheme 'one stone on top of the other' or 'step by step', but rather are dependent on the nature of what is experienced and for the most part arrive suddenly. A single perception and feeling, a sole situation, a single glimpse of a struggle, an impression acquired at home, a scene in front of the window, a perception in the ghetto – from one second to another this can let loose everything in one person, nothing at all in another. Such situations are to be found in a series of auto-biographical testimonies.

If we want to understand the development of the political resistance actions of youths, we must free ourselves of the stepwise model and pay attention to feelings, perceptions and expressions of ideas which are [all] bound up with certain situations. Methodologically such a situational analysis would be bound up with a biographical reconstruction in the case of appropriate authentic materials being available. . . .

Historical research into youth laid out in this manner will establish that often the entire spectrum of motives and forms of action from '*Resistenz*' [defined as 'the reserve, reticence, lack of enthusiasm of individuals and groups which developed out of social conditions of life, milieux and beliefs'] to resistance is to be found in the protest forms displayed by young people. The story of how youths experienced things is especially unsuited to the successful ascent up a stepladder from one concept to the other. Every-thing is involved in his or her action – fun and deep earnestness, direct disruption and 'foolishness' in the literal sense of a 'fool', in a sense of not being so weighed down by [the need to conform] and to be considerate.

Source: W. Breyvogel, 'Resistenz, Widersinn und Opposition', 1991b,
pp. 10–11

For the young, and so presumably for at least some other people too, the decision to resist could be just as much a spontaneous reaction to a particular situation as a protracted development. But the idea that only a detailed biographical under-standing of a resister can render his or her actions totally comprehensible also has consequences.

If we accept that each resister can only really be understood through a careful reconstruction of his or her life, then each tends towards the unique. Under such circumstances, we have to wonder whether the sets of concepts provided by Kershaw and Peukert risk imposing artificial structures on a morass of actions rendered incomparable and entirely distinct by the unique life experiences and character of each actor. Taking an obvious example, Peukert and Kershaw would both define the actions of the Communist group Red Orchestra and of the conservative men of 20 July as 'resistance'. Both were organised and were dedicated to overthrowing the Third Reich as a whole. But is it that useful to push together the work of individuals with such different political agendas? From this perspective, we may be tempted to return to the broadest conceptions of 'resistance' as most likely to help the historian approach his topic with as few preconceptions as possible.

It is a fine ideal to take everyone who stood up to Hitler purely on his or her individual merits, but in practice (and as soon as we move away from assessments about individuals to more general thinking) there is such an expanse of material that some way of ordering it is hard to dispense with. We need a system which, on the one hand, should stimulate our thinking about the topic; and which, on the other hand, should provide a framework within which to compare different historical cases, the better both to understand their critical similarities and differ-ences, and to help identify patterns running through society as a whole. Under the circumstances, while accepting that any system is going to be imperfect, the challenge is to create something as illuminating as possible.

Moving back to a general discussion couched once again in the most general terms of 'opposition' to the Third Reich, we can still recognise that the 'resistance' debate has highlighted key areas to be included whenever we try to understand those who stood up to Hitler and National Socialism. These include the moral worth of action (Jacobsen), the nature and extent of its aims (Kershaw and Peukert), whether it was produced through organised and planned efforts (Kershaw) or individuality and spontaneity (Breyvogel), whether opponents made full use of the sort of opportu-nities open to them (Peukert), the profile of actions within society (Broszat) and, relatedly, whether words or deeds were at stake (Kershaw). We can apply these insights to produce the following table of perspectives on opposition activity.

'IVES ON OPPOSITION TO THE THIRD REICH

Personal motives
Actions which were:

...t a notional political

1 To do with protecting oneself from National Socialism.

...:d on piecemeal political
...is with only elements of
...stem.

2 To protect family and friends.
3 For the good of anyone suffering.

...the creation of a totalitarian, Communist state.
4 Envisaged the creation of an authoritarian, Bismarckian state.
5 Aimed at the creation of an essentially free, democratic state.

Means used
Actions which involved:

1 Personal mental protection.
2 The deliberate carrying on of traditional community life in the face of Nazi preferences to the contrary.
3 Anti-Nazi discussions with close circles of friends.
4 Open dissent.
5 Public protest.
6 Concerted conspiracy using 'low key' means (for example, the secret distribution of leaflets) to subvert Nazi policies.
7 Open rebellion against elements of the Hitler state.
8 Revolution against the whole Hitler state.

Social context

1 Individuals who (a) made use of opportunities for opposition activity only rarely and/or (b) exploited available opportunities only slightly.
2 Individuals who (a) made use of some opportunities for opposition and/or (b) stopped short of exploiting those which were available fully.
3 Individuals who (a) made use of all opportunities and/or (b) exploited their opportunities to the full.
4 Individuals who roughly manufactured opportunities for opposition deliberately.
5 Individuals who planned opposition activity in detail.

There is a *tendency* for each of the four categories to increase in moral worth as the numbers identifying each subheading increase. The same *tends* to be true of the degree of planning and organisation likely to have been behind any given action and of the impact it would have had in society. No implication is intended that people had to progress through stages 1, 2 and 3 etc. of any given category before becoming involved in another type!

Of course we could now try to locate examples of action within the framework and compare what we found. Likewise we could discuss which particular criteria should be applied to define 'resistance' activity and any other number of categories. But, in the light of everything said so far, these are tasks each reader can try for him- or herself. More important is to make explicit that, as complicated as human activity is, an understanding of the varieties of opposition and resistance to the Third Reich is best pursued from more than one angle – in this case, from political, personal, organisational and social–contextual ones.

Nor have we exhausted the problems facing historians of opposition to the Third Reich. Yet even if we apply the very general definitions of 'resistance' offered by Jacobsen and Broszat, it can still be far from clear whether given actions actually constituted opposition to the Third Reich or something rather different. Fifty years after the event, central judgements involved here can be fiendishly difficult, as a number of interrelated examples display well. Take the following political jokes drawn from Germany in the 1930s and 1940s.

Document 8.5 Jokes

1 The ideal German should be: as blonde as Hitler, as tall as Goebbels, as slim as Göring and as chaste as Röhm [leader of the SA and a notorious homosexual].

2 Robert Ley (leader of the German Labour Front) to the manager of a factory:
Ley: Tell me, have you still got any Social Democrats with you?
Manager: Oh yes, about half the workforce.
Ley: How dreadful! But surely no Communists?
Manager: Oh yes, about a third of the men.
Ley: Really! What about Democrats and so on?
Manager: They make up the remaining 20 per cent.
Ley: Good gracious! Haven't you got any Nazis at all?
Manager: Oh yes, of course, all of them are Nazis!

3 Customer: What kind of dogs have you got for sale?
Salesman: Pekinese, dwarf poodles, Yorkshire terriers. . . .
Customer: Stop, stop – haven't you got a dog big enough for a family of five? [The joke is taken from 1943, by which time the hardships of war had started to bite.]

Source: F.K.M. Hillenbrand, Underground Humour in Nazi Germany *1933–45, 1995, pp. 11, 49, 184*

These certainly would not have met with official approval, but did they constitute opposition? The answer has to lie in an assessment of how those telling and listening to the jokes understood what they were doing. Were they enjoying a 'harmless laugh' at the expense of their political leaders (something which even the most loyal of Nazis could do), or were they using jokes as a subversive means to express and bolster up mental protection to National Socialist propaganda (see p. 167, the column entitled 'means used')? So long after the fact, such judgements are particularly hard to make, and would probably have varied from person to person.

A comparable point about the ambiguity of evidence is illustrated in an even more extreme example: the shooting of a Nazi functionary.

Document 8.6 Ambiguity

[The complexity of opposition activity] . . . comes to light clearly in a case which happened on 28 September 1944 at around 9 PM in Cologne-Ehrenfeld: a drunken deserter shot at a NSDAP *Ortsgruppenleiter* who was riding past on his service motorbike. At first he drove on, but then called out 'I am wounded!' and tumbled from the motorbike. A master of the watch was running past with other people straight to an air-raid shelter because the air-raid siren had gone off. He supported the shot man and laid him on the ground.

In the scene which lasted only a few seconds three event sequences were superimposed on each other: people running into an air-raid shelter, an air-raid siren and the shots at the *Ortsgruppenleiter*. In addition the processes happened in darkness and were accompanied by the wail of sirens.

Source: B.-A. Rusinek, 'Desintegration und gesteigerter Zwang', 1991, pp. 278–9

Was this shooting a conscious act of opposition aimed at an accessible symbol of the Third Reich? Or was it an unthinking, alcohol-induced 'lashing out' indicative of little more than a deviant 'will to destroy' given opportunity by the prevailing dark and chaotic circumstances? Once again, so long after the fact, it is hard to attribute a precise meaning to the event because we just don't know what motivated the man to do what he did.

Nor should we ignore that the shooter was a deserter. By virtue of this (never mind that he tried to 'murder' the *Ortsgruppenleiter*), the laws of the time decreed that he was a criminal. In fact deserters are still considered criminals today. In this light we can begin to understand why Melita Maschmann commented in her memoirs that in the postwar world she was left unsure of how to distinguish good and evil **(Maschmann, 1964, p. 220)**. This former SS officer has been far from alone in finding it hard to define clearly the boundaries between opposition and crime. An opinion poll held in West Germany in June 1951 recorded that only 40 per cent of people approved of what the men of 20 July had done when they tried to assassinate Hitler and stage a *coup d'état*. Thirty per cent actually disapproved **(Whalen, 1993, p. 41)**. The statistics spoke of a popular confusion over whether an heroic act or high treason had been committed. Such uncertainties extended well beyond the 1950s and 1960s. In the late 1980s politicians and historians could not decide whether the armed bands of Edelweiß Pirates which attacked Nazi authorities in Cologne in the final stages of the war deserved official recognition as 'resisters', or whether they had been 'criminals'. The debate was all the more highly charged because the Gestapo had hanged a number of teenage members of the so-called 'Steinbrück group' of pirates. An historian summarises how a final evaluation was reached.

Document 8.7 The Steinbrück Group

In order to clarify the facts, the interior ministry of North Rheinland-Westfalia commissioned some research. Its findings are that . . . [many] of the things done by the Steinbrück group . . . would have to be described as criminal, if they had been carried out under normal social conditions. But such conditions did not exist [at the time] and the concept 'criminality' is therefore not applicable to at least the youths [some members of the group were rather older]. The recommendation went on to say that there was nothing to stop the [youths who had been hanged] being recognised as victims of murder by the Gestapo and for compensation to be due to the relatives of the victims.

Source: B.-A. Rusinek, 'Desintegration und gesteigerter Zwang', 1991, p. 272

But does historical context *alone* really determine whether a crime was committed?

To explore the point further, we can stand the criminality issue on its head. Can anybody who did not make themselves into an 'outsider' during the Third Reich actually have been its opponent? More specifically, can somebody who took the decision to join the NSDAP (or a related organisation) ever be recognised as its adversary? In a sense, of course they can. Consider the example of Kurt Gerstein. This devoted Christian wrote the following letter to Pastor Kurt Rehling in 1941.

Document 8.8 Going Under Cover

If you hear strange things about me, don't think that I have changed. Please tell that to (Church) President Koch as well. I shouldn't like him to think badly of me. I have joined the SS and now, at times, I talk their language. I do this for two reasons: the collapse is coming. That is absolutely certain. There will be a Day of Judgement. When that moment comes, these ruthless desperados will do all they can to get rid of anyone left whom they regard as their enemy. At that point, help from outside will be useless. Help then can only possibly come from a person who can suppress orders or deliver them in garbled form. That is where I come in. The second reason is that I am on the trail of so many crimes! My aunt was killed at Hadamar [document 3.12, p. 57]. I want to know where and by whom the orders for these murders are given!

Source: Quoted in S. Friedländer, Counterfeit Nazi, 1969, pp. 80–1

Gerstein came to hold a senior position in the SS. He became responsible for ordering prussic acid, a vital ingredient in the manufacture of the Xyklon-B poison gas which was used in the gas chambers. After the war, Gerstein maintained that he had done what he could to sabotage its production. He had carried out his job so inefficiently that on occasion stocks of the acid had deteriorated and had to be destroyed. Gerstein also provided information to French authorities about people who had known what was being done. He then committed suicide. But was Gerstein's case so extreme as to be unique, or should we be prepared to consider other party men opponents of the Third Reich too?

In a section of her classic study of the relations between Germans and Jews, Sarah Gordon implies that at least some members of the NSDAP were as much anti-Nazis as anyone else.

Document 8.9 Nazis as Opponents?

Opposition among Nazis who aided Jews or criticized persecution was similar to that among non-Nazis, as the following examples demonstrate. Two middle-aged (in their forties) Protestant lawyers who employed Jews in Düsseldorf were purged from the NSDAP for this activity. Another lawyer, a 35-year-old Catholic from Essen, lost his party membership because he opposed Nazi racial ideology. [It would be interesting to be told more details about this case.] Still another lawyer, a 55-year-old resident of Essen, was dropped from party membership because he defended a Jewess in 1936. A 54-year-old small businessman, a Catholic from Düsseldorf, also lost his party membership because he rented to Jews and hid Jews during Kristallnacht. A 39-year-old small businessman in Essen was a member of the SS and had an affair with the non-Jewish wife of a Jew; he too was kicked out of the party and was prohibited from later marrying the German woman because she was 'tainted' by having been married to a Jew. Another independent shopkeeper, a 34-year-old Catholic from Essen, was given strong warning against further purchases from Jews. A 60-year-old small businessman in Essen was kicked out of the party and indicted by the public prosecutor's office because he and his wife hid Jews in 1938 and sold securities to them. A 59-year-old shop-keeper from Essen had extensive business relations with Jews, rented to Jews, warned Jews of deportations, and offered to hide Jews during World War II; he was imprisoned for three months. Another shopkeeper, a 53-year-old Catholic from Essen, gave potatoes and vegetables to Jews during the war; for this she was imprisoned for two weeks. . . .

There were several kinds of opposition among upper level white-collar Nazi workers. One 38-year-old Protestant white-collar worker from Essen was purged from the SA and the NSDAP in 1936 because he socialized with Jews. Another, a 42-year-old white-collar worker from Essen, was also expelled from the party for socializing with Jews in 1937. He was also given nine months in prison in 1943 for making critical remarks about the

Nazi regime. A 25-year-old SA brigade leader from Hagen lost his party membership because he bought from Jews while in uniform. Still another SA man, a 36-year-old electrician from Essen, was expelled from the party because his wife had sexual relations with a Jew, a man with whom he was on friendly terms. . . .

A blue-collar worker, a 36-year-old Catholic from Leverkusen, was expelled from the party for criticizing Kristallnacht. . . .

Source: S. Gordon, Hitler, Germans and the 'Jewish Question', *1984, pp. 271–3*

Certainly these party members did contravene National Socialist expectations and came to the aid of Jews, but in fact Gordon is still wrong to imply that automatically they should be taken as opponents of the Third Reich. Admittedly, some might have been similar to Kurt Gerstein and have decided to take steps to subvert the NSDAP. But others, more simply, might have been committed Nazis who, for one personal reason or another, failed to live up to their own standards. Only detailed evidence about the *thinking* of the individuals involved can decide the point.

A common theme has run through the discussion of documents 8.5 to 8.9. A joke remains just a joke unless the person telling it *intends* deliberately to use it as a subversive tool. A person who breaks the law remains a criminal unless we can be sure that he or she did so in the *secure understanding* that this was not a means to trivial personal gratification but a principled strike against a wicked regime. A Nazi who contravened the party's ideologically-based expectations remains a Nazi unless it can be shown that *he or she honestly held alternative beliefs*. In this context, Broszat's argument outlined earlier in the chapter that the social impact of actions matters more than the intentions which lay behind them simply cannot be accepted. In such complicated historical situations as those outlined here, intention is all-important. If we cannot understand this, we cannot even be sure that we are actually dealing with cases of opposition to the Third Reich or something rather different. This is precisely why 'Perspectives on opposition to the Third Reich' (p. 167) includes a section entitled 'personal motives'. In its widest form and whatever else it may involve, properly understood, opposition to the Third Reich (as opposed to the infraction of a few of its expectations and regulations indicative of personal fallibility or genuine deviancy) had to include a motivation based on the self-conscious knowledge that at least some of the government's values and policies were fundamentally wrong and had to be challenged somehow.

A final topic for debate, and here we are returning to an area replete with inconclusive evidence, involves intelligence and secret organisations. Allegations have been made, for instance, that Admiral Canaris, head of German military intelligence, acted as a British agent **(see Höhne, 1985, p. 405)**. Certainly he did harbour a number of active opponents of the Third Reich in his organisation. These included Helmuth von Moltke (see Chapter 5) and Hans Oster. Oster leaked details of the German western offensive to a Dutch military attaché in Berlin on several occasions in 1939–40. Unfortunately his message was not believed. And yet, other officers under Canaris's command were involved in brutal wartime actions and he himself maintained good relations with Reinhard Heydrich (head of the security police and one of the organisers of the Holocaust). So what was the key to Canaris? Was he a determined opponent of the Third Reich who recognised a need to compromise his principles in order to shield from suspicion a centre for opposition? Or was he a patriot prepared to work alongside National Socialism for as long as it was proving successful, yet ready to 'hedge his bets' by harbouring the germ of 'another Germany' should the Third Reich fail? The extent of the activities carried out by von Moltke and Oster, coupled with Canaris's murder in a concentration camp before the end of the war, suggest strongly that the former is more likely, but the intricacy of the problem coupled with the lack of definitive documentary evidence, not just typical of studies of personal motivation but also characteristic of intelligence matters, makes a categorical conclusion difficult.

This 'intelligence effect' is surprisingly far-reaching. Just after the start of the war in November 1939 a bomb went off in Munich's most famous beer hall shortly after Hitler had finished a speech. Soon after a watchmaker called Georg Elser was arrested trying to cross the border into Switzerland. He was carrying postcards of the beer hall, the membership card of a left-wing organisation and equipment that could have been used to manufacture a timing device for a bomb. So was Elser a dedicated lone bomber, or only the visible side of a more sinister game? Historians L. Gruchmann and E. Calic give very different interpretations.

Document 8.10 Maverick

After his confession of 14 November [1939], Elser was brought to the Gestapo office in Berlin. Although on Himmler's orders he was subjected on several occasions to 'heightened interrogation', i.e., he was physically mistreated, he stuck to the story that he had planned, prepared and carried out the assassination attempt alone. The attempt to weaken him through a confrontation with his mother who was imprisoned temporarily and to move him to make a different statement, simply made Elser cry and he broke down. His relatives, who had already been imprisoned and interrogated as possible conspirators when the suspicion against Elser became strong, were interrogated in Berlin but without success. A commission set up by the state police office in Stuttgart investigated systematically in Elser's Swabian home area the former life, acquaintanceships, relationships and political past of the perpetrator without discovering any proof that he had been egged on by anyone or had been acting on behalf of any foreign power. . . .

The text [of his interrogation and confession] contains no reference to connections of Elser to foreign agents and so in no way corresponded to the wishes of the political powerholder of the time. This fact justifies further the conclusion that it was not manipulated by the Gestapo. The text even contained various statements which were embarrassing to the National

Socialist regime: for example, the references to the worsened material conditions of life of the working class, to the dissatisfaction of the workers, to the reduction of wages and the raising of taxes for carpenters and other professional groups, to the increase of force in the areas of professional and religious life, to Hitler's expansionist foreign policy and to his blame-worthiness over the outbreak of war; – statements which the officials taking the confession would hardly have written on their own initiative.

Source: L. Gruchmann, Autobiographie eines Attentäters, *1970, pp. 13–15*

Document 8.11 . . . or Pawn?

On the night of November 8, 1939, after giving his speech at the Buergerbräukeller in Munich, Hitler left immediately, rather than staying awhile to talk to his old comrades from the early days of the Nazi movement, as he usually did on these occasions. The Nazi leaders who had come with him – Heinrich Himmler, Alfred Rosenberg, Martin Bormann and others – also left; only a few guards and the organizers of the ceremony remained behind. Ten minutes later, at 9:20, a bomb exploded, killing several people and injuring many others.

That night, Christian Weber, a party veteran and not a member of the SS, was in charge of security. This meant that Heydrich and his SD [security service], who ordinarily looked after the Führer's safety, could not be held responsible for what clearly appeared to be an assassination attempt.

The combination of these two circumstances – Hitler's early departure and Heydrich's having turned over the security measures to someone else – prompted several Wehrmacht officers to think and say that the apparent attempt on the Führer's life might have been only a provocation, like the sham attack on the Gleiwitz radio station.

Anyone who carefully examines the incident will reach the conclusion that it was a propaganda operation designed to convince the German people that the British had tried to win the war by an ignoble plot to assassinate the Führer and other important German leaders.

The bomb blast killed seven people. The number of wounded was first announced as about sixty, then reduced by almost half.

Diplomats and journalists in Berlin realized that the Nazi propaganda machine now had enough material to fuel it for several months. Goebbels began constantly denouncing the British as a mob of murderers who wanted to deprive the Germans of their Führer after he had united them into a true national community. The *Vöelkischer Beobachter* said it was 'only by a miracle that the Führer escaped safe and sound from that attempt on his life, which was also a blow struck against the security of the Reich'. . . . The newspapers were filled with photographs showing the devastation of the Buergerbräukeller.

It seemed strange to many observers that in all the vituperative propaganda there was not one reproach against the SS, the organization charged with protecting the Führer, for having failed to take adequate security measures. It was Himmler himself, in fact, who was ordered to form a special commission to investigate the crime. . . .

The perpetrator was said to be a carpenter named Georg Elser, who had acted on orders from two officers of the British Intelligence Service operating in Holland: Major R.H. Stevens and Captain S. Payne Best. . . . For weeks before the crime, he had repeatedly gone into the Buergerbräukeller at night and hollowed out a cavity in the pillar, concealing his work each time by replacing the outside material. Then he installed his time bomb in the pillar so cleverly that it escaped detection. But German borderguards arrested him because of his suspicious behaviour as he was about to leave the country. Two postcards with pictures of the Buergerbräukeller were found in his pocket. The commission took this as an undeniable proof of his guilt. 'Pictures of the Buergerbräukeller in the perpetrator's pocket – isn't that a little too much?' Otto von Heydebreck asked Oster, Canaris's collaborator. . . .

Georg Elser was never tried for the Munich bombing, and after his arrest, he was given relatively lenient treatment. At the Sachsenhausen concentration camp, he had two rooms in a separate building. There he was allowed to play his zither, and he even had a carpenter's bench and tools.

Source: E. Calic, Reinhard Heydrich, *1982, pp. 202–10*

We may favour the latter interpretation for a number of reasons. British and German intelligence and security organisations certainly did play games with each other during the Second World War and it is difficult to be sure where exactly these ended. It also seems unlikely that an individual could have been clever enough to obtain explosives, manufacture a bomb, hollow out a pillar in a public beer hall only weeks before Hitler was due to speak there and then be so stupid as to cross a frontier during wartime carrying incriminating evidence! But this need not have been part of the intelligence game and it is not impossible that Elser made a dreadful miscalculation. In the end our knowledge remains imperfect.

Where do all of these insights into opposition to the Third Reich leave our understanding of German society during this period? In this chapter we have recommended a table analysing opposition activity from multiple perspective rather than a single set of hard and fast conceptual categories, recognised that only personal motives provide the solution to the sort of ambiguous situations encountered in this historical area and acknowledged that historians can face critical deficiencies of evidence. The image is of an historical theme prone to at least as many 'grey' areas as 'black and white'. The summary is apt since the more empirically based chapters of this book have had more than their share of that colour too.

1 In Chapter 2 we found a working class which grumbled, but which enjoyed what model factories and the Strength through Joy movement had to offer.

2 In Chapter 3 there were churches supposedly committed to Christian principles but not always prepared to speak out and act against National Socialist persecutions; we even found Christians ready to implement policies at odds with their beliefs.

3 In Chapter 4 we saw youthful desires for freedom balanced against the glamour and excitement of the Third Reich; we also saw Hitler Youths enjoying banned music and sharing, at times, the youthful rebellion characteristic of the Edelweiß Pirates.

4 In Chapter 5 we found the higher principles and sense of responsibility typical of Germany's traditional élites susceptible to subversion by National Socialism's jingoism.

5 In Chapter 6 some German Jews were seen to go along with National Socialism's demands, either because they could not believe where things were heading or because they felt trapped.

6 In Chapter 7 we saw the failure of popular outrage at the violence of 'Crystal Night' fail to turn into effective protest at wartime persecutions.

It is true that National Socialism never managed to achieve fully its aims for German society; the German people never was transformed into a coherent totality following without question the Führer's every command. But by the same token, and despite Germany's extensive left-wing organisations, strong Christian heritage and aristocratic traditions, neither did a coherent, massed opposition ever look likely to emerge to threaten the position of the government. In part this was certainly a result of the terroristic system of policing, but even the secret police relied on popular support. The strong implication has to be that even if very many people remained less than complete supporters of National Socialism, the movement still touched the lives of by far the majority of Germans in such a way that they were impelled into at least a partial conformity with what was on offer.

In the light of this we can agree with Klemens von Klemperer when he describes anyone who became an outright opponent of the regime as a stranger in his or her own land **(von Klemperer, 1991, pp. 129–31)**. In Germany between 1933 and 1945 the sort of humanitarian ethos we largely take for granted as an 'ordinary' or 'normal' feature of everyday life was at least partially replaced by something we should call 'abnormal'. To understand the nature of this anti-humanitarian abnormality, the place it assumed in people's minds, its connections with German society as a whole, and especially how it prevented the growth of more extensive clear-cut cases of resistance to the obvious injustices of the Third Reich remain as formidable challenges as any in the discipline of history. Even to approach their solution will call for a very careful reading indeed of all the available historical sources.

Further Reading

The assumption is that most readers have no knowledge of German language. Exceptions to this rule should be aware of three books in particular. *Opfer und Täterinnen* (1987), edited by A. Ebbinghaus, explores the experiences of women in Hitler's Germany. It contains a wealth of introspective personal testimony from, as the title says, victims and persecutors alike. *Bremen im Dritten Reich* (1986), a regional study by Marßolek and Ott, draws on a terrific range of original source material. The collection of essays, *Piraten, Swings und Junge Garde* (1991a), edited by W. Breyvogel, focuses on the lives of youths during this period. Each of the volume's contributions has something stimulating to say.

Naturally there is no shortage of worthy material available in English. The trend setting and authoritative overview of conformity and opposition in German society 1933–45, *Inside Nazi Germany* (1993) by Detlev Peukert is not to be missed – especially now it is available in paperback. Less rigorously academic, but more readable, is *Voices from the Third Reich* (1989). Edited by J. Steinhoff et al., the book consists of exerts from interviews with all manner of people who lived through the Third Reich. The immediacy of the recollections brings the historical period to life in a way comparable to Ebbinghaus's book. Classic overviews concerning the nature of National Socialism remain E. Jäckel's *Hitler's World View* (1981) and M. Broszat's *German National Socialism, 1919–1945* (1966). Both, although especially the latter, are full of ideas. Jäckel emphasises the coherence and self-sufficiency of Hitler's ideology, Broszat stresses just about everything else! There are not actually that many good general studies of the character of National Socialism's popular appeal (which of course pulled people into conformity with the movement). Peter Merkl's *The Making of a Stormtrooper* (1980) analyses the Abel sample, a series of essays by SA men in which they explained their reasons for joining the movement. It is worth looking at with a critical eye.

Discussion of the relationship between the workers and Hitler's government can be found in Ian Kershaw's *Popular Opinion and Political Dissent in the Third Reich* (1983). Tim Mason's *Social Policy in the Third Reich* (1993), published posthumously, contains a great deal of information, but his overall argument really has been superseded. In this connection, the essay by Omer Bartov, 'The Missing Years: German Workers, German Soldiers' (1994), and the book by U. Herbert, *A History of Foreign Labour in Germany 1880–1980* (1990), are worthy successors. For a study of specifically the Communist movement, see A. Merson, *Communist Resistance in Nazi Germany* (1985).

Kershaw's *Popular Opinion and Political Dissent in the Third Reich* (1983) once again has much to say on the relationship between churchgoers and the government. Exclusively concerned with church affairs, however, is J.S. Conway's *The Nazi Persecution of the Churches* (1968). It is rather old, but remains a solid introduction to the theme. The experiences of youths have spawned some very accessible memoirs. These conjure up the mood of the time for both conformers and opponents alike. A. Heck's *A Child of Hitler* (1985) provides the memories of a boy who joined the Hitler Youth; Melita Maschmann's *Account Rendered* (1964) is a classic study of a girl's entry into the movement and career as an SS officer. Inge Scholl's *The White Rose* (1983) is a personal recollection of her brother and sister, Hans and Sophie. It also includes the full texts of their protest pamphlets. Works abound on the men of 20 July. *Germans Against Hitler* (1969), edited by H.A. Jacobsen, provides an extensive edited collection of documents about their exploits. Kramarz's biography of von Stauffenberg, *Stauffenberg* (1967), is another book now showing its age. Just available in English is Peter Hoffman's *Stauffenberg: A Family History, 1905–44* (1996). Still weathering the years well are N. Reynolds's biography of General Beck, *Treason was no Crime* (1976) and M. Balfour and J. Frisby's biography of von Moltke, *Helmuth von Moltke* (1972). The latter in particular is an outstanding piece of work.

Accessible studies of the reactions of German Jewry under the Third Reich have not been that numerous. Avrahim Barkai's *From Boycott to Annihilation* (1989) is the most obvious, coherent contender. *The Jews in Nazi Germany 1933–1945* (1986), edited by A. Paucker, is a collection of individual essays and also contains a great deal of information about the way the Nazi policies affected Jewish community life during the period 1933–9. For studies of Jewish resistance to the escalating persecutions of wartime, see Y. Suhl (ed.), *They Fought Back* (1968b) and M.R. Marrus (ed.), *The Nazi Holocaust. Volume 17* (1989). A classic interpretation of German attitudes to Nazi Jewish policy is given in Sarah Gordon's *Hitler, Germans and the 'Jewish Question'* (1984). In *The Germans and the Final Solution* (1992), notwithstanding the title of the book, David Bankier undertakes an in-depth analysis of German popular opinion regarding the Jewish Question. Frances Henry's *Victims and Neighbours* (1984) analyses German–Jewish relations in one village.

The third edition of Ian Kershaw's central text on the Third Reich, *The Nazi Dictatorship* (1993), includes a welcome chapter discussing historiographical aspects of resistance. *Germans against Nazism* (1990), edited by Nicosia and Stokes, provides a set of essays amounting to case studies of different types of opposition activity. *Contending with Hitler* (1991), edited by D.C. Large, is a comparable format and includes contributions by Broszat and Peukert.

Bibliography

Ainsztein, R., *Jewish Resistance in Nazi-Occupied Eastern Europe*. New York: Barnes and Noble. 1974.

Allen, W.S., 'The Social Democratic Underground Movement. The Continuity of Subcultural Values', in J. Schmädeke and P. Steinbach (eds.), *Der Widerstand gegen den Nationalsozialismus*. Munich: Piper. 1985.

——, *The Nazi Seizure of Power. The Experience of a Single German Town 1922–1945*. London: Penguin. 1989.

——, 'Social Democratic Resistance against Hitler and the European Tradition of Underground Movements', in F.R. Nicosia and L. D. Stokes (eds), *Germans against Nazism. Nonconformity, Opposition and Resistance in the Third Reich*. Oxford: Berg. 1990.

Arad, Y., 'Jewish Prisoner Uprisings in the Treblinka and Sobibor Extermination Camps', in M.R. Marrus (ed.), *The Nazi Holocaust. Volume 17: Jewish Resistance to the Holocaust*. Westport: Meckler. 1989.

Arad, Y., Gutman, Y. and Margialot, A. (eds), *Documents on the Holocaust*. Oxford: Pergamon Press. 1981.

Bajohr, F., 'In doppelter Isolation. Zum Widerstand der Arbeiterjugendbewegung gegen den Nationalsozialismus', in W. Breyvogel (ed.), *Piraten, Swings und Junge Garde. Jugendwiderstand im Nationalsozialismus*. Bonn: J.H.W. Dietz. 1991.

Baker, L., *Days of Sorrow*. New York: Macmillan. 1978.

Baldwin, P. (ed.), *Reworking the Past. Hitler, the Holocaust and the Historians' Debate*. Boston: Beacon Press. 1990.

Balfour, M., *Withstanding Hitler in Germany 1933–45*. London: Routledge. 1988.

Balfour, M. and Frisby, J., *Helmuth von Moltke. A Leader against Hitler*. London: Macmillan. 1972.

Bankier, D., *The Germans and the Final Solution. Public Opinion under Nazism*. Oxford: Blackwell. 1992.

Baranowski, S., 'Consent and Dissent: The Confessing Church and Conservative Opposition to National Socialism', *Journal of Modern History*, 59 (1987), 53–78.

Barkai, A., *From Boycott to Annihilation. The Economic Struggle of German Jews, 1933–1943.* London: University Press of New England. 1989.

Bartov, O., *The Eastern Front 1941–45. German Troops and the Barbarisation of Warfare.* London: Macmillan. 1985.

——, 'The Conduct of War: Soldiers and the Barbarization of Warfare', *Journal of Modern History,* 64 (1992), 32–45.

——, 'The Missing Years: German Workers, German Soldiers', in D.F. Crew (ed.), *Nazism and German Society, 1933–45.* London: Routledge. 1994.

Bauer, Y., 'The Judenräte – Some Conclusions', in Yad Vashem, *Patterns of Jewish Leadership in Nazi Europe 1933–45.* Proceedings of the Yad Vashem International Conference, Jerusalem, 4–7 April 1977.

—— 'Forms of Jewish Resistance during the Holocaust', in M.R. Marrus (ed.), *The Nazi Holocaust. Volume 17: Jewish Resistance to the Holocaust.* Westport: Meckler. 1989.

Behrend-Rosenfeld, E.R., *Ich stand nicht allein. Leben einer Jüdin in Deutschland 1933–1944.* Munich: C.H. Beck. 1988.

Beilmann, C., *Eine Katholische Jugend in Gottes und dem Dritten Reich.* Wuppertal: Peter Hammer. 1989.

——, 'Eine Jugend im katholischen Milieu. Zum Verhältnis im Glaube und Widerstand', in W. Breyvogel (ed.), *Piraten, Swings und Junge Garde. Jugendwiderstand im Nationalsozialismus.* Bonn: J.H.W. Dietz. 1991.

Benz, W., *Herrschaft und Gesellschaft im nationalsozialistischen Staat.* Frankfurt-am-Main: Fischer. 1990.

——, 'The Relapse into Barbarism', in W.H. Pehle (ed.), *November 1938: From Kristallnacht to Gënocide.* Oxford: Berg. 1991.

Bergmann, K. and Schörken, R. (eds), *Geschichte im Alltag – Alltag in der Geschichte.* Düsseldorf: Pädagogischer Verlag Schwann. 1982.

Bessel, R. (ed.), *Life in the Third Reich.* Oxford: Oxford University Press. 1987.

Blinkhorn, M. (ed.), *Fascists and Conservatives.* London: Unwin Hyman. 1990.

Boberach, H., *Berichte des SD und der Gestapo über Kirchen und Kirchenvolk in Deutschland, 1934–1944.* Mainz: Matthias-Grünewald. 1971.

Bock, G., 'Racism and Sexism in Nazi Germany: Motherhood, Compulsory Sterilization and the State', in R. Bridenthal, A. Grossman and M. Kaplan (eds), *When Biology Became Destiny. Women in Weimar and Nazi Germany.* New York: Monthly Review Press. 1984.

——, *Zwangssterilisation im Nationalsozialismus. Studien zur Rassenpolitik und Frauenpolitik.* Opladen: Westdeutscher. 1986.

Bracher, K.D., Funke, M. and Jacobsen, H.A. (eds), *Nationalsozialistische Diktatur 1933–1945. Eine Bilanz.* Düsseldorf: Droste. 1983.

Brandt, W., 'Foreword', in F. Henry, *Victims and Neighbours. A Small Town in Nazi Germany Remembered.* Mass.: Bergin and Garvey, 1984.

——, 'The German Resistance Movement', in D.C. Large (ed.), *Contending with Hitler. Varieties of Resistance in the Third Reich.* New York: Cambridge University Press. 1991.

Breyvogel, W. (ed.), *Piraten, Swings und Junge Garde. Jugendwiderstand im Nationalsozialismus.* Bonn: J.H.W. Dietz. 1991a.

——, 'Resistenz, Widersinn und Opposition', in W. Breyvogel (ed.), *Piraten, Swings und Junge Garde. Jugendwiderstand im Nationalsozialismus.* Bonn: J.H.W. Dietz. 1991b.

Breyvogel, W. and Lohmann, T., 'Schulalltag im Nationalsozialismus', in D. Peukert and J. Reulecke (eds), *Die Reihen fast geschlossen. Beiträge zur Geschichte des Alltags unterm Nationalsozialismus.* Wuppertal: Peter Hammer. 1981.

Bridenthal, R., Grossman, A. and Kaplan, M. (eds), *When Biology Became Destiny. Women in Weimar and Nazi Germany.* New York: Monthly Review Press. 1984.

Broszat, M., *German National Socialism, 1919–1945.* Santa Barbara: Clio Press. 1966.

——, 'Hitler and the Genesis of the Final Solution. An Assessment of David Irving's Thesis', in H.W. Koch (ed.), *Aspects of the Third Reich.* London: Macmillan. 1985.

——, 'The Third Reich and the German People', in H. Bull (ed.), *The Challenge of the Third Reich.* Oxford: Clarendon Press. 1986.

——, 'A Plea for the Historicization of National Socialism', in P. Baldwin (ed.), *Reworking the Past. Hitler, the Holocaust and the Historians' Debate.* Boston: Beacon Press. 1990.

——, 'A Social and Historical Typography of the German Opposition to Hitler', in D.C. Large (ed.), *Contending with Hitler. Varieties of Resistance in the Third Reich.* New York: Cambridge University Press. 1991.

Broszat, M. and Fröhlich, E. (eds), *Bayern in der NS-Zeit. Herrschaft und Gesellschaft in Konflikt.* Munich: Oldenbourg. 1979.

Browning, C.R., *The Path to Genocide. Essays on the Launching of the Final Solution.* Cambridge: Cambridge University Press. 1992.

——, *Ordinary Men. Reserve Police Battalion 101 and the Final Solution in Poland.* New York: HarperCollins. 1993.

Bull, H. (ed.), *The Challenge of the Third Reich.* Oxford: Clarendon Press. 1986.

Burleigh, M. and Wippermann, W., *The Racial State. Germany 1933–1945.* Cambridge: Cambridge University Press. 1991.

Calic, E., *Reinhard Heydrich. The Chilling Story of the Man Who Masterminded the Nazi Death Camps.* New York: William Morrow. 1982.

Childers, T. and Caplan, J. (eds), *Reevaluating the Third Reich.* New York: Holmes and Meier. 1993.

Conway, J.S., *The Nazi Persecution of the Churches. 1933–45.* London: Weidenfeld and Nicolson. 1968.

Crew, D.F. (ed.), *Nazism and German Society, 1933–45.* London: Routledge. 1994.

Dahrendorf, R., *Society and Democracy in Germany.* London: Weidenfeld and Nicolson. 1967.

Dawidowicz, L.S., *The War against the Jews 1933–45. Tenth Anniversary Edition.* London: Penguin. 1987.

Denzler, G. and Fabricus, V., *Christen und Nationalsozialisten.* Frankfurt-am-Main: Fischer. 1993.

Deutschland-Berichte der Sozialdemokratischen Partei Deutschlands (Sopade). 1934–1940. Frankfurt-am-Main: Petra Nettelbeck. 1980.

Dirks, W., 'Katholiken zwischen Anpassung und Widerstand', in R. Löwenthal and P. von zur Mühlen (eds), *Widerstand und Verweigerung in Deutschland 1933 bis 1945.* Berlin: J.H.W. Dietz. 1982.

Doll, A. (ed.), *Nationalsozialismus im Alltag. Quellen zur Geschichte der NS-Herrschaft im Gebiet des Landes Rheinland-Pfalz.* Speyer: Landesarchiv. 1983.

Ebbinghaus, A. (ed.), *Opfer und Täterinnen. Frauenbiographien des Nationalsozialismus.* Nördlingen: Delphi Politik. 1987.

Eberhard, F., 'Ilegal in Deutschland – Erinnerung an den Widerstand gegen des Dritte Reich', in D. Peukert and J. Reulecke (eds), *Die Reihen fast geschlossen. Beiträge zur Geschichte des Alltags unterm Nationalsozialismus.* Wuppertal: Peter Hammer. 1981.

Erikson, R.P., 'A Radical Minority: Resistance in the German Protestant Church', in F.R. Nicosia and L.D. Stokes (eds), *Germans against Nazism. Nonconformity, Opposition and Resistance in the Third Reich.* Oxford: Berg. 1990.

Eschwege, H., 'Resistance of German Jews against the Nazi Regime', in M.R. Marrus (ed.), *The Nazi Holocaust. Volume 17: Jewish Resistance to the Holocaust.* Westport: Meckler. 1989.

Fest, J., *Hitler.* London: Weidenfeld and Nicolson. 1974.

Focke, H. and Reimer, U., *Alltag unterm Hakenkreuz. Wie die Nazis das Leben der Deutschen veränderten.* Hamburg: Rowohlt. 1989.

Friedländer, S., *Counterfeit Nazi. The Ambiguity of Good.* London: Weidenfeld and Nicolson. 1969.

Gamm H-J., *Der Flüsterwitz im Dritten Reich.* Munich: Piper. 1993.

Gellately, R., 'Surveillance and Disobedience: Aspects of the Political Policing of Nazi Germany', in F.R. Nicosia and L.D. Stokes (eds), *Germans against Nazism. Nonconformity, Opposition and Resistance in the Third Reich.* Oxford: Berg. 1990.

——, *The Gestapo and German Society. Enforcing Racial Policy 1933–1945.* Oxford: Clarendon Press. 1991.

——, 'Enforcing Racial Policy in Nazi Germany', in T. Childers and J. Caplan (eds), *Reevaluating the Third Reich.* New York: Holmes and Meier. 1993.

Gilbert, M., *The Holocaust. The Jewish Tragedy*. Glasgow: Fontana Collins. 1987.

Goeb, A., *Er war sechzehn als man ihn hängte*. Hamburg: Rowohlt. 1981.

Gollwitzer, H., Kuhn, K. and Schneider, R., *Dying We Live. The Final Messages and Record of Some Germans who Defied Hitler*. London: Collins. 1965.

Golovchansky, A., '*Ich will raus diesem Wahnsinn.' Deutsche Briefe von der Ostfront 1941–1945. Aus sowjetischen Archiven*. Wuppertal: Peter Hammer. 1991.

Gordon, S., *Hitler, Germans and the 'Jewish Question'*. New Jersey: Princeton University Press. 1984.

Gotto, K., Hockerts, H.G. and Repgen, K., 'Nationalsozialistische Herausforderung und kirchliche Antwort. Eine Bilanz', in K.D. Bracher, M. Funke and H.A. Jacobsen (eds), *Nationalsozialistische Diktatur 1933–1945. Eine Bilanz*. Düsseldorf: Droste. 1983.

Gotto, K. and Repgen, K. (eds), *Kirche, Katholiken und Nationalsozialismus*. Mainz: Matthias-Grünewald. 1980.

Graml, H., *Antisemitism in the Third Reich*. Oxford: Blackwell. 1992.

Graml, H., Mommsen, H., Reichhardt, H.-J. and Wolf, E., *The German Resistance to Hitler*. London: Batsford. 1970.

Greiffenhagen, M., *Jahrgang 1928. Aus einem Unruhigen Leben*. Munich: Piper. 1988.

Gruchmann, L., *Autobiographie eines Attentäters. Johann Georg Elser*. Stuttgart: Deutsche Verlags-Anstalt. 1970.

Grunberger, R., *A Social History of the Third Reich*. London: Penguin. 1983.

Gutman, I., 'Jüdischer Widerstand – Eine historische Bewertung', in A. Lustiger (ed.), *Zum Kampf auf Leben und Tod! Das Buch vom Widerstand der Juden 1933–1945*. Cologne: Kiepenheuer and Witsch. 1994.

Hassell, U. von, *The Von Hassell Diaries 1938–1944*. London: Hamish Hamilton. 1948.

Heck, A., *A Child of Hitler. Germany in the Days when God Wore a Swastika*. Frederick, CO: Renaissance House. 1985.

Hehl, U., 'Das Kirchenvolk im Dritten Reich', in K. Gotto and K. Repgen (eds), *Kirche, Katholiken und Nationalsozialismus*. Mainz: Matthias-Grünewald. 1980.

Henry, F., *Victims and Neighbours. A Small Town in Nazi Germany Remembered*. Mass.: Bergin and Garvey. 1984.

Herbert, U., 'Apartheid nebenan. Erinnerungen an die Fremdarbeiter im Ruhrgebiet', in L. Niethammer (ed.), *Die Jahre weiß man nicht, wo man die heute hinsetzen soll*. Berlin: J.H.W. Dietz. 1983.

——, 'Die guten und die schlechten Zeiten', in L. Niethammer (ed.), *Die Jahre weiß man nicht, wo man die heute hinsetzen soll*. Berlin: J.H.W. Dietz. 1983.

——, *A History of Foreign Labour in Germany 1880–1980*. Ann Arbor: University of Michigan Press. 1990.

——, 'Labour as Spoils of Conquest, 1933–45', in D.F. Crew (ed.), *Nazism and German Society, 1933–45*. London: Routledge. 1994.

Heuss, T., Lübke, H., Heinemann, G.W., Scheel, W. and Carstens, K., *Reflections on July 20 1944*. Mainz: Hase and Koehler. 1984.

Heyen, F.J., *Nationalsozialismus im Alltag. Quellen zur Geschichte des Nationalsozialismus vornehmlich im Raum Mainz–Koblenz–Trier*. Boppard: Harald Boldt. 1967.

Hilberg, R., 'The Judenrat: Conscious or Unconscious Tool?', in Yad Vashem, *Patterns of Jewish Leadership in Nazi Europe 1933–45*. Proceedings of the Yad Vashem International Conference, Jerusalem, 4–7 April 1977.

——, *The Destruction of the European Jews*. London: Holmes and Meier. 1985.

Hill, L.E., 'The National Conservatives and Opposition to the Third Reich before the Second World War', in F.R. Nicosia and L.D. Stokes (eds), *Germans against Nazism. Nonconformity, Opposition and Resistance in the Third Reich*. Oxford: Berg. 1990.

Hillenbrand, F.M., *Underground Humour in Nazi Germany 1933–45*. London: Routledge. 1995.

Hitler, A., *Mein Kampf*. London: Hutchinson. 1985.

Hofer, W., *Der Nationalsozialismus. Dokumente 1933–1945*. Frankfurt-am-Main: Fischer. 1989.

Hoffmann, P., *The History of the German Resistance 1933–45*. London: MacDonald and Jane's. 1977.

——, *German Resistance to Hitler*. Cambridge, Mass.: Harvard University Press. 1988.

——, *Stauffenberg: A Family History, 1905–44*. Cambridge: CUP. 1996.

Höhne, H., *Canaris. Patriot im Zweilicht*. Munich. 1976.

——, *The Order of the Death's Head. The Story of Hitler's SS*. London: Pan. 1981.

——, 'Canaris and the Abwehr between Cooperation and Opposition', in J. Schmädeke and P. Steinbach (eds), *Der Widerstand gegen den Nationalsozialismus*. Munich: Piper. 1985.

Irving D., *The War Path. Hitler's Germany 1933–1939*. London: Papermac. 1983.

Jäckel, E., *Hitler's World View. A Blueprint for Power*. Cambridge, Mass.: Harvard University Press. 1981.

——, 'Hitler und die Deutschen', in K.D. Bracher, M. Funke and H.A. Jacobsen (eds), *Nationalsozialistische Diktatur 1933–45. Eine Bilanz*. Düsseldorf: Droste. 1983.

Jacobsen, H.A. (ed.), *Germans Against Hitler. July 20, 1944*. Wiesbaden: Bundeszentrale für politische Bildung. 1969.

Jonca, K., 'Jewish Resistance to Nazi Racial Legislation in Silesia, 1933–1937', in F.R. Nicosia and L.D. Stokes (eds), *Germans against Nazism. Nonconformity, Opposition and Resistance in the Third Reich.* Oxford: Berg. 1990.

Kaplan, M., 'Jewish Women in Nazi Germany: Daily Life, Daily Struggles, 1933–39', *Feminist Studies*, 16 (1990), 579–606.

Kenkmann, A., 'Navajos, Kittelsbach- und Edelweißpiraten. Jugendliche Dissidenten im "Dritten Reich"', in W. Breyvogel (ed.), *Piraten, Swings und Junge Garde. Jugendwiderstand im Nationalsozialismus.* Bonn: J.H.W. Dietz. 1991.

Kershaw, I., 'Antisemitismus und Volksmeinung. Reaktionen auf die Judenverfolgung', in M. Broszat and E. Fröhlich (eds), *Bayern in der NS-Zeit. Herrschaft und Gesellschaft in Konflikt.* Munich: Oldenbourg. 1979.

——, *Popular Opinion and Political Dissent in the Third Reich: Bavaria 1933–45.* Oxford: Clarendon Press. 1983.

——, '"Widerstand ohne Volk?" Dissens und Widerstand im Dritten Reich', in J. Schmädeke and P. Steinbach (eds), *Der Widerstand gegen den Nationalsozialismus.* Munich: Piper. 1985.

——, 'German Popular Opinion and the "Jewish Question", 1939–43. Some Further Reflections', in A. Paucker (ed.), *The Jews in Nazi Germany 1933–1945.* Tübingen: J.C.B. Mohr. 1986.

——, *The Hitler Myth.* Oxford: Clarendon Press. 1987.

——, 'Social Unrest and the Response of the Nazi Regime, 1934–1936', in F.R. Nicosia and L.D. Stokes (eds), *Germans against Nazism. Nonconformity, Opposition and Resistance in the Third Reich.* Oxford: Berg. 1990.

——, *The Nazi Dictatorship. Problems and Perspectives of Interpretation.* London: Edward Arnold. 3rd edn. 1993.

——, 'The Hitler Myth. Image and Reality in the Third Reich', in D.F. Crew (ed.), *Nazism and German Society, 1933–45.* London: Routledge. 1994.

Klemperer, K. von, 'Sie gingen ihren Weg . . . ', in J. Schmädeke and P. Steinbach (eds), *Der Widerstand gegen den Nationalsozialismus.* Munich: Piper. 1985.

——, 'The Solitary Witness: No Mere Footnote to Resistance Studies', in D.C. Large (ed.), *Contending with Hitler. Varieties of Resistance in the Third Reich.* New York: Cambridge University Press. 1991.

——, *German Resistance against Hitler. The Search for Allies Abroad 1938–1945.* Oxford: Clarendon Press. 1992.

Klönne, A., *Hitlerjugend. Die Jugend und Ihre Organisation im Drittehn Reich.* Hannover: Norddeutsche. 1960.

Koch, H. W. (ed.), *Aspects of the Third Reich.* London: Macmillan. 1985.

Kohl, H., 'Introduction', in T. Heuss, H. Lübke, G.W. Heinemann,

W. Scheel and K. Carstens, *Reflections on July 20 1944*. Mainz: Hase and Koehler. 1984.

Kolb, E., 'Die Maschinerie des Terrors', in K.D. Bracher, M. Funke and H.A. Jacobsen (eds), *Nazionalsozialistische Diktatur 1933–1945. Eine Bilanz*. Düsseldorf: Droste. 1983.

Koonz, C., 'Courage and Choice among German–Jewish Women and Men', in A. Paucker (ed.), *The Jews in Nazi Germany 1933–1945*. Tübingen: J.C.B. Mohr. 1986.

——, *Mothers in the Fatherland. Women, the Family and Nazi Politics*. New York: St Martin's Press. 1987.

——, 'Ethical Dilemmas and Nazi Eugenics: Single-Issue Dissent in Religious Contexts', *Journal of Modern History*, 64 (1992), 8–32.

——, 'Eugenics, Gender and Ethics in Nazi Germany: the Debate about Involuntary Sterilization, 1933–36', in T. Childers and J. Caplan (eds), *Reevaluating the Third Reich*. New York: Holmes and Meier. 1993.

Krakowski, S., 'The Opposition to the Judenräte by the Jewish Armed Resistance', in Yad Vashem, *Patterns of Jewish Leadership in Nazi Europe 1933–45*. Proceedings of the Yad Vashem International Conference, Jerusalem, 4–7 April 1977.

Kramarz, J., *Stauffenberg. The Life and Death of an Officer. 15 November 1907–20 July 1944*. London: André Deutsch. 1967.

Kraushaar, L., *Deutsche Widerstandskämpfer 1933–45*. Berlin: Dietz. 1970.

Kroh, F., *David kämpft. Vom jüdischen Widerstand gegen Hitler*. Hamburg: Rowohlt. 1988.

Krüger-Charlé, M., 'From Reform to Resistance: Carl Goerdeler's 1938 Memorandum', in D.C. Large (ed.), *Contending with Hitler. Varieties of Resistance in the Third Reich*. New York: Cambridge University Press. 1991.

Kwiet, K., 'Problems of Jewish Resistance Historiography', in M.R. Marrus (ed.), *The Nazi Holocaust. Volume 17: Jewish Resistance to the Holocaust*. Westport: Meckler. 1989.

——, 'To Leave or not to Leave: the German Jews at the Crossroads', in W.H. Pehle (ed.), *November 1938: From Kristallnacht to Genocide*. Oxford: Berg. 1991a.

——, 'Resistance and Opposition: the Example of the German Jews', in D.C. Large (ed.), *Contending with Hitler. Varieties of Resistance in the Third Reich*. New York: Cambridge University Press. 1991b.

Langbein, H., *. . . nicht wie die Schafe zur Schlachtenbank*. Frankfurt-am-Main: Fischer. 1994.

Langer, L.L., *Holocaust Testimonies. The Ruins of Memory*. New Haven: Yale University Press. 1991.

Lanzmann, C., *Shoah. An Oral History of the Holocaust*. New York: Pantheon Books. 1985.

Large, D.C. (ed.), *Contending with Hitler. Varieties of Resistance in the Third Reich*. New York: Cambridge University Press. 1991.

Lernhoff, F.G., *The First Thirty Years. An Autobiographical Study*. Shrewsbury: Shotton Hill. 1975.

Linsert, L., 'Aus meiner Widerstandarbeit', in R. Löwenthal and P. von zur Mühlen (eds), *Widerstand und Verweigerung in Deutschland 1933 bis 1945*. Berlin: J.H.W. Dietz. 1982.

Löwenthal, R., 'Widerstand im totalen Staat', in R. Löwenthal and P. von zur Mühlen (eds), *Widerstand und Verweigerung in Deutschland 1933 bis 1945*. Berlin: J.H.W. Dietz. 1982.

Löwenthal, R. and Mühlen, P. von zur (eds), *Widerstand und Verweigerung in Deutschland 1933 bis 1945*. Berlin: J.H.W. Dietz. 1982.

Lustiger, A. (ed.), *Zum Kampf auf Leben und Tod! Das Buch vom Widerstand der Juden 1933–1945*. Cologne: Kiepenheuer and Witsch. 1994.

Mark, B., 'The Herbert Baum Group. Jewish Resistance in Germany in the Years 1937–42', in Y. Suhl (ed.), *They Fought Back. The Story of the Jewish Resistance in Nazi Europe*. London: MacGibbon and Kee. 1968.

Marrus, M.R. (ed.), *The Nazi Holocaust. Volume 17: Jewish Resistance to the Holocaust*. Westport: Meckler. 1989.

Marßolek, I. and Ott, R., *Bremen im Dritten Reich. Anpassund–Widerstand–Verfolgung*. Bremen: Carl Schünemann. 1986.

Maschmann, M., *Account Rendered. A Dossier on My Former Self*. New York: Abelard-Schumann. 1964.

Mason, T.W., *Arbeiterklasse und Volksgemeinschaft*. Opladen: Westdeutscher. 1975.

—— 'Arbeiteropposition im nationalsozialistischen Deutschland', in D. Peukert and J. Reulecke (eds), *Die Reihen fast geschlossen. Beiträge zur Geschichte des Alltags unterm Nationalsozialismus*. Wuppertal: Peter Hammer. 1981.

——, *Social Policy in the Third Reich. The Working Class and the 'National Community'*. Oxford: Berg. 1993.

Mengus, R., 'Dietrich Bonhoeffer and the Decision to Resist', *Journal of Modern History*, 64 (1992), 134–46.

Merkl, P., *Political Violence under the Swastika*. Princeton: Princeton University Press. 1975

——, *The Making of a Stormtrooper*. Princeton: Princeton University Press. 1980.

Merson, A., *Communist Resistance in Nazi Germany*. London: Lawrence and Wishart. 1985.

Michalka, W., *Das Dritte Reich Vol 1*. Munich: DTV. 1985.

Mommsen, H., 'Social Views and Constitutional Plans of the Resistance', in H. Graml, H. Mommsen, H.-J. Reichhardt and E. Wolf, *The German Resistance to Hitler*. London: Batsford. 1970.

——, 'Resistance against Hitler and German Society', in J. Schmädeke and

P. Steinbach (eds), *Der Widerstand gegen den Nationalsozialismus.* Munich: Piper. 1985.

——, 'What did the Germans Know about the Genocide of the Jews?', in W.H. Pehle (ed.), *November 1938: From Kristallnacht to Genocide.* Oxford: Berg. 1991.

Mosse, G.L., *Toward the Final Solution.* London: Dent and Sons. 1978.

Nicosia, F.R. and Stokes, L.D. (eds), *Germans against Nazism. Nonconformity, Opposition and Resistance in the Third Reich.* Oxford: Berg. 1990.

Niemöller, M., *Die Evangelische Kirche im Dritten Reich.* Bielefeld. 1946.

Niethammer, L. (ed.), *Die Jahre weiß man nicht, wo man die heute hinsetzen soll.* Berlin: J.H.W. Dietz. 1983a.

——, 'Heimat und Front. Versuch zehn Kriegserinnerungen aus der Arbeiterklasse des Ruhrgebietes zu verstehen', in L. Niethammer (ed.), *Die Jahre weiß man nicht, wo man die heute hinsetzen soll.* Berlin: J.H.W. Dietz. 1983b.

Noakes, J., 'German Conservatives and the Third Reich: an Ambiguous Relationship', in M. Blinkhorn (ed.), *Fascists and Conservatives.* London: Unwin Hyman. 1990.

Otto, H.-U. and Sünker, H. (eds), *Politische Formierung und soziale Erziehung im Nationalsozialismus.* Frankfurt-am-Main: Suhrkamp. 1991.

Overy, R., *War and Economy in the Third Reich.* Oxford: Clarendon Press. 1994.

Paucker, A. (ed.), *The Jews in Nazi Germany 1933–1945.* Tübingen: J.C.B. Mohr. 1986.

——, 'Jüdischer Widerstand in Deutschland', in A. Lustiger (ed.), *Zum Kampf auf Leben und Tod! Das Buch vom Widerstand der Juden 1933–1945.* Cologne: Kiepenheuer and Witsch. 1994.

Peczorski, A., 'Ha-Mered be-Sobibor', in Y. Arad, Y. Gutman and A. Margialot (eds), *Documents on the Holocaust.* Oxford: Pergamon. 1981.

Pehle, W.H. (ed.), *November 1938: From Kristallnacht to Genocide.* Oxford: Berg. 1991.

Peukert, D., *Die KPD im Widerstand. Verfolgung und Untergrundarbeit an Rhein und Ruhr 1933 bis 1945.* Wuppertal: Peter Hammer. 1980.

——, 'Youth in the Third Reich', in R. Bessel (ed.), *Life in the Third Reich.* Oxford: Oxford University Press. 1987.

——, *Die Edelweiß Piraten. Protestbewegungen jugendlicher Arbeiter im 'Dritten Reich'.* Bonn: Bund. 1988.

——, 'Working Class Resistance: Problems and Options', in D.C. Large (ed.), *Contending with Hitler. Varieties of Resistance in the Third Reich.* New York: Cambridge University Press. 1991.

——, *Inside Nazi Germany. Conformity, Opposition and Racism in Everyday Life.* London: Penguin. 1993.

Peukert, D. and Reulecke, J. (eds), *Die Reihen fast geschlossen. Beiträge zur Geschichte des Alltags unterm Nationalsozialismus.* Wuppertal: Peter Hammer. 1981.

Pikarski, M. and Uebel, G., *Der Antifaschistische Widerstandskampf der KPD im Spiegel des Flugblattes 1933–1945.* Berlin: Dietz Verlag. 1978.

Pocket Oxford Dictionary. Oxford: Clarendon Press. 1969.

Rauschning, H., *Hitler Speaks.* London: Thornton Butterworth. 1939.

Rebbentisch, D., 'Die politische Beurteilung als Herrschaftsinstrument der NSDAP', in D. Peukert and J. Reulecke (eds), *Die Reihen fast geschlossen. Beiträge zur Geschichte des Alltags unterm Nationalsozialismus.* Wuppertal: Peter Hammer. 1981.

Reynolds, N., *Treason was no Crime. Ludwig Beck, Chief of the German General Staff.* London: William Kimber. 1976.

Ritter, G., *The German Resistance. Carl Goerdeler's Struggle against Tyranny.* London: Allen and Unwin. 1958.

Robertson, E.H., *Christians against Hitler.* London: SCM Press. 1962.

Robinson, J., 'Introduction: Some Basic Issues that Faced the Jewish Councils', in I. Trunk, *Judenrat. The Jewish Councils in Eastern Europe under Nazi Occupation.* London: Macmillan. 1972.

Roon, G. van, *German Resistance to Hitler. Count Moltke and the Kreisau Circle.* London: Van Nostrand Reinhold. 1971.

Rosenfeld, A.H., *Imagining Hitler.* Bloomington: Indiana University Press. 1985.

Rothfels, H., *The German Opposition to Hitler. An Appraisal.* Chicago: Henry Regnery. 1962.

Rusinek, B.-A., 'Desintegration und gesteigerter Zwang. Die Chaotisierung der Lebensverhältnisse in den Großstädten 1944/45 und der Mythos der Ehrenfelder Gruppe', in W. Breyvogel (ed.), *Piraten, Swings und Junge Garde. Jugendwiderstand im Nationalsozialismus.* Bonn: J.H.W. Dietz. 1991.

Schewick, B. von, 'Katholische Kirche und nationalsozialistische Rassenpolitik', in K. Gotto and K. Repgen (eds), *Kirche, Katholiken und Nationalsozialismus.* Mainz: Matthias-Grünewald. 1980.

Schiedecki, J. and Stahlmann, M., 'Die Inszenzierung totalen Erlebens. Lagererziehung im Nationalsozialismus', in H.-U. Otto and H. Sünker (eds), *Politische Formierung und soziale Erziehung im Nationalsozialismus.* Frankfurt-am-Main: Suhrkamp. 1991.

Schlabrendorff, F. von, *The Secret War Against Hitler.* Boulder: Westview Press. 1994.

Schmädeke, J. and Steinbach, P. (eds), *Der Widerstand gegen den Nationalsozialismus.* Munich: Piper. 1985.

Schmidt, D., *Pastor Niemöller.* London: Odhams. 1959.

Scholl, I., *The White Rose. Munich 1942–43.* Middleton, Col.: Wesleyan University Press. 1983.

Schörken, R., 'Jugendalltag im Dritten Reich – Die Normalität in der Diktatur', in K. Bergmann and R. Schörken (eds), *Geschichte im Alltag – Alltag in der Geschichte*. Düsseldorf: Pädagogischer Verlag Schwann. 1982.

Schulte, T., *The German Army and Nazi Policies in Occupied Russia*. Oxford: Berg. 1989.

Sherman, A.J., 'Eine Jüdische Bank in der Ära Schacht: M.M. Warburg + Co. 1933–38', in A. Paucker (ed.), *The Jews in Nazi Germany 1933–1945*. Tübingen: J.C.B. Mohr. 1986.

Simmert, J. (ed.), *Die nationalsozialistische Judenverfolgung in Rheinland-Pfalz 1933 bis 1945*. Koblenz: Landesarchivverwaltung, Rheinland-Pfalz. 1974.

Sopade, see *Deutschland-Berichte der Sozialdemokratischen Partei Deutschlands*.

Steffahn, H., *Stauffenberg*. Hamburg: Rowohlt. 1994.

Steinbach, P., 'The Conservative Resistance', in D.C. Large (ed.), *Contending with Hitler. Varieties of Resistance in the Third Reich*. New York: Cambridge University Press. 1991.

Steinberg, J., *All or Nothing. The Axis and the Holocaust 1941–43*. London: Routledge. 1990.

Steinberg, L., *Not as a Lamb. The Jews against Hitler*. Farnborough: Saxon House. 1970.

Steinhoff, J., Pechel, P. and Showalter, D. (eds), *Voices from the Third Reich. An Oral History*. Washington: Regnery Gateway. 1989.

Stern, J.P., *Hitler. The Führer and the People*. Glasgow: Fontana. 1975.

Stokes, L.D., *Kleinstadt und Nationalsozialismus. Ausgewählte Dokumente zur Geschichte von Eutin 1918–45*. Neumünster: Karl Wachholtz. 1984.

Suhl, Y., 'Introduction', in Y. Suhl (ed.), *They Fought Back. The Story of the Jewish Resistance in Nazi Europe*. London: MacGibbon and Kee. 1968a.

——, (ed.), *They Fought Back. The Story of the Jewish Resistance in Nazi Europe*. London: MacGibbon and Kee. 1968b.

Szepansky, G., *Frauen leisten Widerstand: 1933–1945*. Frankfurt-am-Main: Fischer. 1994.

Tausendpfund, W. and Wolf, G.P., *Die jüdische Gemeinde von Schnaittach*. Nürnberg: Verlag Kornt Berg. 1981.

Taylor, S., *Prelude to Genocide. Nazi Ideology and the Struggle for Power*. London: Duckworth. 1985.

Trial of the Major War Criminals before the International Military Tribunal. Nuremberg. 1947.

Trunk, I., 'The Attitude of the Judenrats to the Problems of Armed Resistance Against the Nazis', in Yad Vashem, *Jewish Resistance During the Holocaust*. Jerusalem: Yad Vashem. 1971.

——, *Judenrat. The Jewish Councils in Eastern Europe under Nazi Occupation*. London: Macmillan. 1972.

Wagner, K. and Wilke, G., 'Dorfleben im Dritten Reich: Körle in Hessen', in D. Peukert and J. Reulecke (eds), *Die Reihen fast geschlossen Beiträge zur Geschichte des Alltags unterm Nationalsozialismus.* Wuppertal: Peter Hammer. 1981.

Waite, R.G.L., *The Psychopathic God. Adolf Hitler.* New York: Da Capo Press. 1993.

Weinberg, G.L. (ed.), *Hitlers zweites Buch: Ein Dokument aus dem Jahr 1928.* Stuttgart: Deutsche Verlags-Anstalt. 1961.

——, *Germany, Hitler and World War II.* Cambridge: Cambridge University Press. 1995.

Welch, D., *The Third Reich. Politics and Propaganda.* London: Routledge. 1993.

Wenzel, H., 'Widerstandsmythen und Anpassungsrealität. Das Beispiel der Naturfreundejugend', in W. Breyvogel (ed.), *Piraten, Swings und Junge Garde. Jugendwiderstand im Nationalsozialismus.* Bonn: J.H.W. Dietz. 1991.

Whalen, R.W., *Assassinating Hitler. Ethics and Resistance in Nazi Germany.* London: Associated University Press. 1993.

Wheeler-Bennett, J.W., *The Nemesis of Power. The German Army in Politics 1918–45.* London: Macmillan. 1964.

Yad Vashem, *Jewish Resistance During the Holocaust.* Jerusalem: Yad Vashem. 1971.

——, *Patterns of Jewish Leadership in Nazi Europe 1933–45.* Proceedings of the Yad Vashem International Conference, Jerusalem, 4–7 April 1977.

Yahil,L., 'Jewish Resistance – An Examination of Active and Passive Forms of Jewish Survival in the Holocaust Period', in Yad Vashem, *Jewish Resistance During the Holocaust.* Jerusalem: Yad Vashem. 1971.

Zahn, G.C., *German Catholics and Hitler's War. A Study in Social Control.* London: Sheed and Ward. 1963.

Zipfel, F., *Kirchenkampf in Deutschland 1933–45.* Berlin: de Gruyter. 1965.

Zuelzer, W., 'Recollections of a Non-Aryan Emigrant from the Third Reich', in W.H. Pehle (ed.), *November 1938: From Kristallnacht to Genocide.* Oxford: Berg. 1991.

Index

Himmler, Reichsführer-SS Heinrich 174; Globocnik's fiancée 5, 6; religion 59

Hitler, Adolf: assassination attempts 93–116, 164–5, 173–5; Beck 98–9; Czechoslovakia 104–5; euthanasia 58, 63; ideology 3; Jews 12–13, 119, 121–3; *Mein Kampf* 46; Niemöller 47–8; Nuremberg rally 1938 72; racism 12–13; religion 46–8, 53, 54, 65; workers 23; youth 68

Hitler Youth: brutality 82; camps 78–9; Catholic Youth 50; 'Crystal Night' 145; drummers 86, 87; Edelweiß Pirates 85–6, 89; Friends of Nature 77; Law of Dec 1936 77–8; propaganda 4; religion 74–5; schools 74–6; structure 78; 'Swing' group 88; youth rebellion 69

Hoffmann, Erich 129–30

Hoffmann, P. 97, 98, 113, 178

Höhne, H. 7, 172

Holocaust: Globocnik 5; Jewish response 118–19, 126–34; public cooperation 149–50, 154–7; public knowledge of 144–5, 150–3; sabotage 170–1; SS 148–9

homosexuality 9–10, 11

Huber, Kurt 89

industrial sabotage 37, 38

informers 141–2; children 81–2; Communists 35; personal vendettas 18

interrogation: Elser 173–4; Gestapo techniques 7–8; torture 27–8

Irving, D. 12

Italian army, Jews 153

Jäckel, Eberhard 12, 13, 177

Jacobsen, H.A. 8, 96, 104–5, 107, 109–10, 178; 'resistance' 162, 166, 168

Jäger, August 50

Jews 117–36; assimilation 119; Christian Church 63–5; Communists 126; 'Crystal Night' 117, 144, 145, 146–7, 161, 171, 172; definition 117; deportations 102, 126–8, 131, 139–40; discrimination against 14; emigration 124–5, 147; escapes 131–2; executions 118–19, 130–1, 144–5, 148–9; Galicia 148–9; ghettos 128–9, 132–3, 148–9; Hitler's views 12–13; killing units 19–20, 153; lack of resistance 117–18; Nuremberg Laws 117, 144; Orthodox Jews 119, 120; public indifference 21; public opinion 66, 138–48; self-help groups 122–4; Soviet Union 153; Star of David 140, 147; youth associations 76; *see also* anti-Semitism; Holocaust

Joachim, Hans 135–6

jokes 166, 172

Jonca, K. 121–2

Judenräte 128–9, 132–3

Kaplan, M. 119

Kenkmann, A. 83, 89

Kershaw, Ian 23, 91, 161, 177–8; 'resistance' 162–3, 164, 166

Kittelbach Pirates 83, 84–5

Klemperer, Klemens von 98, 111, 176

Klönne, A. 76, 78

Kochmann, Sala 135

Kohl, Helmut 115–16

Kolb, E. 8

Koller, Martin 151–2

Koonz, Claudia 16–18, 125

KPD *see* German Communist Party

Kraft durch Freude 41–4

Krakowski, S. 132

Kramarz, J. 106, 178

Kreisau Circle 96–7, 100

Kreuzmann, Heribert 129–30

Kristallnacht (Crystal Night) 144, 145, 146–7, 161, 171, 172